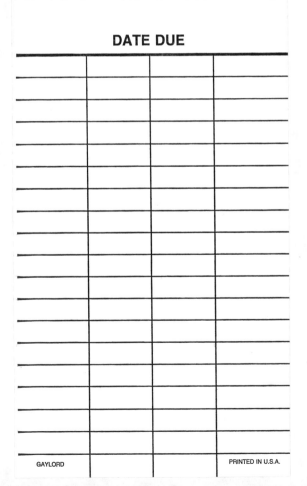

DATE DUE

GAYLORD			PRINTED IN U.S.A.

Contemporary Criminology and Criminal Justice Theory

Contemporary Criminology and Criminal Justice Theory

Evaluating Justice Systems in Capitalist Societies

Geoffrey R. Skoll

palgrave
macmillan

CONTEMPORARY CRIMINOLOGY AND CRIMINAL JUSTICE THEORY
Copyright © Geoffrey R. Skoll, 2009.

First published in 2009 by PALGRAVE MACMILLAN® in the
United States - a division of St. Martin's Press LLC, 175 Fifth Avenue,
New York, NY 10010.

Where this book is distributed in the UK, Europe and the rest of
the world, this is by Palgrave Macmillan, a division of Macmillan
Publishers Limited, registered in England, company number 785998,
of Houndmills, Basingstoke, Hampshire RG21 6XS.

Palgrave Macmillan is the global academic imprint of the above
companies and has companies and representatives throughout the world.

Palgrave® and Macmillan® are registered trademarks in the United
States, the United Kingdom, Europe and other countries.

ISBN-13: 978–0–230–61598–4

Library of Congress Cataloging-in-Publication Data
Skoll, Geoffrey R., 1948–
    Contemporary criminology and criminal justice theory : evaluating justice
    systems in capitalist societies / Geoffrey R. Skoll.
        p.   cm
    Includes bibliographical references and index.
    ISBN 0–230–61598–8
    1. Criminal justice, Administration of.   2. Criminology.   I. Title.
    HV7419.S59 2009
    364—dc22   2009006413

Design by Integra Software Services

First edition: September 2009

10 9 8 7 6 5 4 3 2 1

Printed in the United States of America

Dedicated to Jenny Peshut who makes all things possible

Contents

1

Introduction

Theories of Justice in Late Capitalism

This study casts a critical eye on criminal justice through a sociological lens. It focuses primarily on the United States but also on other capitalist countries. Two terminological problems arise. First, *sociology* should be understood in the broadest sense. It does not refer just to the academic discipline but to a viewpoint on humans and their works in collective action. The term *criminal justice* also has two usages. One points to the policies and practices of criminal justice institutions, the other to the study of those institutions by the academic discipline of criminal justice. Unfortunately, this second confusion of usage remains less easily clarified, so the reader will have to rely on context.

For Socrates in Plato's *Republic*, justice was harmony. In the *Nichomachean Ethics*, Aristotle characterized it as moderation—the golden mean. Questions of justice under late capitalism take many forms and include a wide swath of social phenomena and institutions. A slice of the swath covers justice relating to severe normative violations—that is, crime, hence criminal justice.

Four aspects of criminal justice interact reciprocally and sometimes dialectically: crime, criminality, criminalization, and policy and practice. Studies of crime include its ontology, prevalence, incidence, and variation. Who commits crimes, when, how, and why are the questions relevant to criminality. Examinations of criminalization ask how a society comes to designate something as criminal, whether that something is a person, a thing, or a behavior. Policy studies analyze those organizations, usually governmental, that administer criminal law—cops, courts, and corrections.

Since the foremost task of theory is to tackle explanation, theories about criminal justice should explain one or more of its four aspects.

The more useful theories explain all four aspects along with how those aspects affect each other. Too often crime theory predominates. This kind of crime theory makes unwarranted and unquestioned assumptions, especially about the definitions of crime, how institutions shape crime, and how policies create a criminal class. By way of illustration, most theorizing by criminologists and scholars of criminal justice offers accounts of street crime—robbery, rape, murder, theft, and so forth. Few, if any, theories treat war crimes, terrorism, and crimes of high finance in the same way. Ask criminologists to explain, say, burglary, and they can turn to a host of theoretical essays. Ask them to explain burglary in the same way as they might explain the gargantuan banking frauds leading to the world financial crisis of 2008, and they would find themselves at a loss. Then add the crime of aggressive war such as the U.S. invasion of Iraq, and they would probably look askance, perhaps thinking they had misheard the question. The criminologists' perplexity arises from the domination of crime theory by a very narrow understanding of crime and little appreciation of the dynamic, interactive, and dialectical relationships among crime, criminality, criminalization, and policy. The narrow focus arises from the role of criminal justice practices under late capitalism, which have shaped if not completely determined theories of criminal justice.

Theory in Criminal Justice

In 2006 Peter Kraska decried the lack of criminal justice theory in the flagship journal of the Academy of Criminal Justice Studies, the main academic society for the field of criminal justice in the United States: "Criminal justice/criminology does not have a recognized and readily accessible theoretical infrastructure about the criminal justice system and crime control..." (168). Twenty-two years earlier, in the inaugural issue of the same journal, Frank P. Williams III (1984) said much the same in his "Demise of the Criminological Imagination," although he confined his criticism to the decade of the 1970s. Seemingly, a burgeoning bevy of academics in the field failed to generate usable theories in almost a quarter century. According to Williams, one could not blame a lack of good starts. He cited important work by Richard Quinney (1970a, 1970b), Graeme R. Newman (1978), Harold E. Pepinsky (1976), Jack P. Gibbs (1975), David O. Friedrichs (1979), Steven Spitzer (1975), Austin T. Turk (1976), Michel Foucault (1979), and Donald Black (1976) (Williams 1984:92). Using the list illustratively instead of exhaustively, Williams opined that potentially seminal theoretical advances occurred in conflict, labeling, and social control theoretical frameworks, but that none led to continued development.

Instead of theory, Williams said, scholars in criminology had concentrated on methodological tools and tautological explanations for correlations in data sets. The problem seemed to be not lack of ideas but lack of interest in theoretical work. In a similar vein, Joachim Savelsberg and Robert Sampson said that criminology failed to become a discipline because it lacks an intellectual core, and it has relied too heavily on state financing, thereby making it a hostage to state interests (Savelsberg and Sampson 2002). Their diagnoses apply even more forcefully to criminal justice. For this condition to continue for so long, one suspects a systemic defect.

In fact there are four. First, the criminal justice field does not lack theories, but ideology causes a few theories to obscure and crowd out new additions. Second, criminal justice theories do not rely on, or limit themselves to, theories about crime; just the opposite. They give too much weight to criminality and policy while denying their implicit reliance on theories of criminalization. Third, the theories do not lack creativity, but they show little of the honest craft C. Wright Mills identified with the sociological imagination (1959), from which Williams got his title and theme. The fourth systemic flaw comes from the treatment of theories, or how the discipline deals with theoretical work. Conspicuously, there is much so-called theory-testing, which betrays a misunderstanding of theory's role in the human sciences. All these obstacles to fruitful theorizing stem from the nature of the field of criminal justice itself. Therefore, the long-observed lack of theory will likely continue to prevail unless the discipline radically alters itself or outside pressures force it to change.

Criminal justice studies in late modern capitalism

By the time the study of criminal justice entered academe, criminology already had a substantial history. Sociology and sociology departments in universities usually provide a home for criminology. Unlike the field of criminal justice, criminology also has theoretical foundations first laid down in the first three decades of the twentieth century by social scientists at the University of Chicago, and hence identified as the Chicago School. The sociological base of Chicago School criminology drew on the work of Emile Durkheim, Georg Simmel, and George Herbert Mead. Later, in the 1930s, criminological theories used Robert Merton's work, especially his 1938 article "Social Structure and Anomie." Georg Rusche and Otto Kirchheimer, émigrés from the Frankfurt School, published *Punishment and Social Structure* in 1939 in the United States, which added a Marxian and Weberian perspective to American criminology. Subsequent theoretical work in the middle decades of the twentieth century built on this foundation and informed empirical investigations.

Academic criminal justice did not spring fully formed from the head of criminology. Instead, money, politics, and policy at the level of the U.S. federal government gave birth to the discipline. Academic criminal justice, typical of altricial offspring, has not strayed far from its parentage. Consequently, the theories in criminal justice largely conform to policy expectations of the criminal justice apparatus. That apparatus has required devotion to applied research, especially on topics such as crime control, police organization and management, corrections organization and management, and analyses of legal and juridical processes. Criminal justice scholars followed the money. They studied criminal justice policy and practice with little attention to theory development, even dismissing theory as not very relevant to their work.

As any social scientist should know, strictly empirical work is impossible. All empiricism, in the social sciences especially, is theory laden, even if its practitioners do not always recognize the often-implicit theories guiding their observations. Because it was implicit, even unconscious, the theoretical molding of criminal justice scholarship relied less on explicit scientific theory construction, and more on political and administrative ideology. Moreover, the ideology that increasingly dominated criminal justice, along with other public policy areas after 1970, reflected a program of reconquest by the elite in the United States, a shoring up of capital and its owners, and a concomitant suppression of parts of the population who challenged the supremacy of the elite. Criminalizing challengers of the status quo fit with an overall strategy of reasserting control of the political economy, suppressing dissent, and managing the potentially unruly masses. The central role of the criminal justice apparatus in this strategy has meant that criminal justice scholarship cherry-picked criminological theories supportive of crime control. Such theories pay little attention to the study of crime as a social fact—its character, extent, prevalence, and variation. Criminal justice theories of crime, to the extent that they are theories at all, try to explain criminality and policies designed to control criminals, who are usually treated as a self-evident subpopulation. Therefore, much that has passed as criminal justice theory purports to explain crime but really focuses on criminals and their assumed criminality along with theories about how to control them. A corollary to this theoretical and ideological orientation rules out of court theories of criminalization.

Beginning with the birth of criminal justice studies in the 1970s, criminal justice diverged from criminology. Criminology continued its theoretically promising trajectory as suggested by the work cited by Frank P. Williams in the seminal writings of Foucault, Pepinsky, Quinney, and

Turk, to name just a few. Later, in the 1990s and beyond, criminology has developed theoretical work using late modernity and postmodernism, critical race and critical gender perspectives, and some orientations that are not so easy to categorize, such as peacemaking criminology. As criminal justice diverged, it isolated itself from criminological innovation as it continued to bind itself to increasingly authoritarian criminal justice policies and apparatuses.

Criminal justice as a commodity

A 1976 lecture by Stanford law professor Lawrence M. Friedman provides a point of departure. In 1900 a London court convicted a young woman, Ellen McDermott, for habitual suicide attempts. Clearly a recidivist for that offense, she had seven previous convictions. The court sentenced her to six months at hard labor (Friedman 1977:257). Friedman went on to compare the state of criminal justice in three historical cultures: colonial Massachusetts; early twentieth-century England; and Oakland, California, in the late nineteenth century. He concluded by saying: "Law and order, it turns out, is a commodity, like oil, sugar, or Maine lobsters; if demand increases too fast and the supply cannot keep pace, the price goes up ... Conceptions of crime are rapidly changing" (274). Conceptions of crime were rapidly changing in the United States in the 1970s, while commodification of law and order took increasingly diverse forms. At the same time, the academic discipline of criminal justice was maturing from infancy to childhood. It was not coincidence.

Theoretical shallowness in American criminal justice studies intertwined with changing conceptions of crime in the 1970s and 1980s. More than just interconnecting, the discipline of criminal justice helped promote and legitimize the changing conceptions. The discipline did not pick up on the theories of people like Michel Foucault, Harold Pepinsky, Richard Quinney, and Austin Turk, among others mentioned by Frank P. Williams, because their ideas did not fit the direction of change in conceptions of crime. Those theorists had proposed critical analyses, often at a fundamental level, of the connection between social arrangements, kinds of crime, and the criminal justice system. In contrast, ideas focusing on a reputed criminal class came to the fore as explanations for crime along with recommendations for policy responses.

Instead of critical theory, American criminal justice since the 1970s elevated what Frank P. Williams (1984) called empirical tautologies. The main academic journals in criminal justice over the last thirty years show repeated recourse to so-called theories of "rational choice," "broken windows," and "self-control." There are exceptions, but empirical work and theory development using other theoretical frameworks remain in a definite minority. Moreover, these exceptions use long-established theories deriving from the 1930s, which John P. Crank (2003:20–21) rightly called conservative. Robert Sampson (Sampson 1986; Sampson and Laub 1993; Laub and Sampson 2003) and Ronald Akers (1985, 1990; Akers and Jensen 2003) are leading examples. It is not that scholars are not doing new and critical research in criminology and criminal justice, but that their work is marginalized, confined to niches, or pursued outside the United States (Crank 2003:109–162). The main thrust of the discipline reiterates ideas that gained currency in the 1970s and 1980s.

When Mills described the sociological imagination, now almost half a century ago, he warned of a trend in the social sciences and lamented its probable triumph. He called it abstracted empiricism.

> The most conspicuous—although not necessarily the most important—of its characteristics have to do with the administrative apparatus that it has come to employ and the types of intellectual workmen it has recruited and trained. This apparatus has now become large scale, and many signs point to its becoming more widespread and influential. The intellectual administrator and the research technician—both quite new types of professional men—now compete with the more usual kinds of professors and scholars. (Mills 1959:55)

The natal origins of criminal justice guaranteed the powerful influence of abstracted empiricism as the discipline matured. This does not deny earlier roots, for instance August Vollmer's police academy associated with the University of California – Berkeley even before the United States entered the First World War. Nonetheless, modern academic criminal justice was conceived in the mid-1960s (Morn 1995). The Law Enforcement Assistance Act of 1965 (79 Stat. 828) used government money to promote the kinds of social scientific workshops providing what C. Wright Mills would have called "...employment for semi-skilled technicians...This style of research, in brief, is accompanied by an administrative demiurge which is relevant to the future of social study and its possible bureaucratization" (1959:56). Practitioners in the abstracted empirical style show an obsession with method and instrumentation. Mills cited Paul F. Lazarsfeld as exemplary, noting that he "is among the most sophisticated spokesmen of this school" (Mills 1959:59). Mills interpreted Lazarsfeld as favoring psychologism, statistical analytics, repetitive studies of structurally similar social action so as to permit statistical analysis, and presentism—which elevates ahistorical understanding to scientific preeminence. The approach relies on data sets of individualistic information as it "reduces sociological realities to psychological variables" (63).

Some years after Mills's forecasts and forebodings, Weston LaBarre noted that

> ... most contemporary sociologists would prefer to think of themselves as quantifying scientists with "testable" hypotheses. Now any such hypothesis derives from common sense, a basic "insight" (unwitting awareness of his own culture)... But the plausible hypothesis must derive from that covert consensus, unexamined local ethnography. Thereupon the sociologist sets out to "collect his data"... to be calibrated against the opinions of his selected "subjects." Next he brings heaps of protocols, puts them on punch-cards, and lays them at the feet of the Truth Machine untouched by human mind. Finally he pushes the button and science emerges... But he does not seem to realize that his results have already been programmed by a far more sophisticated (or sophistic) computer, his mind—the unexamined, motivated, enculturated, time-serving human mind.
>
> If the sociologist is lucky, his results will indicate an overlap of two intersecting circles—never concentric, unless he has produced an authentic tautology, though the more tautological the more impressive—the common area of which can be expressed statistically (if the circles are not even tangent he has flubbed it)... He has discovered the obvious, however pretentiously, to which all can agree. (LaBarre 1978:260–261)

The fears of Mills and LaBarre for sociology defined the discipline of criminal justice. Coincident with the triumph of abstracted empiricism, leading lights in academia joined with bureaucrats in an increasingly federalized criminal justice administration. In their united front they set out to reverse changes in norms of civil behavior and the trend toward material equality in the American political economy. Their immediate fear was social revolution.

They put the criminal justice system at the forefront of social control. Within the discipline of criminal justice and its abstracted empiricist style, everyone was too busy refining methodologies and testing hypotheses to notice. Scholars from the older discipline of criminology waned in influence or moved on to other research. Meanwhile, a new generation bent substantial theories developed in the 1930s and 1940s into new forms. For example, Robert Merton's thoroughly sociological anomie theory turned into a psychologized strain theory studying persons rather than situated role adaptations (Agnew 1985, 1992, 2001).

The power elite's Reconquista originated in the early 1970s. It battled on three fronts: in the streets, in the media, and in academe. The discipline of criminal justice articulates all three. The project has been successful. As

Bernardine Dohrn, a leader of the revolutionary impetus of the 1960s and 1970s, puts it about today's conditions,

> [it is] a moment of U.S. triumphalism, permanent war, global domination, and reactionary fundamentalism so deliberately intimidating we are meant *not* to see. The gritty consequences of empire at home include economic collapse, job flight, a national security state, unprecedented caging of people of color, renewed assaults against women, gays, and fundamental liberties, ecological plunder, barricaded and isolated North America as a fortress against immigrants, and the pandering of fear. (Dohrn 2005:xiii)

It may seem overly expansive to include such large forces as globalization in a critique of a single academic discipline, but the centrality of the discipline to those very forces should not be underestimated. Depicting the theoretical status of American academic criminal justice requires a broad canvas.

American Academic Criminal Justice

Briefly, three leading approaches are found in the main American criminal justice journals—rational choice, broken windows, and self-control. Rational Choice says that crime comes from individuals who make cost-benefit analyses on whether to do something prohibited by law. Broken Windows claims that disorderly neighborhoods, or signs of such disorder—the distinction is not always made pellucid—cause serious crime, by which its proponents mean individualized violent acts such as murder, rape, or robbery. Self-Control explains crime according to individuals' differential abilities to act rationally and control emotional impulses. That is, it says crime comes from people who cannot control themselves. At a superficial level, these accounts differ. One says people are too rational, another says they are not rational enough, while a third blames crime on the environment. More basically, however, these three ideas have much in common. Their similarity draws on popular feelings about crime and criminals. These ideas are not objectively, scientifically rational, but they are understandable. What makes them problematic for the field of criminal justice is that they are treated as if they were rational, scientific theories. In fact they are nontheories. They resemble primitive beliefs found among certain tribal peoples as well as those in industrialized complex societies of the West.

Irrational, absurd, primitive beliefs abound in the United States (Spradley and Rynkiewich 1975). H. O. Mounce (1973) used those terms in his discussion of the conundrum of Azande witchcraft versus Western science. After E. E. Evans-Pritchard described Azande witchcraft (1937), Peter Winch (1964) took up the issue in terms of the philosophy of science. Winch concluded that Azande witchcraft and Western science were incommensurable because they participated in different language games as described by Ludwig Wittgenstein in his *Philosophical Investigations* (1953). Azande witchcraft pertained to social relations and existential morality, whereas science applied to pragmatic manipulation of the material world. Bronislaw Malinowski (1948, 1965) made a similar point with respect to the Trobriand Islanders. Magic, according to Winch and Malinowski, applies in realms not amenable to science or other kinds of pragmatic technology. Although Mounce disputed Winch's interpretation of Wittgenstein's language games, Mounce's (1973) conclusion makes headway toward understanding the role of nontheories in criminal justice. The following steps in his argument cite well-known American social practices.

> Married couples often feel upset at the loss of a wedding ring. This feeling... is neither rational nor irrational. It is just the way that many people, at least, happen to feel. There comes a point however at which the feeling passes into what is plainly absurd. For example, one can find oneself thinking "This is a bad sign. If we don't find that ring soon I'm sure something will go wrong with our marriage". (353).

> . . .

> What we have here is a belief which is crazy... this is not because it is a distortion of some previously existing activity... On the contrary, it is rooted in reactions that are as primitive as almost any. (355)

> . . .

> My action does not have a purpose in the sense of bringing something about; it is merely the expression of a wish. (356)

> . . .

> What gives rise to these beliefs is not, for example, a deficiency in intellect, but certain tendencies or reactions which in connexion with certain deep human emotions such as love of a friend or fear of an enemy are likely to mislead us all. (362)

Mounce described beliefs in which causally unrelated symbols are believed to effect actions or policies not as rational solutions to problems but expressions of wishes, which themselves are formulations of deep human emotions connected to friends and enemies. Azande witchcraft, then, along with wedding ring worries and the public burning of effigies (355), are expressions of wishes taken in social forms. They are what Freud (1900) said dreams represent for psychological processes. They are also how George Herbert Mead (1918) explained systems of criminal justice.

Mead argued that punitive criminal justice systems make no sense either as deterrence or as retribution. Retribution, he said, is absurd because commensurability does not exist between sin and suffering. We recognize its validity "only in resenting and condemning injury, not in rendering justice for the evil done" (Mead 1918:583). As for deterrence, he said what should be obvious even to casual observers. "... [A] system of punishments assessed with reference to their deterrent powers not only works very inadequately in repressing crime but also preserves a criminal class" (583). Mead suggested looking at one particular element of the criminal justice process, criminal court procedure. Three characteristics stand out: the solemnity of the proceedings, the majesty of the law, and the impersonal character of justice. These characteristics reveal the purpose of law, which is defense of the social group. Mead argued that crime and criminals represent threats to the social order. "In this attitude we are defending the social structure against an enemy with all the animus which the threat to our own interests calls out" (585). Nonetheless, the institutions defended by the law are valued not for their functionality but for their symbolic meaning expressing attachment to the group. The criminal is one who becomes an outsider, a barbarian at the gates. Mead illustrated by reference to "Property [which] becomes sacred not because of its social uses but because all the community is as one in its defense ..." (589). The institutions of society perform essential existential functions for its members as they allow them to transcend their purely biological forms, enabling humans to transcend their inevitable death despite its certainty. They are a wish fulfilled collectively. Criminals are enemies because they represent existential threats. A punitive criminal justice system treats them as enemies by constructing identities for them as deadly foes. They are made into the other, not just individual community members who have transgressed. In Mead's view, the currently operative criminal justice system cannot be understood on rational and pragmatic grounds. The system operates on a war footing not because of a deficiency of collective intellect but because it taps into deep human emotions about friend and foe, power and dependency, life and death.

Mead's analysis distinguishes between social actions emerging from rational discourse and those emanating out of primitive emotions. The distinction parallels the point made by Mounce and Malinowski. Those things people can control through practical technology, they will. Those they cannot, bring forth magical solutions. Often, the same activity includes both strategies.

Robert Cover (1982) made a distinction that, while not exactly the same, extends the argument. Cover used a sixteenth-century commentator on the Torah to illustrate how cultural values bind people through a system of moral ties into a community. "These 'strong' forces—for Caro, 'Torah, worship, and deeds of kindness'—*create* the normative worlds in which law is predominantly a system of meaning rather than an imposition of force" (12). Cover called this kind of system "paideic." In paideic systems, discourse is initiatory, celebratory, expressive, and performative, rather than critical and analytic. Alternative to the paideic, Cover wrote of what he called the "imperial." In the imperial model, norms are universal and enforced by institutions. The imperial discourses gain validity through external objectivity—that is, practical effects on a material world. Relatively simple societies, like the Azande, exhibit many practices that are paideic. Simple societies tend to have something approaching a unitary value system. Complex societies, the modern nation-state, are predominantly imperial where there are many competing value systems, but a few are enforced by law. Cover found a radical dichotomy between these two systems, the paideic and imperial. The many values in complex societies that are not enforced by law have a "destabilizing influence upon power" (18). Complex societies have many countercultures that tend to destabilize social structures through which elites exercise power, of which the state is the paramount structure.

> The state's claims over legal meaning are, at bottom, so closely tied to the state's imperfect monopoly over the domain of violence that the claim of a community to an autonomous meaning must be linked to the community's willingness to live out its meaning in defiance. Outright defiance, guerrilla warfare, and terrorism are, of course, the most direct responses. They are responses, however, that may—as in the United States—be unjustifiable and doomed to failure. (52)

Challenges to reigning values and norms accompany social upheaval. The 1960s in the United States, indeed around the world, were a time of upheaval. The heretofore underground, countercultural discourses gained increasingly outward expression. The civil rights movement challenged the values of American racism and the laws supporting it. The anti-Vietnam War movement challenged the military-industrial complex (Eisenhower 1961) and imperialistic force. Controls over sexual and reproductive behavior, the pharmacopeia, and the regulation of labor all came under attack. Values, views, and attitudes, along with norms of behavior that had been taken for granted as enforceable and enforced, seemed no longer so stable. Of course norm violation appeared rampant at all levels of behavior.

Sundry politicians and others with access to public voice promoted the belief that the country faced a crime wave of unprecedented proportions. A reaction against the challenges and violations was as inevitable as it was far reaching.

On August 23, 1971, two months before his nomination to the U.S. Supreme Court, Lewis Powell wrote a memorandum to his friend and neighbor Eugene Sydnor, chairman of the Education Committee of the U.S. Chamber of Commerce, formalizing his thoughts arising from several of their conversations about the state of America. Powell's diagnosis focused on the economy, but he said the attack was not limited to economic matters.

> Rather, the assault on the enterprise system is broadly based and consistently pursued. It is gaining momentum and converts... A frontal assault was made on our government, our system of justice, and the free enterprise system... The foregoing references illustrate the broad, shotgun attack on the system itself. (Powell 1971)

Powell's prescriptions to fight the attack were a program for wish fulfillment. After organizing the ruling class, which Powell euphemistically called "businessmen," the first target was higher education, and especially social science faculty. Powell called for support for scholars "who do believe in the system." He also recommended a broad public relations campaign, gaining influence and ultimately control of print media, including scholarly journals, along with other more traditional political and legal maneuvers.

Powell's memorandum is instructive, because it brings out what Winch, Mounce, Mead, and Cover left out—a class analysis. Powell enunciated the elites' fears that their system would fall to assaults by the lower classes. The elites could use their wealth and power to realize their wishes, and they did. Dario Melossi (1993) calls this the moral gazette and social whip they use when they perceive threats to their privileges. Wealth and influence supported efforts to realign scholarship, and concomitantly policy, in criminal justice, along with other fields, of course.

Three criminal justice wishes

Three leading theories in mainstream criminal justice derive their preeminence from the effectuation of Lewis Powell's prescriptions for taking back control of America. Their roots predated Powell's memo, but the success of the theories needed leverage from ruling class money and influence. Lewis Powell had recommended that those who had a stake in keeping control of America should financially support scholars and writing that conveyed conservative ideas. Further, they should use their influence on such things as universities' boards of trustees to make sure the right kind of scholars achieved prominent positions.

Broken Windows appeared in 1982, Rational Choice in 1986, and Self-Control in 1990, but their publication merely put the finishing touches on theoretical developments going back to the late 1960s. As Ronald Akers (1990) pointed out, Rational Choice owes its paternity to Gary Becker's enunciation of the economy and criminal law perspective in his 1968 article "Crime and Punishment: An Economic Approach." Becker proposed using a typical device in abstract economics—the rational man—to explain criminality and, with the usual economistic legerdemain, crime as well: "Some persons become 'criminals,' therefore, not because their basic motivation differs from that of other persons, but because their benefits and costs differ" (Becker 1968:176). Economists use this device to plug in active agents to drive their mathematical models. Their rational actors are inventions having no real-person referents. When applied to criminal justice, where one occasionally encounters real people, they become, in Baudrillard's (1981) terms, simulacra, copies without an original.

Broken Windows traces its lineage through James Q. Wilson. Basically, "Broken windows policing is merely the professional model on steroids" (Herbert 2001). The professional model is what James Q. Wilson called the legalistic style in his 1968 *Varieties of Police Behavior* (Langworthy 1985; Sampson and Cohen 1988; Wilson and Boland 1978. In that earlier work he appeared to describe a type of policing associated with certain kinds of urban political economy, especially western cities such as Los Angeles. In the 1982 *Atlantic Monthly* article where Broken Windows first appeared, he advocated the model in its extreme form. Nonetheless, the same advocacy is between the lines in his 1968 book on police, and in the context of his work with Edward C. Banfield and Wilson (1963) along with other works on urban politics (Wilson 1968a). In these earlier writings, Wilson took what has become known as a neoconservative position: a main goal of policing is controlling the potentially disruptive elements in urban society.

Self-Control theory derives from earlier ideas of Travis Hirschi, who was known for his social bond theory as described in his 1969 book *Causes of Delinquency*. Despite his own protestations to the contrary in his introduction to the 2002 reissue of the book (Hirschi 2002), Self-Control theory is just a stripped-down version of his social bond theory without obfuscatory claims to anything social about the theory. It appears to be purely psychologistic. It explains crime by explaining criminals, who are a distinct breed in this theory because they lack self-control. Careful reading, however, reveals something sociologistic. Those who lack self-control have other characteristics besides criminality. They also tend to smoke, drink, gamble, have extramarital sex, prefer exciting recreations, enjoy physical pursuits (as opposed to professorial mental ones), and generally fit a particular class-based stereotype. The core of Self-Control theory turns out to be a stereotyped middle class.

> Cohen's [1955] description of middle-class values is quoted at length because it is a detailed conceptualization of what we mean by self-control. In fact, just as we suggest that crime is a by-product of a tendency to seek immediate pleasure ... (Gottfredson and Hirschi 1990:143)

Taken at its word, Self-Control theory could serve a useful purpose in that it could be used to explain the street criminality of the *lumpen* and the suite criminality of the upper class. It does not fit, however, because Gottfredson and Hirschi have not used *middle-class* in any social scientific way, but in the popular American way that really means "people like us." That is what makes Self-Control theory sociologistic instead of sociological.

Broken Windows, Rational Choice, and Self-Control are not theories in a meaningful, scientific sense, no matter how often the criminal justice academy proclaims them as theories, or how often researchers say they are testing them. They are authoritarian programs grounded in irrational beliefs. What makes them authoritarian is their reliance on that apparatus of the state power that ultimately relies on physical force to carry out its mission—police power. They are also conservative in their aim, at least as applied in criminal justice: preservation of hierarchy within the polity.

The moral life of criminal justice

All three also espouse a particular morality that helps maintain the social, political, and economic status quo. They treat morality as prescriptive, not descriptive or analytic. A basic part of their program is deontological. Despite their deontological bent, they devote little discussion to analyzing contemporary morality or ethical systems.

In the case of Broken Windows, the clearest view of the morality is through the lens of James Q. Wilson's association with neoconservatism. A principle tenet of neoconservative philosophy is an abhorrence of moral relativism. Although woven throughout his writings, Wilson's views were most explicitly and expansively stated in his 1993 book *The Moral Sense*. In that extended essay, Wilson refers to Aristotle's *Nichomachean Ethics* often enough that one might think he is Aristotelian. Unfortunately, he uses Aristotle much as Leo Strauss used Plato—in a most peculiar way. Much of the thrust of Aristotle's ethical argument refuted the Platonic inclination to find an overarching moral principle toward which all ethical systems must aspire. Instead, Aristotle says, ethics is all about gaining happiness, and the way to be happy is for every person to realize his (and Aristotle did mean *his*) potentials. The best way to do that was through moderation—the well-known principle of the golden mean.

Aristotle also made ethics and morality a political matter in which the citizens of the polis devised laws to help everyone live a full life and be happy. If anything, the moral relativists Wilson so dislikes—he singles out Richard Rorty in particular—could use Aristotle as their foundation. Nonetheless, Wilson is up to something else. He uses Aristotle to further his argument in favor of legislating morality. The morality, however, is not one of self-realization, but an inborn sense; it is part of human biology. Wilson even makes a distorted Darwinian argument for innate morality, saying that it has survival value. It does not occur to him, at least not explicitly in his writings, that human constructions of moral systems are adapted to our biological heritage as social primates. Morality is human rationalization for the norms we create to go on living in groups, a necessity for such creatures as ourselves. He avers an innate moral sense that not only shores up hierarchy but supports an inherited disposition, and by implication, the right to rule. In this respect, Wilson joins the main ideologues arguing for a reaction against Enlightenment liberalism. Wilson's philosophy, and the analyses and policy proposals that flow from it, have the same neoconservative roots.

Morality, so-called middle-class values (*supra*), undergirds Self-Control, but there it is not a biological condition. Gottfredson and Hirschi explain that it comes from child-rearing practices (1990:97). That is, parents with low self-control do not instill self-control in their children. Inherited hierarchy is maintained socially rather than biologically. Gottfredson and Hirschi devote about ten pages to linking their ideas to the so-called classical theories. In their discussion of those Enlightenment thinkers, they neglect the main point: Beccaria, Bentham, and others stressed common human rationality not as a psychological theory, but as a political theory. Rational constraint was meant to apply to government. They mention the utilitarianism of Cesare Beccaria and Jeremy Bentham, but the reader searches in vain for an explicit statement of ethics from Gottfredson and Hirschi. Is it Aristotelian, Humean, Spinozist; do they follow some contemporary ethicists, say Alasdair McIntyre or Thomas Nagel? They give no clue. Neither do their moral interests lie in some empirical evaluation of values, belief systems, and public policies such as those studies carried out by Harold Grasmick and others (1992) or Brandon Applegate, et al. (2000).

Finally, they do not pursue a well trod path of sociohistorical studies of religion in the tradition of Max Weber (1952, 1958a, 1958b) or the analytic *The Sacred Canopy* by Peter L. Berger (1967), to name just a few. Instead, they forge their simulated theories on templates of implicit value systems supportive of invidious hierarchy.

Rational Choice seems an unlikely candidate for moral embedment, but its applications speak otherwise. Consider the basic concept of criminality as a cost-benefit calculation. One would think a Rational Choice analysis would suit white-collar crime best. The rational choices of transnational corporate executives along with government officials and financiers devoting long hours to calculating the relative costs and benefits of stripping the resources from central Africa, promoting ethnic enmities, and providing weapons to fanatic military leaders would seem ideally suited to applying a Rational Choice analysis. Instead, Rational Choice more typically finds application to petty burglars and similar lower-level, and lower-class, miscreants.

These three programs outline ways to stop and even reverse the direction of social change associated with the 1960s. They embody diagnoses of social ills and prescriptions for their cure. They enunciate views of the power elite (Mills 1956) or ruling class (Domhoff 1967, 1979, 1983), but, as Paul Fussell (1983:15) points out, "the idea of class is notably embarrassing" in America. Social class has been banished from polite conversation for a long time, if not always. "That is, the ideological effort ... has been to eradicate class consciousness from the political realm, all the better to control the economic realm and hide its objective operations" (Smith 2007:88). Broken Windows, Rational Choice, and Self-Control are statements of political ideology with a moral underpinning, which serve ruling class interests while eliding their class origins. They resemble theatrical masks; they express one image in gross and simplistic terms while hiding, or at least disguising, their underlying import. That import is both a consequence and a condition for the other aspect of law and order, besides change, that Lawrence Friedman mentioned—commodification.

Commodifying law and order

Start with language. It articulates law. Going back to the Laws of Manu and Hammurabi's Code, law uses the linguistic code to codify social norms. Law and language share a highly abstract quality, and both come from people doing things with one another. They are the products of social interaction, or as Georg Simmel (1908a, 1908b) called it, sociation. Speaking people make language, so language is an abstraction from speaking. The products of linguistic interaction—words, sentences, and similar paraphernalia—take material form, in sound; in the case of writing, as ink on paper; in the case of Internet blogs, as electronic patterns; and so on. Language consists of linguistic interactions in space and time. Libraries house much language, collected through time and, of course, arranged spatially. People who speak do so in particular times and particular spaces. There is a good deal of contemporaneous speaking, even sometimes simultaneously. As people speak they recreate language, changing it ever so slightly all the time. The linguistic products they create, the words and other formations, are congealed interactions connected with people in relation to one another, to social relations.

People also make commodities through interactions in certain kinds of relation to one another. They produce things like oil, sugar, and Maine lobsters, cited by Lawrence M. Friedman as examples of commodities to which he likened law and order. What makes oil, sugar, and Maine lobsters commodities is not their intrinsic characteristics, but their role in a meaning-filled, human world. People extract petroleum and refine it for use, mainly as fuel, and sell it for that ultimate purpose. Without elaborate social institutions, including but not limited to political economies, oil would not be a commodity; neither would sugar, nor would Maine lobsters. The last minimally requires a State of Maine. All the interactions involved with making commodities make society, or at least a big part of it. That is, they *are* society, not just social. People doing things to, with, and against one another are the fabric of the social. Commodities, then, are congealed interactions associated with definite social relations, much as words are congealed linguistic interactions. In the case of the current, dominant system of capitalism, the wage system defines the social relations.

Commodification of law and order means the production of laws and the ordering of people. Once produced, laws and order enter the market for use and sale. Marx argued that commodities differ from other sorts of useful things in their relation to money. His famous construction of C-M-C, commodity-money-commodity, is the exchange of a useful product on the market. The seller realizes payment, and the buyer gets a useful product in return for the purchase. The buyer then uses up the commodity. This is what happens when people buy a house. They pay for a use value. The problem occurs because of what Marx calls mystification. Many house buyers think they can become little capitalists through their purchases. They think this because houses often increase in price. They forget that to become capitalists they must convert their money into capital, and that they cannot do if they want a place to live.

As Marx points out, the conversion to capital needs a different circuit, not C-M-C, but M-C-M. "Here it is not the piece of money that changes its place twice, but the commodity ... such a reflux is not dependent on the commodity being sold for more than was paid for it" (1867:147). The commodity must be resold to complete the M-C-M circuit. The point for the capitalist—the real estate developer, banker, or refinance company that sells the homeowners' debts—is to use the monies gained from buying and selling houses to buy more commodities and convert them to money so as to buy more commodities. These other commodities need not be, in fact usually are not, limited to houses, but include oil futures, sugar cane fields, or Maine lobsters, for example. That is because, "in the circulation M-C-M, both the money and commodity represent only different modes of existence of value itself, the money its general mode, and the commodity its particular, or, so to say, disguised mode" (151–152). The relevance for law and order as commodities, therefore, is to see them not for their use values, but for their exchange values, because that is where the investment can turn into capital. When capitalists purchase laws by, for instance, bribing legislators, or when they sell law-and-order services as do firms such as Wackenhut or Blackwater, use value is not their goal. The goal is capital accumulation. Therefore, what seem to be social relations among people (law and order) are material relations among things—that is, the fetishism of commodities.

> A commodity is therefore a mysterious thing, simply because in it the social character of men's labour appears to them as an objective character stamped upon the product of their labour; because the relation of the producers to the sum total of their own labour is presented to them as a social relation, existing not between themselves, but between the products of their labour. This is the reason why the products of their labour become commodities. (77)

In the case of law and order, there is a double mystification. It is presented as a social relation, but it is really a commodity, which originated as a social relation. Of course, people produce law and order when they enter into relations with each other. Those relations are sold back to them as commodities. Eliminate the capitalists and the (bribed) legislators, and the scales would fall from all our eyes. In Thesis 11 of his "Theses on Feuerbach" (1845/1983) Marx famously said, "The philosophers have only *interpreted* the world, in various ways; the point, however, is to *change* it." Yet he also pointed out that theory can be a material force if it is radical and speaks to the needs of people (Marx 1844). What is needed, then, is a radical theory of crime, law and order.

A Theory of Crime, Law and Order

As the explananda are social phenomena, the theories should be social scientific—not in a restrictive, purely sociological sense, but admitting the broadest kind of explanations. These may include psychological or biological phenomena. They will be theories about humans and what they do to, for, with, and against each other. Social scientific theories must recognize humans as social primates.

That is enough for the social part, at least for now. The scientific part has more complexity and perhaps more controversy. As one philosopher of science, Mary Hesse, observed over a quarter century ago, the scientificity of knowledge has been changing. The work of, among others, Thomas Kuhn, Paul Feyerabend, and W. V. O. Quine challenges previously held assumptions of science: naïve realism, the possibility of a universal scientific language, and the correspondence theory of truth (Hesse 1980:vii).

Science offers truth claims. Science is one of several human endeavors wherein those who work within it follow certain procedures and do so based on certain unquestionable assumptions. Social scientific theories, therefore, must also use the general assumptions of science and rely on the scientific method. To say one uses science means one assumes that external reality exists regardless of anyone's awareness of it, that humans gain access to that reality through their senses, and that the universe operates according to discoverable regularities. These assumptions underlie all scientific inquiries. Scientific method also displays certain characteristics. First, science relies on a combination of reason and observation working in concert. Second, scientific observers use controls. Third, scientific method aims at objective knowledge. Fourth, the truths discoverable by science are objective as opposed to subjective, which is to say that they are true not just for their discoverer, but for all those who follow the method, because they are correct accounts of external reality. The foregoing assumptions and characteristics distinguish science from other approaches offering truth claims, such as religion or the arts.

Scientific theories explain observed phenomena. The explanations also have to use systematic and consistent logic; not haphazard, idiosyncratic, or coincidental. These requirements distinguish science from magic, as the latter practices a technology relying on extraordinary logic (Bronowski 1978; Malinowski 1926, 1948, 1965). Scientific theories must not only use a consistent logic but also comport with regularities or scientific laws, both those internal to the theory and other well-established observational regularities.

One such regularity is more in the nature of a model of human nature. Most clearly explicated by Clifford Geertz (1965), this model rejects the uniformitarian view associated with the European Enlightenment. The Enlightenment view holds humans to be of a piece with nature such that all have some core that is the same the world over. Differences in time, place, and circumstance pile on top of this essential core in a sort of layer cake fashion. The Enlightenment model of uniformitarian nature clashes with the regularity that humans are always and everywhere enculturated, else they are not human. Geertz put it this way:

> Whatever else modern anthropology asserts—and it seems to have asserted almost everything at one time or another—it is firm in the conviction that men unmodified by the customs of particular places do not in fact exist, have never existed, and most important, could not in the very nature of the case exist. (96)

Two important implications follow. First, the Cartesian mind-body dualism disappears. Second, reductive explanations of humankind reduced to chemical, biological, or other similar explanations run afoul of having no empirical referents, as simply physical humans do not exist. "We are, in sum, incomplete or unfinished animals who complete or finish ourselves through culture..." (112–113), particular cultures we ourselves create. "Our ideas, our values, our acts, even our emotions, are, like our nervous system itself, cultural products..." (114). The chemistry, biology, psychology, sociology, and culture of humans does not resemble a layer cake, but a multidimensional process in which all these natures interact, producing not things but dynamic and semiopen systems.

The foregoing dynamic, nonuniform model of humanity does not, however, negate the psychic unity of humankind. Just as all humans have the innate capacity for speech, but individual humans speak particular languages, so all have the capacity for thought, reason, and observation, but the particulars vary as much as languages. We are not bound by the language or languages we first learned; humans can and do learn other languages. Humans do not have an essential character, but we share a common heritage and therefore share common capacities, among which are those that permit learning foreign cultures and thereby gaining empathy. Simply stated, we can understand each other, because we are human. As Harry Stack Sullivan said, we are all more human than anything else (1953:33).

Furthermore, the dynamic, open system model means that all human endeavors—beliefs, institutions, practices, and so on—share the same characteristic dynamism. Human works are recursive and reflexive. All human products operate dialectically with positive and negative feedback producing an ever-changing social, cultural, and historical landscape.

Therefore, objective knowledge of human products cannot assume fixity of its object. Physicists discovered the Heisenberg uncertainty principle, in which the act of observation limits what they can describe about sub-atomic particles. Social scientists face a vastly more complicated problem in that the very nature of what they study constantly changes, not just by the fact of their study of it, but because of other ongoing forces, which they cannot control. There are implications here for criminal justice theorizing.

In a now undeservedly neglected 1969 article, Leroy Gould used chang-ing patterns of bank robbery and automobile theft to illustrate a larger theoretical point. He noted that explaining bank robbery by looking at bank robbers or car theft by looking at car thieves merely showed that over time different kinds of people engaged in these felonious pursuits. In addi-tion, characteristics of the loot changed, as did the victims, the detectors of crime, and of course the penal system that processed the cops' catch. To be worthy of the name, criminal justice theory will have to explain four things, all in continual dynamic relation to each other: crime, criminal-ity, criminalization, and criminal justice institutions. Patterns of crime do not change without changes in who commits them, how the act came to be deemed criminal, and the institutional arrangements dedicated to deal-ing with such activity. Gould's perspicacity remained unrecognized even in Martin Killias's 2006 article that tried to integrate crime patterns and social change. There are more complications in store.

C. Wright Mills (1959) maintained that any social study must explain biography, history, and their intersections in society. He elaborated with three questions: 1) What is the structure of a particular society? 2) Where does it stand in human history? 3) What varieties of people prevail in a par-ticular society at a particular period? Crime, criminality, criminalization, and criminal justice institutions are always socially situated. Criminal jus-tice theories should not ignore that fact by treating crime as an abstract evil, criminals as essentially wicked, criminal legislation as a mainly unques-tioned assumption, and criminal justice institutions as embodiments of political ideals. Unfortunately, that is what the main current of American criminal justice theory and research has done, beginning in about 1970 and increasingly ever since. Its cause lies with changes in two of Mills's three questions. American social structure has changed by becoming more hierarchical, and related to increasing inequality and hierarchy, certain kinds of people have come to prevail. Those changes have caused changes in the third. The United States has become the most incarcerated society in human history, far outpacing such paragons of imprisonment as Nazi Germany, Stalinist Russia, and apartheid South Africa.

The troubles in criminal justice theorizing are directly linked to particular historical changes in American society over the last third of the twentieth century. Moreover, criminal justice theoretical shortcomings also connect with a particular strain in social and political philosophy, which itself is closely associated with the historical changes. Two exponents of the strain of thought have been influential—one directly, the other less so. They are Leo Strauss at the University of Chicago and the former Nazi jurist and legal and political philosopher Carl Schmitt. Strauss taught and influenced a group of currently influential policy makers and academics known as the neoconservatives. He influenced James Q. Wilson through his friend and Wilson's mentor, Edward Banfield. Schmitt was recently rediscovered, oddly or perhaps not so oddly, by self-identified leftist intellectuals, especially those with a continental bent. In 2003, for instance, Telos published a new translation of Schmitt's *The Nomos of the Earth*, originally published in 1950 with a second German edition in 1974. I will argue that recent social and political changes in the United States, of which criminal justice institutions are integral, owe their theoretical and philosophical foundations to Strauss's neoconservatism and Schmitt's neofascism.

America and the world are not without alternatives. Interesting and potentially influential criminal justice theorizing can move from the margins to center stage. Social and political philosophies and theories opposing those of Strauss and Schmitt can form foundations for new kinds of theories about crime, law and order. Jeffrey T. Walker (2006:556) referred to John H. Laub's lament that "criminal justice/criminology was unable to properly utilize scientific method to examine issues of crime and justice." Laub (2006) had an axe to grind inasmuch as he advocated the adoption of his own, presumably multidisciplinary life-course theory in favor of overreliance on sociology. Walker went on to say that Laub did not go far enough; criminology/criminal justice ought to be radically transdisciplinary. Walker proposed using nonlinear analysis or chaos theory, and he called this new theoretical framework Ecodynamics Theory. I would say Walker did not go far enough.

The last part of the book will employ several approaches to sketch out some templates for new theoretical frameworks in criminal justice. They include world-systems analysis, chaos theory, and a new view of historical semiotics. The last extends Eric Havelock's (1983) insight that consciousness changed when logos replaced mythos as the dominant form of discourse. I argue that since about the middle of the twentieth century, an equally momentous change has been under way, transforming our writing-based discourse into one built on icons. The transition is roughly as follows: *mythos* (to ca. 550 BCE), *logos* (550 BCE to 1950 CE), and *iconos* (1950 CE on). The field of criminal justice is an apt place to study and employ the concept of a transition from logos to iconos, as the centrality of the Willie Horton icon implies, and various studies in cultural criminology explore. This iconic foundation, heretofore just a part of a media or cultural analysis, can take a basic and formative role in new criminal justice theorizing.

2

History of Criminal Justice Theory

With the exception of a few pockets such as classical Athens and ancient Rome, theories about criminal justice outside the modern West rely mainly on inference from the societies' laws. Prehistoric societies require a double inference, since archaeology cannot say much about criminal justice practices, let alone theories. For those societies, contemporary kinship-based societies have to serve as an inferential model. The classic study remains Arthur S. Diamond's 1971 *Primitive Law Past and Present*. It covers ancient civilizations such as Egypt, the classical period, medieval Europe, and contemporary tribal or kinship-based societies. Diamond categorized societies' laws according to their types of political economy, so his analysis has a strong social evolutionary bias. Nonetheless, it is a serviceable approach as it permits both generalizations about the functions of criminal justice and inferences about their rationales—that is, the theories.

For most of human history, until the Neolithic revolution about ten thousand years ago, people lived as nomadic foragers in small bands of a few hundred at most. Kinship, age, and sex marked the only persistent social divisions. Laws in such societies pertained to dispute resolution, as social cohesion was so important for both group and individual survival. Crimes with punishments revolved around kinship, for example incest and other sexual delicts. Punishment lay with injured parties except when an individual persisted in offensive behavior. Ejection from the group in such cases was tantamount to capital punishment.

Intervening in the reproductive cycles of plants and animals increases sedentary living and produces larger social groupings. Horticulture, pastoralism, and semisettled foraging typify the emergence of social control through laws with collectively enforced sanctions. A distinction emerged between offenses against all and those against a particular individual, parallel to the distinctions between crime versus tort and public versus private law. In addition to the kinship type of crimes, these societies often add witchcraft and crimes against good order such as interfering with mass gatherings, like buffalo hunts among the plains Indians (Llewellyn and Hoebel 1941; Lowie 1927; MacLeod 1927; Provinse 1937). Generally, the more complex and sedentary the society, the more that criminal laws and criminal justice institutions exert social control.

Early Imperial States

Several social institutions and cultural practices co-emerge: class-based stratification, state political organization, writing, and law codes. One could say law codes are the first written literature, although the first writing usually records taxes and movements of astronomical bodies. Early states came about through conquest. The ensuing imperial government replaced clan-controlled territories, and the extant law codes reflect this history and the needs of an urban-centered empire. The most complete of the ancient codes come from the Middle East, Mesopotamia, and Anatolia during the second millennium BCE. They contain prescriptions regarding behavior, often with consequences for not following the code. A typical example is from the Hittite code ca. 1500 BCE: "§59 If anyone steals a ram, they used to give 30 sheep: he shall give 5 ewes, 5 wethers and 5 lambs. And he shall look to his house for it" (Hoffner 1997:71). Clause 259 in Hammurabi's Code of ca. 1780 BCE states: "If any one steal a water-wheel from the field, he shall pay five shekels in money to its owner" (*Ancient History Sourcebook: Code of Hammurabi*). A final example comes from Assyria ca. 1075 BCE: "I.13. If the wife of a man go out from her house and visit a man where he lives, and he have intercourse with her, knowing that she is a man's wife, the man and also the woman they shall put to death" (*Ancient History Sourcebook: The Code of the Assura*).

These examples show two characteristics. First, they are addressed universally; the laws apply to everyone. Second, they specify exact consequences. In some cases the injured party must be compensated; in others, the miscreant must also compensate the king. Capital and corporal punishment are common. Corporal punishment sometimes called for dismemberment; in other cases for whipping, beating, or the like. The more complete codes, like that of Hammurabi, contain commercial regulations. Unlike modern systems of punishment, their rationale does not rest on an ideology of retribution, deterrence, or reform. Criminal justice in the ancient empires served the needs of the empire and its ruler. Ruling an empire meant keeping it cohesive so that competing clan leaders did not challenge imperial authority. The law codes specified exact consequences to prevent feuds and self-help retaliation, which could lead to a break-down of central authority (Diamond 1971). They also ensured the integrity of status groups and kinship, hence the law against adultery quoted from the Assyrian code. The codes provided for class divisions so that nobility, for instance, faced different consequences than commoners for violations. The early imperial state law codes reflect pragmatism and secularism. Unlike later natural law ideologies, references to the gods remain limited to invoking them, and the codes avoid prescriptions regarding religion.

The Classical Period

In the early classical period, from the seventh to the third century BCE, legal thinking and criminal justice made a turn toward the ethical as the basic rationale for identifying crimes and imposing punishments. Arguably this development connects with movements of religious reform that swept through the Old World at the time. Whether admitting of religious beliefs or a secular philosophy, classical Greek, Hebrew, Indian, and Chinese cultures tied law to the concept of justice. In addition, the promulgation of codes and workings of legal apparatuses carried with them explications and explanations of laws in terms of moral imperatives instead of bare pragmatic commands as in the codes of the early imperial states. The Greek and Hebrew traditions have the most extant accompanying literature. Additionally, they form the ethical and philosophical basis for current Anglo-American criminal justice.

In his study of Athenian homicide law, Edwin Carawan pointed to a cornerstone of the ethical turn in criminal justice, namely that "What constitutes right and wrong is now defined by a fixed standard to which all members of the community have access—justice is no longer dependent on the wisdom or the whim of 'bribe-devouring kings' (as Hesiod called them, WD [*Works and Days*], l.39)" (Carawan 1998:5). The reference is to Draco's code calling for a grand jury to decide interclan disputes. Carawan also argued that Draco's code brought into legal proceedings the concept of mind and intention, now called by its Latin name, mens rea. Prosecutors had to prove intent. Under Athenian law, they proved it procedurally by showing that the prosecution had availed itself of all witnesses and swearing their belief in their assessment of the defendant's intentions. Modern principles of the greater good or fairness did not guide the judges and juries of Athens; instead "The prosecutors must show that they have undertaken every reasonable measure to validate the evidence and eliminate other theories . . ." (387–388). The guilty mind depended on proofs of negligence and malice (389).

The codes of Draco, and later of Solon, institutionalized a system of laws, procedures, and decision making that realized through courts what ancient empires sought to achieve by authoritarian edicts. After Draco, the Athenian courts became the forum for self-help to redress wrongs and grievances, thereby providing a place where rhetoric rather than force resolved disputes. Aristotle (384-331 BCE) said Draco had set out his code in 621 BCE. By Aristotle's own time, Athenian institutions produced a semblance of justice, which he said was not in the laws but came from what people did in deciding matters. The decisions came from using reason and rhetoric (*Rhetoric* I.15.4-5) in the courts. The laws set the procedures, but justice in the abstract came from the virtue of the people living in the city, the polis. Urbanity is politics in this Aristotelian sense. The city makes possible the meting out of justice in the courts and other public bodies through collective action according to principles of justice and virtue. "[The virtue of] justice is a thing belonging to the city. For adjudication is an arrangement of the political partnership, and adjudication is judgment as to what is just" (*Politics* 1253a38). Aristotle articulated the first theory of criminal justice, tying it to his theories of ethics, rhetoric, and politics.

At about the same time Athens was institutionalizing a criminal justice, Nebuchadnezzar's Babylonia conquered Judah (586 BCE), one of the kingdoms of the Hebrews in Palestine, south of Israel, the other kingdom to the north. Leading citizens were taken to Babylon, hence the term "Babylonian captivity or exile." This event coincided with the destruction of the First Temple of Jerusalem. After the overthrow of Babylonia by the Persian Empire, in 537 BCE, the Persian ruler Cyrus the Great gave the Jews permission to return to their native land, and more than 40,000 are said to have availed themselves of the privilege, as noted in the Biblical accounts of Jehoiakin, Ezra, and Nehemiah. The latter two, Ezra and Nehemiah, served as Cyrus's emissaries as the Persians set up a new Hebrew state to serve as a frontier buffer. Ezra and Nehemiah had the task of bringing order in that state, and out of their, and others' efforts, the Jewish Torah was codified. While including older traditions, much as did Draco's code, the Ezra-Nehemiah mission gave rules of living to ensure domestic tranquility among the Jews and to secure a defensible territory for the Persian Empire. Arthur Diamond (1971) said that in the post-exilic period of the Second Temple the priestly order became more involved in the secular administration of justice. Diamond argued that the two kinds of justice, secular and religious, were separate: "... in the Hebrew mind law was one thing and *toráh* was another, and while the *toráh* was the province of the priest, the law and its administration belonged to the civil rulers" (138). Diamond's position confuses the pre-exilic with the post-exilic. The Torah was the basis for law and justice, whether administered by priests or secular administrators under Persian tutelage, and the Great Assembly made political, legal, and religious decisions.

The Jewish Great Assembly acted legislatively and judicially. This admixture of politics and adjudication typified Jewish legal institutions in the period of the Second Temple much as did the courts and assemblies of Athens. Ethical principles underlay both politics and law. Furthermore, the same kinds of public forums dealt with interpersonal disputes and wrongs along with collective decision making for the respective communities of Jews and Athenians. Public and private law had indistinct boundaries. For instance, treason to the polis was a public crime among Greeks. Those accused were tried in public courts, often the same courts that tried serious individual or private crimes such as murder. The classical civilizations politicized criminal justice.

Ancient Rome relied on Greek philosophy and borrowed many Greek forms for political and legal institutions. Roman innovations tended toward the bureaucratization of Greek ideas and forms. In keeping with the trend, Roman criminal justice compartmentalized public and private law. Roman law distinguished between *delicta privata*, which covered theft, bodily injury, and robbery, for example, and *crimina publica*, involving such acts as treason and assassination. Roman governmental offices prosecuted the latter as crimes against the state. Procedures and penalties varied according to whether an offense fell into the *crimina* or *delicta* category. Nonetheless, in practice the demarcation between public and private law was far from clear (Mousourakis 2003:140).

Roman Law and Medieval Europe

Several competing systems governed Europe after the fall of the Western Roman Empire. The Eastern Roman Emperor Justinian collected Roman law in the *Corpus Iurus Civilis* in three parts: the Codex (529 CE), containing statutes and imperial decrees; the Digest (533 CE), incorporating writings of learned jurists; and the Institutes (534 CE), which was a sort of textbook for law students. The Roman Catholic Church followed Roman conceptions of law for religious and ecclesiastical interests. The Church claimed universal application throughout western Christendom. A third kind of law rose from feudalism.

Feudal law came from an initially Roman conception of nexus, which was the bond between the lord and vassal. At first personal, it evolved into a bond between lineages. Feudal law gave the lord command of the law and decision-making power. A patchwork of law and lords' courts spread throughout medieval Europe as the feudal, manorial system replaced the imperial system of Rome. By 800 CE criminal justice became similarly localized. The laws and procedures followed regional traditions, clan interests, and often the whim of the lord. With the slow rise of monarchical power after the crusades of the twelfth and thirteenth centuries, royal law increasingly competed with feudal law. Moreover, an early merchant class of bourgeoisie favored Roman law, because of its recognition of commercial interests. Against the feudal barons, the bourgeoisie and kings allied themselves, albeit with mutual suspicion.

England followed the pattern, with merchants and the Tudors both seeking suppression of feudal controls and restrictions. By about 1600 the English throne under Elizabeth had gained the upper hand over the barons. The bourgeoisie turned to England's common law as protection against royal overreach. Edward Coke (1552–1634) argued for a common law based on what was really a feudal document, the Magna Carta. His argument, however, modernized it, by saying the principles applied not just to feudal barons but to all citizens of England. That is, the common law protected the rights of all, even against king and Parliament. Coke's writings and ideas traveled with the first English colonists to North America, forming a basic text for colonial legal thought.

English Roots and American Criminal Justice

By the middle of the eighteenth century, the American colonists' conception and practice of criminal justice reflected principles of English law. First, what had been private delicts under ancient Roman law became crimes against society, as they broke the king's peace. Second, those accused of crimes had the right to due process of law, which essentially meant notice of the charge against them and the opportunity to answer it. Third, juries played an important role: grand juries for investigations and indictment; petit juries to try facts. Fourth, basic rights of common law applied to all persons, especially habeas corpus, the protection from self-incrimination, and limitation on arbitrary searches and seizures. The politicians and jurists who led the American Revolution, wrote the Constitution, and organized politics and law in the early republic combined these English common-law principles with the works of three widely read authors: Cesare Beccaria (1738–1794), William Blackstone (1723–1780), and Jeremy Bentham (1748–1832).

Beccaria's 1764 *Of Crimes and Punishments* influenced such American luminaries as John Adams and Thomas Jefferson. Translated into English in 1767, it was the first to offer a comprehensive penal theory, which influenced reforms throughout continental Europe and especially in the American colonies. The book derived its main theories from European

Enlightenment philosophers such as Thomas Hobbes and John Locke. In keeping with them, Beccaria asserted rationality as definitive of all humanity, something that the philosophy and practices of the ancien régime denied to the lower classes. Since all citizens were rational, so must their government and laws be organized and applied rationally. A key part of his penology treated punishments as deterrents. He based his argument on an early version of utilitarian psychology—namely that people are motivated by the seeking of pleasure and avoidance of pain—and that a rational system of punishments should use rational and predictable punishments to deter crime generally and specifically. Beccaria also argued that the best deterrents were those minimally necessary to prevent crime. He therefore included in his treatise attacks against torture and capital punishment on the grounds of humanity and, theoretically more important, grounds of rationality and scientificity.

Blackstone's *Commentaries on the Laws of England* was published in four volumes between 1765 and 1769. Among the framers of the U.S. Constitution, lawyers and nonlawyers alike, knowledge of English common law as expounded by Blackstone was de rigueur (Bailyn, 1967; Rutland, 1955; Schwartz, 1977). In the early years of the republic, legal treatises and U.S. Supreme Court decisions are rife with references to Blackstone. Joseph Story is exemplary. Story was an early Supreme Court justice (1811–1845) and Harvard Law School professor, named to the Dane chair in 1829. His *Commentaries on the Constitution* (1987) have continued to influence legal thought into the twentieth century. Lest it be thought that Blackstone and his veneration of the common law faded away in the last century, a 2005 decision by the U.S. Supreme Court set aside a death sentence because the defendant had been shackled during the sentencing phase of the trial. In his per curiam decision Justice Breyer noted that shackles are permitted only by special need, saying, "This rule has deep roots in the common law..." Breyer went on, saying, "American courts have traditionally followed Blackstone's 'ancient' English rule..." (*Deck v. Missouri* 2005:630–631).

Jeremy Bentham wrote extensively on legal and political matters. He mainly influenced American thought in the early republic, although some of his ideas on penal reform such as the Panopticon were not put into practice until later in the nineteenth century. He fully developed, and is known as the basic expounder of, utilitarian philosophy. He associated himself with radical bourgeois political groups. Both a rationalist and pragmatist, his ideas diverge from the common-law tradition on two main points. First, he utterly rejected social contract theory, often referring to governments rising and falling through power rather than agreement. Second, he was suspicious of using case law as legislation and argued that positive law should be legislated by representative bodies, not judges. In this he offered a counterweight to Blackstone. These ideas fit with the American view that the most democratic and effective law-making bodies were republican legislatures.

The legacy of the three thinkers helped produce an American criminal justice system built around deterrence theory and criminal adjudication heavily weighted toward proceduralism. The systemization of American criminal justice throughout most of the nineteenth century reflected theories of crime and criminality that were rationally understandable and public policy that set up predictable sanctions. In effect, this predictability expressed expectations about how state power in the form of organized violence would be used. The penal laws and rules of procedure also carried within them justifications of the legitimacy of the exercise of that violence (Tigar and Levy 2000:251–252).

The Influence of European Science in the Nineteenth Century

Scientific criminology in the nineteenth century built on Beccaria's foundational assertion for a rational system. Evidence was to replace inquisition. Lockean empiricism formed Beccaria's epistemology, which challenged the assumption of volitional criminality of the ancien régime and its proclivity for cruel punishments and tortured inquisitions (Beirne 1993:40 ff). The social statistical studies of Adolphe Quetelet and André-Michel Guerry provided an auspicious beginning for criminology in nineteenth-century Europe. That their work subsequently suffered from distortion and disregard reflects the political ideologies of later times.

Quetelet's major work, *A Treatise on Man* (1835/1842) set forth five main propositions: (1) While individual behavior is too varied for law-like predictability, human behavior in the aggregate follows fixed laws. (2) Measures of central tendency reveal those laws. (3) Crime rates are predictable according to causative factors. (4) "Society includes within itself the germs of all the crimes committed . . . and the criminal is merely the instrument to execute them" (1835/1842:6). (5) Public policy can ameliorate crime and improve public morality. Putting them slightly differently, Piers Beirne (1993:155–156) commented that these propositions constituted virtually the only sociological analysis of crime until the 1880s. Conceptually similar, but using an obverse statistical analysis (Lindesmith and Levin 1937:657), Guerry, Quetelet's contemporary, introduced crime mapping correlated with social factors. Guerry mapped crime and related data according to geographical and temporal distribution. Both Guerry and Quetelet influenced the Chicago School criminologists

Clifford R. Shaw, Henry McKay, and Edwin Sutherland, as these twentieth-century researchers cite them (Whit 2002:xxvi). Emile Durkheim relied on their work for both conceptual and empirical support.

While Quetelet and Guerry enjoyed respect among social scholars in Europe, Darwin's work in biology beginning with his 1859 *On the Origin of Species* quickly found a distorted application in what became known as social Darwinism. Darwin's cousin Francis Dalton helped found and promote the eugenics movement, which applied principles of biological selection to management of human populations and became influential in American and British social and political policy. Herbert Spencer (1820–1903) popularized an evolutionary view of society based more on Lamarckian principles than Darwin's theory of natural selection. Famous for coining the term "survival of the fittest," Spencer's philosophy found an eager audience in Britain and the United States for reasons related less to its inherent worth and more to the political economies of those two countries. Both eugenics and Spencer's social Darwinism supported neocolonialism and laissez-faire economics, with the rationale of racial superiority of northern Europeans and justification for imperialist conquest and exploitation. These intellectual currents prepared the ground for the work of individualistic criminology associated with Cesare Lombroso's 1876 *L'Uomo delinquente*, later disseminated with modifications, editing, and translation into English by his daughter Gina Lombroso-Ferrero (1911). Richard L. Dugdale (1877), Arthur H. Estabrook (1916), and Henry H. Goddard (1912) espoused similar views. This biopsychological criminology became dominant in the United States by the early twentieth century, but it did not go unchallenged. Continental criminologists attacked it (e.g., Aschaffenburg 1913; Ferri 1896; Goring 1913; Tarde 1890), and even in America other voices had some influence. Although eclipsed in the middle third of the twentieth century in America, it returned in the last third of the century.

Emile Durkheim worked against the Lombrosian approach while promoting his scientific sociology. His *Division of Labor in Society* (1893), *Rules of the Sociological Method* (1895), and *Suicide* (1896) provided the main framework for American, sociologically oriented criminology for the Chicago School and related theorists such as Robert Merton and Thorsten Sellin. Durkheim's sociology contributed foundational concepts to criminological theory. First, by asserting that sociology is a science, he said that empirical social facts, such as the rate of homicide or suicide, were things that could be studied much as geologists study rocks, zoologists study fauna, or astronomers study planetary motion. Second, societies are people bound in their relationships by different types and degrees of solidarity, which is measurable, albeit indirectly. Durkheim operated with a theoretical framework of social evolution that had a definite direction from earlier, more primitive, simple societies with a type of solidarity he called mechanical, to more advanced, complex, civilized societies—such as France in the 1890s—with organic solidarity. All societies have crime, as it is functionally necessary for social change, norm clarification, and boundary setting. Moreover, according to him, each society has its own normal amount and kind of crime, according to its phase in social evolution. Simpler societies with mechanical solidarity tend to have repressive law using repressive sanctions and enforced by society as a whole. Complex, civilized societies with organic solidarity and increased individualism tend increasingly to practice restitutive law. Although Durkheim most famously applied his concept of anomie to suicide, later criminologists used it for analyzing crime. Anomie refers to social conditions in which norms break down, or become unclear or ambiguous. Like laws, Durkheim (1901) said, punishment covaries with social evolution such that less-developed societies tend to use intense and corporeal punishment, while advanced societies rely on deprivation of liberty. Durkheim is known for functionalism and evolutionism, and he should be known for his eminently bourgeois biases. All three colored his own work and therefore much of criminological thought that relies on it.

American Criminology

The first and most influential school of criminology in the United States emerged from the Chicago School of sociology at the University of Chicago. University of Chicago sociology began with Albion Small, who established the first department in 1892. Chicago sociologists used Chicago as a laboratory for study. Their theoretical base relied on the European thought of Durkheim and Georg Simmel, and on two Americans, the pragmatic philosophers George Herbert Mead and John Dewey, also at the University of Chicago. Another important connection and focus of research came from Jane Addams's Hull House near the Chicago stockyards. This last gave Chicago sociology a reformist bent that later showed in the criminologists' association with the Chicago Area Project designed to prevent juvenile delinquency. Methodologically diverse, the Chicago School under Robert E. Park and Ernest W. Burgess (1925) tethered their research to the theory of social ecology. In broad terms, social ecology linked kinds of social relationships, institutions, and subcultures to geographically defined areas of the city, which in turn grew from a stagelike urban growth and development.

The City of Chicago provided the context for Chicago School criminology, especially after World War I, although Thrasher published his famous study of gangs in 1915. The university criminologists worked with and in the Chicago Crime Commission founded in 1919. Chicago in the 1920s gained notoriety for its gangsters and their exploits, such as Al Capone and the St. Valentine's Day Massacre of 1929. Chicago criminologists notably disputed the then reigning understanding of crime as rooted in individual pathology—psychological, physiological, and often genetic. Instead, they argued for understanding crime in social terms. The most prominent of them in the early years were Clifford R. Shaw, Henry McKay, and Edwin Sutherland. Collectively and through a number of publications they laid the basis for important perspectives, concepts, and theories in criminology. The Chicago criminologists wrote of the criminal career concept, which recognized criminality as a learned process rather than an individual character trait. Cultural transmission theory argued that criminality follows generational communication—that is, one generation passes it on to the succeeding one. They argued that value conflict typifies criminogenic social conditions. Edwin Sutherland proposed his differential association theory, which associates crime with those situations in which social definitions favor criminality. The Chicago School is best known for social disorganization theory, correlating crime with communities where the basic social institutions—economy, education, family, politics, and so on—function poorly.

Two other sociologically oriented theorists stand out in contributing to American criminology during the interwar period: Robert K. Merton and Thorsten Sellin. Although neither was part of the Chicago School proper, their ideas were not incompatible. Merton made many contributions to sociology in general. His main criminological work came in 1938 in his article "Social Structure and Anomie," where he applied Durkheim's anomie concept to social structural constraints. Sellin, a sociologist at the University of Pennsylvania, developed the idea of cultural conflict as causative of crime.

Another influence came from Frankfurt School émigrés Georg Rusche and Otto Kirchheimer, whose 1939 *Punishment and Social Structure* argued that penal regimes follow structures and functions shaped by the reigning political economic forms. For instance, imprisonment with hard labor arose when factories and factory discipline emerged in the nineteenth century; slavery served as punishment in slave economies, corporal punishment in medieval and early modern Europe, and so on. When Marxist criminologists first applied their insights, they tended to use them in a limited way doing correlational studies between incarceration and unemployment rates. Later, with Foucault's (1975) recuperation of their ideas, their basic theory again spawned a variety of productive theoretical offspring.

The criminological writing of Erich Fromm, another Frankfurt School émigré, was translated into English in 2000. Fromm's psychoanalytic orientation offers an interesting connection between the Marxist analysis of Rusche and Kirchheimer and George Herbert Mead's (1918) social psychological critique of punitive mass psychology. Mead had said that the two main rationales for punishment, deterrence and retribution, make no sense. Punitive regimes merely create a criminal class, thereby refuting the deterrence argument, and retribution is defeated by the observation that a given punishment can never exactly equal the harm of the crime. Instead, Mead said, criminals are seen as threatening the social order, and people therefore respond to them as enemies rather than errant citizens. Fromm added to this that the role of the state in psychology resembles that of the father: "Criminal justice is like the rod on the wall, which is supposed to show even the well-behaved child that a child is a child, and a father a father" (1930:126). That is, criminal justice serves state control of the masses. Moreover, "The 'sense of justice' [Gerechtigkeitsgefühl] of the people, their legal-moral views are to a large extent nothing but the expression of an unconscious need for revenge and retribution" (Fromm 1931:146). The need arises, Fromm said, because the class system and exploitive nature of capitalism forces renunciations on the mass of people. Therefore, "Criminal justice is an indispensable psychological requirement for a class society" (147).

While social and social psychological theories developed at the University of Chicago, Columbia (with Merton), and Penn (with Sellin), at Harvard the biopsychological maintained a stronghold. Ernest A. Hooten, a physical anthropologist, carried on the Lombrosian tradition linking various phenotypes with criminality. The child psychiatrist William Healy mentored Sheldon and Eleanor Glueck (1930, 1943, 1950, 1956, 1968) (Snodgrass 1972), who carried on the biopsychological tradition. In a series of books beginning in 1930 and running through the 1960s, they linked delinquent propensities to body type and temperament. Criticized by criminologists at the time, they nevertheless proved a congenial source for the ideas of the criminal justice reaction in the 1970s.

The Emergence of Academic Criminal Justice

About 1970 the new academic field of criminal justice emerged to challenge criminology for theories and research on crime, criminality, criminalization, and criminal justice policy in the United States. The field had humble beginnings. Originating with federal monies for police education, most criminal justice departments were in community colleges and consisted of police science. As more money became available through the U.S. Law Enforcement Assistance Administration, the academy followed Parkinson's Law (1958). Throughout the 1970s and 1980s, criminal justice gained academic prestige with journals, Ph.D. programs, and the usual accoutrements of academic institutionalization. During this same period, criminology and criminal justice diverged. Originally many of the professoriat had been recruited from criminology, but criminal justice always habited itself as interdisciplinary, whereas criminology usually found itself in sociology departments.

Criminology in the 1970s and into the twenty-first century expanded on the theories first put forward during the interwar period. It also incorporated new perspectives. Theoretical criminology reflects developments in public health, geography, and linguistics and semiotics, to name a few fields. Critical criminology has branched out from basic Marxist and labeling approaches to include critical race theory, critical feminism of both radical and Marxist bent, postmodern criminology, and so on. Nonetheless, its connection with, and influence on, the practice of criminal justice waned as the academic field of criminal justice waxed. While criminal justice gained institutional success, its theoretical base has remained shallow. This phenomenon is explored in subsequent chapters.

3

The Nature of Theory

Confusion about the nature of theories plagues the field of criminal justice. An article by Michael Tonry serves as an example. "Looking Back to See the Future of Punishment in America" (Tonry 2007) contains, inter alia, a discussion of penological theories. The reason for choosing this article has much to do with what it and its author are not. First, Michael Tonry is not an ideologue masquerading as a scholar. He is an estimable academic light in criminal justice, a researcher, theoretician, critic, and editor of others' work. The article offers an enlightening and potentially useful appraisal of the past, present, and possible future for penal policy in the United States. It also contains what purports to be a discussion of theories, but they are not theories. They are penal philosophies, or ethics, or even ethos, but not theories.

Among the so-called theories, Tonry identified utilitarian, retributive, and restorative. Penal programs based on the liberal doctrine of Beccaria and Bentham constitute the utilitarian category. They aim at incapacitation, deterrence, and education or rehabilitation. Those of a retributive character follow some form of just deserts. Making good the harm characterizes the restorative theory.

Arguably, Beccaria and Bentham operated with theories, but their suggestions and programs were not theoretical. They were normative. They described what those Enlightenment writers believed *should* be done, based on their theories of government, human psychology, and so on. For the retributive approach, Tonry identified the work of Andrew von Hirsch (1976, 1985, and 1993) as exemplary. Similar to Beccaria and Bentham, von Hirsch's penal proposals doubtless rely on various social and political theories, but they are not themselves theoretical. Finally, the discussion of restorative justice programs refers to such things as drug courts, offender rehabilitation, and reentry programs. They suffer from theoretical lag: as Tonry says, "Practice has moved well ahead of theory" (Tonry 2007:371).

Unfortunately, there is no indication of what a theory of restorative justice might look like. The reason for the lack is not Tonry's failure of theoretical imagination. It is instead that restorative justice advocacy is not a penal theory.

So what kind of thing is penal theory? It would be something that explained penal practice. At least that is what a theory of what humans do through collective action would resemble. One such theory was that of George Herbert Mead, whose 1918 article explained why punishment is popularly supported in democratic societies. He said crime and criminals threaten social structures and relations in a way people perceive as existential. They therefore respond as if the criminals were enemies—barbarians at the gates. Mead's theory could be instructive in exactly the sort of discussion Tonry offered in his 2007 article. Penological theory, to be worthy of the name, has to explain the hows and whys of penal policies and practices. More generally, criminal justice theories have to explain the institution of criminal justice. The following describes several ways to accomplish that goal.

Theorizing Scientifically

It is tempting to begin by saying that criminal justice theories should be scientific, if only to make clear that the sense of the word *theory* is meant in a formal way. Nonetheless, asserting scientificity for criminal justice theories runs into a problem. The problem is what moved Susan Haack to write a new preface to her *Defending Science—Within Reason* (2006). The problem is misunderstanders; readers who leapfrog from a narrow, deferentialist view of science, as Haack called it, to read in claims that are not there. The deferentialist view conjures up images of science replete with massive, electronic, and usually very expensive equipment. With such images an aura of authority swirls around theories and the rest of science production. This is an honorific sense of science in which its findings must be right because they are scientific. It is also what made C. Wright Mills (1959) shy away from calling what he did social science, preferring the term social study. Along with Haack, I want to stress that the meaning of science employed here does not defer to science's aura of authority. On the contrary, what I mean by science is what Haack, borrowing from Charles Sanders Peirce, calls critical common sense.

> The core idea of Critical Common-sensism is that inquiry in the sciences is like empirical inquiry of the most ordinary, everyday kind—only conducted with greater care, detail, precision, and persistence, and often by many people within and across generations; and that the evidence with respect to

scientific claims and theories is like the evidence with respect to the most ordinary, everyday claims about the world—only denser, more complex, and almost always a pooled resource. (Haack 2006:iv)

Science is a main way of getting the truth about the world and the human condition. At least two other ways are religion and art. These three methods make truth claims. They promise we will find the truth if we follow their procedures. Each of these methods has important differences from the others.

Religion makes truth based on faith. No matter what else the religious method involves, at its base is that we accept what it reveals as true based on faith. In contrast, science is not faith based. Science is a logico-empirical method. Scientific methods depend not on faith but on human reason, the "logico" part, and observation, the empirical part. Empiricism limits our source of knowledge to that which we gain through our senses. Although scientific observation may use instruments that aid our observation, for example telescopes and microscopes, eventually all empirical knowledge comes through one or more of our senses. In contrast, certain kinds of religious knowledge, especially revelatory knowledge, may depend on mystical ways of learning things. Mysticism uses knowledge gained directly, immediately. The knowledge is gained in ways not mediated by the senses.

The difference between science and art is not the same kind of difference as that between science and religion. Whereas the difference between science and religion lies in the ways of gaining knowledge, the difference between science and art pertains to differences in the kind of knowledge. Art, in the sense I am using it, should be understood broadly. It includes music, painting, literature, drama, sculpture, dance, and so on. Art too offers truths about the world and human condition. Consider, for instance, the painting *Mona Lisa*. Gazing at it informs us about being human. So does seeing *Hamlet* performed, or reading the play. The same can be said about experiencing a variety of art forms. They tell us something that purports to be true about the world, our lives, or other people's lives. These artistic expressions help us make meaning and make our experiences more meaningful. Like science, artistic knowledge relies on empiricism. Our artistic knowledge comes through our senses. Art also appeals to human reason, and here I am not distinguishing between reason and emotion. Logic or rationality and feelings are both part of human reason broadly understood. The difference between science and art is that the truths we gain from them are different kinds of truths, different kinds of knowledge. Knowledge gained from gazing at the *Mona Lisa* or seeing a performance of *Hamlet* depends on the viewing subject. It is subjective knowledge. It is potentially different, if only slightly, for each viewing subject, whereas the kind of knowledge gained from a laboratory demonstration of the boiling point of water, to take a very simple example, should be the same for all who see the demonstration. That is, the boiling point of water is the same for any and all viewing subjects. It is objective knowledge. This is the difference between the truths of science and art. Science offers objective truth. Art's truths are subjective.

All methods of gaining knowledge have certain basic assumptions. As Kurt Gödel demonstrated in 1931 for arithmetic, all formal systems, of which scientific method is one, necessarily contain elements unprovable within the system. Science has at least four, which are its basic assumptions. They are as follows: First, reality exists. Second, it exists independently of mind. Third, it is accessible through the senses. Finally, reality has discoverable regularities; it is not random. The existence of a reality outside our own thoughts is not provable by the scientific method. Nonetheless, science cannot operate without this assumption. This reality is postulated as knowable through human senses, the requirement of empiricism. The scientific project holds out the hope that its researches will yield covering laws or regularities for all observed phenomena. The truth of this hope is not something science can ensure, but the project depends on striving toward it.

The scientific method yields truths through research. The research consists of systematic observation and reasoning about the observations. Scientific research has four possible goals: exploration, description, correlation, and explanation. Each goal is appropriate to a level or stage of knowledge. Each stage has its set of appropriate methodological techniques.

Consider an example of a famous bit of scientific research, that undertaken by Charles Darwin. The first stage of his research was exploratory. He set off on the HMS *Beagle* December 27, 1831, to survey the natural history (as science was called then) of South America. Initially, Darwin's purpose was to explore. As part of his exploration he brought instruments and accoutrements, perhaps chief among them his notebooks, to record what he observed. That is, Darwin prepared himself to record his observations by describing them—the second goal of research. In particular he noted the great variety of species of various organisms, especially finches in the Galapagos Islands. He correlated his observations of species' varieties with current ideas about change and similarities. Drawing on ideas from geology, paleontology, and other areas of science, Darwin correlated his observations of finches and other creatures, noting less differentiation within species than between them—a form of correlation. Finally, Darwin explained his observations and correlation by his theory of natural selection, which is an account of speciation over time. Simply stated, the theory of natural selection is that speciation is the result of organisms adapting to different ecological niches. The variety of niches correlates with the variety of organisms.

While all organisms are in complex, reciprocal relationships with their environment, the human organism is especially complicated. Humans' primary ecological niche is culture, which is a human invention. Therefore, the scientific study of humans has to contend with reciprocal relationships in ecologically dynamic systems but also the dialectics of human intervention. Studying human sociation includes more difficulties than studying physical or chemical dynamics because of the added complexities. Unlike carbon atoms, people decide to do things. Unfortunately, social scientists sometimes take their measure from physicists. They try to do science in the same way, and consequently miss or misconstrue the most important part, as the following illustrates: "The likelihood of a criminal act is the sum of a person's criminalistic tendencies plus his total situation, divided by his resistance . . . $C = (T + S)/R$" (Haack 2006:168 quoting Abrahamsen 1960:37). Haack meant to demonstrate absurdity, but as readers of criminal justice literature should recognize, this sort of reasoning currently passes for important theoretical insight.

Theories

While the word *theory* is often used casually, here is a formal definition of scientific theories. Theories are systematic explanations of observations in a framework of regularities. First, they are systematic, not haphazard. Theories explain a range or type of observations, and they are universal explanations for the type. So an explanation for why a particular person committed a particular crime is not a scientific theory, although it may be a "theory" of the crime.

Second, theories are explanations. They are not guesses or speculations. They are not predictions. They are not statements having a truth value—that is, theories are neither true nor false. They explain. Writing about theories in the natural sciences, Wilfrid Sellars (1961:71–72) said,

> Theories about observable things *do not explain empirical laws, they explain why observable things obey, to the extent they do, these empirical laws*; that is, they explain why individual objects of various kinds and in various circumstances in the observation framework behave in those ways in which it has been inductively established that they do behave.

Some theories may explain more, others less. Some may be more comprehensive, more general, more specific, more concise, and so on. Theories themselves are not falsifiable, and they are by definition not testable.

Fruitful theories provide a framework for hypotheses, which do have a truth value and are testable.

Third, what theories explain are observations. Scientific theories imply scientific observations, which are planned and controlled. By "controlled" I mean that the observational procedure is such as to exclude variations in the observation coming from differences in the way things are observed. Controls might mean using the same instrument, a microscope for example, possibly varying other conditions such as temperature or time of day, and so on.

Finally, theories must fit into one or more frameworks of regularities. Theories explain types of observations through models. Models are representations of reality. Models in turn are activated by laws, laws in the sense of regularities. To explain the rising and setting of the sun, for example, we would construct a model of planetary motion. The working of the model would follow the laws or regularities of mechanics, mainly Newton's laws of motion. The same applies to explaining human phenomena. Models represent social reality, and the workings of the model would follow established regularities of human, social behavior.

The basic building blocks of theories are concepts. Concepts are ideas with empirical content. Not all ideas have empirical content. Ideas about unicorns, for example, lack empirical content. Therefore, they are not concepts, because unicorns are not observable, although representations of ideas about unicorns are observable. A theory about unicorns would not be a theory about an animal, but a theory about ideas.

The conceptual building blocks are linked logically, often anchored in axioms or postulates. Axioms are basic assumptions. The four basic assumptions of science underlie all scientific theories. They operate as "givens," and therefore usually they are not explicitly articulated in theories. Axioms or postulates more specific to the theory and its subject matter often are explicitly stated in the theory. For example, in a theory about the rising and setting sun, it is not necessary to assert the existence of matter, of which the sun and planets are composed, but it would be useful to postulate that the earth and other celestial bodies have mass.

Theories embody the two faces of science, reason and observation. Theories are made of concepts, which include reference to empirical data, and the concepts are linked together by logic to form coherent statements.

Applying theories to research

The relation of theories to research is dialectical. That is, scientific research alternates between induction and deduction. At an inductive moment, researchers are gathering particular observations about which they generalize. They then apply the generalizations to new ways of observing; that is deduction. Charles Sanders Peirce called this process abduction.

All observations occur within one or more theoretical frameworks or orientations. They are always already theory laden (Feyerabend 1975; Quine 1960). Researchers strive to identify the theoretical orientations within which they are working, and the process of theorizing is helpful in illuminating otherwise implicit theories. A theory of criminality must have as part of it a theory of human motivation. If it appears to be lacking, it merely means the motivational theory is implicit—that is, hidden.

Theories also give meaning to data. The observation that the crime rate rose or fell during some duration of time is meaningless without a theory of crime. Usually there is more than one theory, and science demands that all theories should be explicit. In this case of crime rates, for instance, the measure of crime, say the Uniform Crime Reports, contains a theory about what constitutes crime.

Having formulated a theory, researchers then apply that theory in planning observations. The application process involves converting the general explanatory statements of the theory into applications to empirical observations. This conversion process results in more or less formal hypotheses.

Hypotheses are statements having truth value. The truth of them should be measurable. Hypotheses, then, are statements with a testable truth value. Following Alfred Tarski's 1933 essay on truth in formal languages, truth is defined by the following: The statement "snow is white" is true if and only if snow is white. "Snow is white" is a hypothesis. In order to test its truth value—that is, measure how true it is—researchers must specify how to define "snow" and "white" and measure whiteness, which is the variable in the hypothesis. Subjecting the hypothesis to empirical test requires finding some snow and measuring its whiteness. An adequate test involves controlled observations. One would observe snow under a variety of conditions. Some snow is whiter than other snow. In the presence of dogs, some snow is yellow. On city streets, snow turns various shades of gray, depending on how long since it snowed. Having found degrees of truth in the hypothesis, the researchers turn back to the theory, which explains why snow is white. Is it necessary to modify or elaborate on the theory based on empirical observations? Perhaps. This model illustrates the scientific method, and relations among theories, hypotheses, operationalization, and empirical observations.

Important to note is that even if the snow researchers found no snow that was white, their finding would not make the theory—the explanation of why snow is white—false. Or, if they found all snow to be white, their findings would not prove the theory true. A lack of white snow would, at worst, make the theory not very usable. The theory would be disregarded, perhaps to be revived when someone found white snow. Alternatively, findings of only white snow cannot prove the theory true, because there may be some exception not yet found.

Sometimes theories entail a model of reality that is so different that the theories are what Thomas Kuhn (1970) called incommensurable. In Kuhn's terms, the theories represent different paradigms. One of his main examples used Newton's mechanics and Einstein's relativity. Edwin Hung (2006:9) illustrated Kuhn's notion with a parable.

> There is a group of children living in a room with a huge wall mirror. They can see that there are two types of (real) people: those who live in front of the mirror and those who live behind it. They call the latter kind persons-in-mirror, or PIMs. Soon, they notice that for each person in the room there is a PIM that looks exactly like him or her. In other words, each child has a counterpart PIM and vice versa. They further notice that as they move their counterparts move as well, always copying their movements.

In seeking an explanation for these observations, two consultants offer two different theories. One, a folk psychologist, according to Hung, says that PIMs have a disposition for mimicking behavior. The other consultant, a physicist, says the concept of PIMs has no empirical referent—that is, the physicist denies their ontological status. The physicist says that what appear to be PIMs are light images, and so their movements should be explained in terms of the laws of optics.

Hung's parable reveals several important principles. First, the physicist's theory is not of the deductive-nomological, or covering law, model of scientific theories following Carl Hempel (1965). Hempel's model says that observations of phenomena are explained by an initial condition through a law of nature. A body at rest is observed to begin moving. The deduction, using Newton's laws of motion, concludes that some force caused the movement. The physicist, according to Hung, does not deduce anything about the movement of PIMs, because the physicist denies their reality. Instead, the physicist shifts conceptual framework; a paradigm shift.

Second, the parable shows the solution to the problem of induction, the validity of which David Hume (1748) and Karl Popper (1959) denied. Popper said scientific discovery works by the hypothetical-deductive method using deduction alone, with falsification to test for the truth of theories. By Popper's lights, much of social studies could not be scientific, but his approach also would rule out a good deal of natural science. In the parable, the psychologist faces the problem of induction, because the psychological explanation has to account for the contingency of non-mimicking behavior by PIMs. The problem of induction simply states that there can never be enough observations to establish the truth of a regularity or theory. Logically, there could always be a PIM who did not mimic. The physicist's explanation does not try to explain why PIMs always are observed to mimic, or why there are no observations of nonmimicking behavior. Implicit in the physicist's theory is a theory about epistemology: " 'Why is the possible (namely, PIMs not mimicking') not actual?' as it is, can't be answered ... [Instead], 'Why is the possible *thought* to be possible? Why is the possible *thought* to be non-actual?' " (Hung 2006:12). The physicist turns an ontological question into one that is epistemological.

A great many criminal justice theories, especially Broken Windows and Self-Control, resemble the psychologist's explanation for PIMs mimicking behavior. They ask why criminals commit crimes or why some people are criminal. They then have to account for noncriminal behavior. Usually they account for noncriminal behavior by ignoring the fact that most, by far the overwhelming amount, of behavior by noncriminals (cf. non-PIMs) and criminals (PIMs) does not violate legal prohibitions. Just as the physicist's theory implied an epistemological question about why people *thought* PIMs mimic, so effective criminal justice theories ask why people *think* there is a category of people, criminals, who produce crime by their behavior.

In Hung's parable a limited, nonfruitful, and weak social science theory is replaced by an expansive, fruitful, and robust natural science theory. Nonetheless, the problem does not lie in the psychological theory. The problem has to do with the observations. The children in the parable fail to account for a variety of observable differences between themselves in the room and the images in the mirror. In effect, they fail to notice that what they call PIMs are images, representations. So despite Hung's apparent invidious comparison between natural and social science, we need social science to study humans and their works.

Explanation in Social Sciences

The social sciences, or as C. Wright Mills preferred, social studies, use four different kinds of explanation. The first is causal. Following Sigmund Freud's ideas (1895), causality for the social sciences recognizes four kinds of causation. These four kinds are beyond the two-type model of causation featuring necessary and sufficient causes. The four-cause model includes preconditions, specific cause, co-occurring, and triggering. Preconditions are equivalent to necessary causes; the specific cause is equivalent to the sufficient. Co-occurring causes are those that accompany the specific cause and may condition it, but are not sufficient in and of themselves to produce the effect. Triggering causes are those final events that directly precede the effect but do not explain it. For instance, that the First World War was caused by the assassination of Archduke Ferdinand would be a triggering cause. In many cases in the social sciences, there is no identifiable specific cause. There are only multiple co-occurring causes, all of which contribute to the effect, and some or all of which affect each other. In most cases multiple causation reigns in the social sciences; single, specific causes are rare. Real events among humans are overdetermined.

To explain why a match bursts into flame, there are certain necessary conditions such as an oxidant, fuel in the match head, and heat. The oxidant is supplied by oxygen in the air. The fuel is the chemical compound in the match head, and heat is supplied by friction. These are necessary and sufficient conditions to explain the match flame in the abstract world of chemistry and physics. They are woefully inadequate to explain why Paul Henreid struck a match to light the two cigarettes in his mouth, handing one lit cigarette to Bette Davis in the famous scene in the 1942 movie *Now, Voyager*.

Social science explanations use not just causal, but three additional kinds of explanation, according to Gupreet Mahajan (1997). The additions to causal explanations are reason-action, hermeneutic, and narrative. Reason-action explanations focus on actors. They try to give objective reasons why people act within a context of social forces. Reason-action explanations bring together objective covering laws of the social sciences with the recognition that history proceeds not by the abstract laws of social structures alone, but also by individuals taking certain courses of action. It brings human agency back into the causal equation.

Hermeneutic explanations also recognize human agency but pay less attention to objective laws. Instead, they focus on the agents' worldviews. Hermeneutic explanations are those that try to discern the world the way the actors experience it. In effect, they put the researchers in the shoes of those whom they study.

The fourth kind of explanation, narrative, offers yet another method of accounting for things. Narrative explanations explain events in their specificity. For example, they can give the story of the beginning of the First World War as they recount the way events unfolded for the main actors. They help researchers understand why the leaders of the great powers of Europe pushed their countries into war in 1914. Narrative explanations bridge the divide between *Verstehen* and *Erklärer*, between understanding and explanation in the narrower, causal sense. Narrative adds a dimension to deterministic explanations that underscores alternatives. Researchers use narrative to understand why actors chose particular paths when other paths were possible.

Bourdieu: The construction of social space-time

Pierre Bourdieu's theory of social space-time draws on the foregoing kinds of explanation, causal and noncausal. Recall the space of the children in the room who discovered persons-in-mirrors, PIMs. They divided the room in two: in front of the mirror and behind the mirror, and identified two classes of people according to their position with respect to the mirror. The PIM parable brings out a central problem in social science theory and research, the so-called Thomas theorem (Merton 1995): "If men define situations as real, they are real in their consequences" (Thomas and Thomas 1928:571–572). As Merton noted (1995:383), George Herbert Mead made a similar pronouncement. "If a thing is not recognized as true, then it does not function as true in the community" (Mead 1936:29).

Closely related problems involve Marx's fetishism and Korzybski's non-Aristotelian logic exemplified by the paradigmatic aphorism that the map is not the territory. Marx's fetishism (1867) is a form of hypostatization in which products of thought appear as objective phenomena. Alfred Korzybski (1958) developed a non-Aristotelian logic that distinguishes objects from their representations (maps) and any particular object at different points in time, as in $Object^{T1}$ ... $Object^{T2}$ ... $Object^{T3}$ and so on. The problem posed by the Thomas theorem was summed up by Bruce Lincoln: "categorizers come to be categorized according to their own categories" (1989:137).

Bourdieu advocated for a social analysis using a topology of social space. "The social field can be described as a multi-dimensional ... [in which] agents are distributed ... according to the overall value of the capital they possess [and] ... according to the composition of their capital—i.e., according to the relative weight of the different kinds of assets within their total assets" (Bourdieu 1985:724). Bourdieu's topology adds the distinction of social power, which he calls capital, to the ability to represent reality and have those representations taken for reality. Using the parable of the children in the room again, distinctions of power among the children would make some more influential than others. Some would identify persons-in-mirrors, and the rest would accept them as real, because of their different distributions in the social space.

The social space looks different depending on the observer's position within it—the perspective of a factory worker, a physician, a corporate CEO, and so forth. People move within social space by altering their social relationships. This social space and the relationships are real phenomena, not PIMs, not fetishes; territories instead of maps.

> What does exist is *a space of relationships* that is as real as a geographical space, in which movements are paid for in work, in efforts and above all, in time (moving up means raising oneself, climbing and acquiring the marks, the stigmata, of this effort). Distances within are also measured in time (time taken to raise or convert capital, for example). (726)

Bourdieu's social space-time is a kind of Einsteinian universe where points of observation are relative to one's acceleration and where the weight of capital bends the fabric of social space. People construct their views of reality according to a double structuration, objective and subjective. Objective structuration follows from the fact that properties of people and institutions do not offer themselves independently of perception (the Thomas theorem). For example, "possessors of substantial cultural capital are more likely to be museum-goers than those who lack such capital" (727). Subjective structuration depends on the schemes of representation available at any given time, especially those deposited in language, which are themselves the products of previous social struggles. The meaning of *freedom* varied enormously when uttered by a slave in the antebellum South versus by plantation owners ca. 1860, to use an extreme and historical example. "The categories of perception of the social world are . . . the product of the internalization, the incorporation, of the objective structures of social space" (728). This is why most social perceptions seem normal; they correspond to existing patterns of social relations. It also makes social analysis difficult. Varying perceptions lead people to act on the social world, and change it by their actions. Social analysis cannot rely on a kind of Newtonian differential calculus in which movements occur within stable frameworks of space and time. Instead, it must use an Einsteinian relativity and quantum mechanical calculation, because the basic frameworks are changed by the very things the analysts are trying to measure.

Lyotard: Postmodern space-time

"Thus the society of the future falls less within the province of a Newtonian anthropology (such as structuralism or systems theory) than a pragmatics of language particles" (Lyotard 1979:xxiv). Jean-François Lyotard popularized the term *postmodern* probably more than anyone else. Unfortunately, it and his associated ideas are too easily lost in translation. While recognizing a break with high modernism, which he identified as based on metanarratives, Lyotard did not mean to say that modernism had ended. Scholars in the humanities, especially literary and artistic critics, have made extensive use of Lyotard's work, but it is at least equally applicable to the social sciences. In that usage, his postmodernism should be understood politically. It is the postmodernism of the post – *Evenements de Mai, 1968*, a postmodernism of the failed revolution of 1968, and the reaction against it. Postmodernism here means a turn to the right-wing politics so evident in American criminal justice. The metanarratives are those stories legitimizing the prevailing regime. They are the often-implicit assumptions, the taken-for-granted ways of the world. Lyotard opposed postmodernism with the modernism in which such metanarratives legitimized knowledge, as in the case of philosophies of history, which implicitly inform the political science of democracy as the story of elections. Under a regime of metanarratives, what counts as truth, justice, law and order are all part of a grand narrative. "I define *postmodern* as incredulity toward metanarratives" (xxiv). He went on to define his question: "is a legitimation of the social bond, a just society, feasible in terms of a paradox analogous to that of scientific activity? What would such a paradox be?" (xxv). Lyotard's paradox is that "Scientific knowledge cannot know and make known that it is the true knowledge without resorting to the other, narrative, kind of knowledge, which from its point of view is no knowledge at all" (29).

Postmodernism's quarrel is not with modernity, but with modern*ism*— that is, an ideology of the modern. Its exemplars are David E. Apter (1965) and Walter W. Rostow (1960). They preached a kind of imperialism with a velvet glove, where development would bring world peace and prosperity so long as it took the form of so-called free enterprise capitalism coupled with Western-style parliamentary democracy. For Apter and Rostow, modernism contained a discourse with scientific trappings. They spoke in terms of laws of social change, which dictated a natural path for development. The kind of approach used by Apter's and Rostow's modernization theory showed up in artistic and literary developments of the mid-twentieth century as well. There one glimpses a modernism in architecture as in the international style of Le Corbusier and Frank Lloyd Wright, in literature such as John Updike and Saul Bellow, in abstract expressionism, and so on. In these fields of the humanities there was a canon, which indirectly expressed metanarratives about the story of the arts. The metanarratives implied a linear development, much like the linear development envisioned by modernization theory in political economy. The postmodernism of Lyotard is a reaction against this kind of high modernism. It took two opposing directions, which makes discussions about postmodernity doubly confusing. One direction was reactionary. It reacted against modern liberalism in the broadest sense of the term, not just politically but in all areas of life and culture. The other direction continued a radical critique of liberalism associated with the critical theory of Theodore Adorno and Max Horkheimer, among others.

Postmodernism appeared more as a caesura rather than a break with modernism. Lyotard advocated a postmodernism as a return to the fundamentals of modernity. Beginning more or less with the twentieth century, modernity put metanarratives to the question. Modernity continually challenges claims to a privileged position, hence the modernity of Einstein's relativity, Picasso's cubism (Miller 2001), Freud's psychology, George Herbert Mead's social psychology, and so on. Lyotard's assertions have to be understood as a dispute with Jürgen Habermas who argued, insofar as Lyotard was concerned, that legitimacy and justice come from consensus obtained through discussion. That is, once everyone agrees about the ways of the world, they can put into practice plans to improve them. It is a view that disregards both the Thomas theorem and Bourdieu's corollary to it. It disregards the fact that beliefs come from social arrangements, and unless the social arrangements, the sum of social relations, are already just, no amount of discussion can alter the inherent injustice of the ways of the world.

The paradox of science, then, comes down to a recognition that all science is part of human endeavor, and all human endeavor is bound by culture and history. Narratives forever entangle science. For example, the modernity of the twentieth century came from a cultural and historical milieu described in the 1848 *Manifesto of the Communist Party*.

> The bourgeoisie cannot exist without constantly revolutionising the instruments of production, and thereby the relations of production, and with them the whole relations of society. Conservation of the old modes of production in unaltered form, was, on the contrary, the first condition of existence for all earlier industrial classes. Constant revolutionising of production, uninterrupted disturbance of all social conditions, everlasting uncertainty and agitation distinguish the bourgeois epoch from all earlier ones. All fixed, fast-frozen relations, with their train of ancient and venerable prejudices and opinions, are swept away, all new-formed ones become antiquated before they can ossify. All that is solid melts into air, all that is holy is profaned, and man is at last compelled to face with sober senses his real conditions of life, and his relations with his kind. (Marx and Engels 1848:207).

The rise of bourgeois social relations brought a new way of looking at the world, modernity. All is change, there is no fixed point, no privileged position. Metanarratives are always questioned, all frameworks are contingent, all patterns ephemeral. This kind of world makes the Thomas theorem a Gricean implicature (Grice 1975). In a world of ever-changing social relations together with constant renewal of the material conditions of life, people will deconstruct and reconstruct according to their "real conditions of life," which are, in part, their own creation. Science cannot escape these conditions, but it can interrogate them. That Einstein discovered relativity at a time and place where social relations had largely eliminated "fixed, fast-frozen relations" should come as no surprise.

Debord's spectacular space-time

Politically, the high modernism of modernization theory coupled with postcolonial anticommunism laid the groundwork for the world revolution of 1968, its failure, and the subsequent reaction. John F. Kennedy's "Alliance for Progress" was emblematic. Focused on Latin America, the Alliance program supported improvements in education, public health, housing, and general social conditions through aid money and expertise. It raised expectations of peasants and urban workers, and it weakened control by traditional elites. The elites saw their centuries-old privileges eroded and the basis for the political power undermined. They believed the programs of the Alliance attacked the integrity of elites' control of large rural estates. As part of the Kennedy anticommunism program in general, and the reaction to the Cuban revolution in particular, the United States also shifted its emphasis in military assistance. Counterinsurgency replaced hemispheric defense as the main goal (Loveman and Davies 1997:23–27). The Kennedy policy combined foreign aid with counterinsurgency. The former weakened traditional political elites and encouraged popular demands for democracy and equality. The latter supported Latin American military and police apparatuses. The various indigenous revolutionary movements, whether inspired by Cuba or not, posed threats to political stability, which were met with militarized repression and often military coups and the installation of military regimes in Argentina (1976), Bolivia (1964), Brazil (1964), Chile (1973), Peru (1968), and Uruguay (1973).

With important national and regional differences, the pattern was repeated during the crisis of high modernism. In the Soviet Union and the Warsaw Pact countries, post-Stalinist liberalization coupled with exigency to expand the military during an increasingly expensive Cold War created demands for greater freedoms, decreasing control by traditional elites, and finally repressive measures by military force—for example the Prague Spring of 1968 followed by Soviet invasion. In France, the uprisings of 1968—*Les Evenements de Mai 1968*—preceded a Gaullist reaction. These were worldwide patterns, and they produced similar responses: high modernist liberalization, political instability, repression by force. In the United

States, they took forms directly related to the institution of the repressive criminal justice regime beginning in the 1970s.

Support for the civil rights movement from certain elements of the American ruling elite—in effect the high modernist, liberal wing of the ruling class (Domhoff 1979)—helped ensure eventual government support, vaguely under Kennedy, clearly under Johnson. Once again, this kind of liberalism weakened traditional elites in the South especially. It encouraged rising expectations everywhere, North and South. It came coupled with a major Cold War military effort in Vietnam. The reaction led by traditional elites in the South and the conservative wing of the ruling class led to the criminal justice reaction beginning with the 1968 election of Richard Nixon and its institutionalization with growing federal support throughout the 1970s and subsequent decades (Beckett 1997; Beckett and Sasson 2004).

The uprisings of 1968, identified by Immamuel Wallerstein (2004) as the failed world revolution, were truly worldwide: Chicago, Mexico City, Paris, and Prague, to name a few. On their threshold, Guy Debord (1967) proffered a critical theory that foresaw them and their repercussions. In his 1992 preface to the third edition, he noted that what he called the Great Schism ended with the collapse of the Soviet Union. The Communist regimes of the East had, in his estimation, merely been a "substitute ruling class for the market economy . . . an undeveloped type of ruling class" (Debord 1967:9). The postmodern political reaction against liberalism after 1968 shattered the liberal consensus forged in the advanced capitalist centers in the nineteenth century. The collapse of the Soviet Union ended the old Stalinist policing which had managed perceptions through force. "The ideology that took on material form did not transform the world economically, as capitalism in its affluent stage had done; it succeeded only in using police methods to transform *perception*" (74). Despite the death of liberalism and the end of bureaucratic state capitalism in the East, Debord pointed to the persistence of "The same formidable question that has been haunting the world for two centuries . . . How can the poor be made to work once their illusions have been shattered . . . ?" (10).

According to Debord the society of the spectacle has become both the means of control and the goal of control.

> All that once was directly lived has become mere representation . . . The spectacle in its generality is a concrete inversion of life . . . The spectacle is not a collection of images; rather, it is a social relationship between people that is mediated by images . . . It is far better viewed as a weltanschauung that has been actualized, translated into the material realm—a world view transformed into an objective force. (12–13)

The spectacle is the mirror image of the ruling economic order. It is the mirror image because, just as with the PIMs, the persons-in-mirrors, the actual world is inverted and reversed. In Debord's society of the spectacle, commodities articulate social relations. That is, people do not use commodities in carrying out their social lives, but their social lives conform to the needs of commodities. People adapt their lives to automobiles, televisions, and cell phones, for instance. It is a world where PIMs have changed places with the children in the room, now determining rather than mimicking their movements. Today's globalization merely recognizes that commodities have infiltrated and invested even those areas that had once been most remote from the centers of production and the market.

Criminal Justice as Semiotic

Criminals, like PIMs, become theoretically viable when treated as representations, signs. Summarizing otherwise scattered writings into a single chapter, "Logic as Semiotic: The Theory of Signs," Justus Buchler's edited volume of Charles Sanders Peirce's *Philosophical Writings* (1955) sets out Peirce's theory of signs, or semiotics. What recommends Peirce's semiotics as opposed to Ferdinand de Saussure's semiology is that the former uses a materialist metaphysics, and the theory posits a dynamic process of representation. Saussure's semiology is idealist and static. Therefore, semiotics meets the need for an analytic system that reflects the continual change and reflexivity of social reality.

Briefly, Peirce described a semiotic process involving three positions or moments: object, sign, and interpretant. "A sign, or *representamen*, is something which stands to somebody for something in some respect or capacity" (Peirce 1955:99). The sign stands for an object to somebody; it is interpreted as a sign of the object, and that interpretation is the interpretant of the sign linking the sign and object. This is a true triad, which is not resolvable into sets of dyads. The sign is not a sign without both an interpretant and an object. What is a sign at one point in time can be an object at another, and an interpretant in the next. Thus, a stop sign signifies cross traffic at an intersection. It is an object of various traffic regulations, and it interprets the actions of drivers. Peirce also identified three kinds of sign relations: icon, index, and symbol. An iconic sign relation comes from characteristics of the sign that make it "like that thing [object] and [is] used as a sign of it" (102). An indexical sign relation depends on contiguity rather than similarity; there is some connection between the index and object as in smoke and fire. The symbolic sign relation comes about through convention, and it carries meaning. Symbolic sign relations are peculiar to human usage, whereas iconic and indexical sign relations about throughout biology (Sebeok 1968). Ants follow pheromone trails and bees follow directions of the honey dance without attributing meaning to the signs. While Peirce introduced far more complexity in his complete theoretical treatment, those complexities are not necessary at this stage to show the theory's relevance for social analysis.

Applying the theory to Hung's parable of PIMs yields fruitful questions. If the PIMs are signs, where do they stand in the semiotic process? What are their objects and interpretants? What kind of sign relations prevail? Are they iconic, indexical, or symbolic? What kinds of information are needed to answer these questions? Do different standpoints offer different answers to the questions? And so on.

Now, apply the same kind of analysis to criminals. Do criminals signify some object (persons) to other persons? What kind of interpretant completes the semiotic chain? What is the ground or context for the semiotic triad of "criminals"? Peirce's semiotics is not a theory of criminal justice any more than quantum mechanics is a theory of physics. Both are analytic methods that allow theoretical formulations. Semiotics helps overcome problems posed by the Thomas theorem. It helps clarify distinctions between criminal justice theories and other sorts of things like normative statements or advocacy of policies such as those confusions about the formulations of Beccaria, Bentham, and von Hirsch mentioned at the beginning of the chapter. Treating the stuff of criminal justice—crime, criminals, courts, prisons, and so on—as signs opens up analytic pathways and clarifies potential confusions.

4

The Nature of Law, Order, Crime, and Criminal Justice

Bronislaw Malinowski (1926) provides a point of departure. Arguing against Maine (1861) and others including Durkheim, Malinowski averred that the Trobiand Islanders had law although theirs was a society based on kinship, a tribal society, or as he put it a "savage" society. First, he found that crime and custom coexisted. They were different, if not always distinctly separated. Second, law did not merely reflect a unified sentiment. In Malinowski's view, law was something that emerged from social relations. Most Trobriand law would fall into the American classification of civil law, yet they also had criminal law. That law and order were only matters of criminal law was a view he attributed to a number of his contemporary anthropologists.

> Law represents rather an aspect of tribal life . . . Law is the specific result of a configuration of obligations, which makes it impossible for the native to shirk his responsibility without suffering for it in the future. (59)
>
> . . .
>
> We have to abandon now definitely the idea of an inert, solid, 'crust' or 'cake' of custom rigidly pressing from outside upon the surface of tribal life. Law and order arise out of the very processes which they govern. (Malinowski 1926: 122–123)

Malinowski found Trobriand law conservative. He argued that law, especially criminal law, served to maintain the social system. Legal institutions could and did allow for variation, both by law evasion and law breaking, but only within limits that would not change basic social structures. The conservative, tradition-preserving nature of law can apply to any level of social complexity. Logically, of course, the one seems entailed by the other through definition. Since laws regulate society, they must maintain it, its internal organization, and its boundaries bordering an external world.

In some contrast to Malinowski, Stanley Diamond (1971) argued, in agreement with Maine, that the formation of the state and law are mutually dependent, and "The relation between custom and law is, basically, one of contradiction, not continuity." He noted that Paul Bohannon (1968) claimed that law grows from custom, but in agreement with Malinowski, Diamond saw two separate categories. According to Diamond, the formation of the state and law are mutually dependent processes (1978:251). There is no state without law and no law without a state. He contrasted social rules in nonstate societies where custom reigns. A distinguishing characteristic of nonstate societies is alternative social formations— corporate kin groups, age-grade sets, secret societies, and so on—and corporate responsibility for delicts and debts. State formation is a process. States do not just come into being and then carry on business. States, whenever they may have first appeared, continually re-form in a dialectical process where law is always involved.

This processual view applies to all states, from those that are nascent and fragile to mature, cohesive states such as those of Western Europe and North America, and to decrepit or disintegrating states. As states extend their authority throughout a society they override and subsume alternative sources of authority—corporate kin groups, religious organizations, and whatever stands in the way of total hegemony. A principal means by which they gain hegemony is law. The state makes laws that create and take account of individualized, legal persons. The law substitutes these persons for families, religious orders, and so on. Instead of corporate responsibility, the state creates several, or individual, responsibility under law. State formation relies on individualization through law, which is most apparent when examining archaic proto-states. Emerging states characteristically create a census-tax-conscription system. The state enumerates individuals, taxes them, and conscripts them into armies and public labor. Individuals become assets of the state (Diamond 1978).

Courts of state law appear as states emerge. Courts settle social conflicts that previously relied on customary ritual cycles ratified by councils of elders. During early state formation laws slowly supplant customs as the rules for conflict resolution. Diamond cited the case of the emerging proto-state of Dahomey to illustrate. The Dahomean king would send a certain category of his women to reside in villages. Local men who had sexual intercourse with the women were charged with the crime of rape. After a summary trial, the men were conscripted into the king's army as punishment. The crime of rape served the state's purpose, whereas before the emergence of the state, the wrong would be corrected by composition—ritualized giving of goods to the injured party (Diamond 1978:251). Usually the injured party was a corporate kin group. Other punishments in nonstate societies include ritual purification, ridicule, and ultimately banishment for severe recidivists. These kinds of punishments are easily recognizable as typical for nonstate societies governed by custom rather than law. They do not serve the economic or political needs of the state. As states begin to emerge, laws vie with customs as arbiters of social conflict. Criminal law replaces tort.

> The intention of the civil power is epitomized in the sanctions against homicide and suicide, typical of early polities; indeed they were among the first civil laws. Just as the sovereign is said to own the land, intimating the mature right of eminent domain, so the individual is ultimately conceived as the chattel of the state. In Dahomey, persons were conceived as *les choses du monarchque*. (Diamond 1978:252)

This process does not represent some enlightened and progressive development in human rights, but the assertion of authority by a new political form—the state. Without a state, societies treat homicide as a tort, but once the state emerges, the blow striking down a person becomes the deprivation of a political, economic, and military resource to the sovereign. Unlike societies where corporate groups sought compensation, the state resorts to its definitive response, that of retaliation, hence the law of the talion so characteristic of early states. State ideology rationalizes *lex talionis* as punishment. Nonetheless, the process of an emerging concept of criminal law and punishment does not occur without conflict, often violent. Laws create the individual subject of the law, often with grades or variations of rights and obligations depending on the subject's status. As Max Weber put it, the content of law is determined by status (1925:144).

In societies stratified by class, which coincide with state-level political institutions, the state distributes rights according to class. Malinowski saw "conflict . . . between strict law and legalized usage, and it is possible because the former has the strength of more definite tradition behind it, while the latter draws force from personal inclinations and actual power" (Malinowski 1926:123). Malinowski summed up his theory of law with a methodological caveat. "The true problem is not to study how human life submits to rules; but the real problem is how the rules become adapted to life" (127). In the case of law in industrialized societies such as that of the United States, the preponderant adaptation preserves class hierarchy and facilitates capitalist social relations at the cost of law determined by status. It is a hallmark of rationalizing modernism to separate status and class. Equality before the law increasingly means abolishing status distinctions regarding rights and obligations. American law no longer distinguishes rights and obligations based on race, those based on gender are fast diminishing, and various other status designations lose legal expression. The trends in law are toward regulating class-based social relations. Consequently, the American criminal justice system keeps order by applying criminal law to the lowest classes, civil law to the middling classes—the professions, technicians, managers, and the like—and corporate law to the ruling classes. In this case corporate law refers to the business corporation along with the older sense of corporate referring to kin groups and similar structures. The content of the law changes, and so does the ontological status of those subject to the law (Chambliss 1964:77; Weber 1925:144).

In the kinds of societies exemplified by the Trobriand Islanders the law restrains people according to customary rationales. "The justification for conforming to law is not that it makes sense, but that '*that is what our ancestors said we should do*'" (Leach 1977:30–31). Relatively important criminal laws, often in the form of taboos with supernatural sanctions, tend to focus on sex and kinship. "*Incest* rather than *murder* is the ultimate prototype of a public crime" (31). Note that such crimes are those pertaining to status violations with the subjects of the law defined by corporate membership in clans, lineages, and similar kin-based institutions. In modern, industrialized, capitalistic societies, prototypical public crimes are homicide and theft, which validate the importance of individual life and property (32). They reflect individualized rights and obligations; atomized, as opposed to corporate, social relations; and of course property—the sine qua non of capitalist political economy. Crimes in modern societies are those of class, and they apply to subjects of the state—that is, citizens.

Law and Ideology

Whether in kinship or capitalist societies, the key to law's authority is forgetting. The legal scholar Ronald Dworkin (1986), polemicizing against the positivist theory of law, argued that law is more than a set of rules. Going even further, law can be conceived as a formal expression of ideology. The law is an encyclopedic compendium of the way things are and what people ought to do about them. Its encyclopedic nature opposes any sort of legal grammar or dictionary as representing the law. Dictionaries and grammars follow the logical structure as Porphyrian trees, a bidimensional hierarchy of categories. They record usage and act as authoritative references. Other than their origin in usage, dictionaries and grammars are self-referential. Dictionaries define words with other words; grammars state rules with reference to other rules and grammatical categories. Oliver Wendell Holmes

Jr. in *The Common Law* (1881/1991) famously marked the move away from thinking about law in the way of dictionaries and grammars. The law, in the post-Holmesian view, cannot just be the logical working out of the will of the sovereign, as the formalist followers of John Austin (1832) would have it. Instead, the "law evolves in response to changing conceptions of public policy, and therefore cannot be captured by a purely logical scheme" (Novick 1991:ix). The logical arrangement of law according to positivist philosophy sought to bring order to the common law by dividing the law into a taxonomy based on rights. It followed the utilitarian philosophy of Jeremy Bentham (1789/1823). Accordingly, government and laws secured the rights of the community as measured by the greatest good for the greatest number. Holmes rejected such a transcendental view of the law and came closer to Malinowski's observation that the law emerges from social relations. Consequently, any legal taxonomy, or any conception of the law modeled on taxonomic logic, is doomed to miss its nature. The law is like an encyclopedia, not a grammar.

Anyone who has ever delved into the law soon discovers the difference. Checking a point of grammar or the meaning of a word using grammars and dictionaries usually takes little time. Look up the word or the grammatical rule; then close the book. Checking a point of law can become a lengthy and labyrinthine journey. The legal code, the statute book, leads out into a variety of pathways. First, there is the legislative history, then case law—a thicket filled with brambles only Br'er Rabbit would relish—commentaries, and so on. The law is not simply a code, much as language is not simply a code. Furthermore, differences in legal codes do not come from simple differences in the laws, the individual statutes. The law has different structures in different jurisdictions. Laws of the State of Virginia, the laws of England, and the penal code of France reflect basic differences in logic, and these all share a common Western heritage!

To explicate encyclopedias, Michel Foucault (1966/1973:xv) adverted to a passage from Jorge Luis Borges, who began his 1952 essay by noting an omission in the fourteenth edition of the *Encyclopaedia Britannica*. It concerned one John Wilkins (1614–1672), an early natural scientist who tried to identify and order all human thought, beginning the task around the year 1664, according to Borges. Wilkins set up various tables to contain the information, but though the code for accessing his tables was easy to learn, the code led to a disguised encyclopedia. Borges illustrated by reference to a certain Chinese encyclopedia, the *Celestial Emporium of Benevolent Knowledge*.

On these remote pages it is written that animals are divided into (a) those that belong to the Emperor, (b) embalmed ones, (c) those that are trained,

(d) suckling pigs, (e) mermaids, (f) fabulous ones, (g) stray dogs, (h) those that are included in this classification, (i) those that tremble as if they were mad, (j) innumerable ones, (k) those drawn with a very fine camel's hair brush, (l) others, (m) those that have just broken a flower vase, (n) those that resemble flies from a distance. (Borges 1952:103)

The logic of this encyclopedia largely escapes modern, Western readers. That is because encyclopedias are rooted in their historically specific cultures. Encyclopedias are multidimensional labyrinths. They are structured as networks of interpretants, which are virtually infinite because they take into account multiple interpretations realized in different times and places (Eco 1986:83). When courts settle the law, the settlement is always contingent. The law has to be encyclopedic. Instead of the well-ordered analytic system envisioned by the nineteenth-century jurists who were the targets of Holmes's critique, the legal taxonomy

> blows up in a dust of differentiae, in a turmoil of infinite accidents, in a non-hierarchical network of *qualia*. The dictionary [or law book] is dissolved into a potentially unordered and unrestricted galaxy of pieces of world knowledge. The dictionary thus becomes an encyclopedia, because it was in fact *a disguised encyclopedia*. (Eco 1986:68)

The law, then, records a piece of a given historically situated culture's weltanschauung. The law is always part of the ideology of a society. People, most people most of the time, follow the law because they believe in its imperatives. In the realm of beliefs, the law exercises hegemony or ideological domination. Hegemony is a dynamic process as developed by Antonio Gramsci (1971) to explain domination in liberal democracies where the social order is dependent on consent. Gramsci begins with *The German Ideology*: "The ideas of the ruling class are in every epoch the ruling ideas . . . The ruling ideas are nothing more than the ideal expression of the dominant material relations" (Marx and Engels 1864:59). These ruling ideas take systematic form through various authoritative discourses, scientific, political, economic, and, of course, legal. In modern, technologically developed societies, they seem to rely on objective truth.

> Ideologies, then, are belief systems distinguished by the centrality of their concern for What Is and by their world-referencing "reports." Ideologies are essentially public doctrines offering publicly scrutable evidence and reasoning on their behalf; they are never offered as *secret* doctrines . . . Ideologies are intended to be believed in by those affirming them publicly and by all men, because they are "true," and they thus have a universal character . . . With the waning of traditionalism, there is now an increasing struggle over "ideas."

> This means a greater struggle over which definitions of social reality (or reports) and which moral rules (or commands) are dominant. Social struggle in part takes the form of contention about What Is and what should be done about it. (Gouldner 1976:33–34.)

The concept of hegemony or ideological domination takes into account social struggle as an intrinsic part of the formation of ideology. A dominant ideology is never simply arrived at; it emerges from social struggle. As Malinowski commented, there is always some leeway, some space to adapt to systemic needs. So, during times of challenges to class power, or when the ruling class is more divided than unified on certain matters or particular areas, the law becomes more flexible, bending without breaking. At times when a more unified ruling class is asserting power and control, the law gets stiffer (Piven 1981). Ideology defines and frames problems that become matters of social conflict. It allows, in fact requires, critique of discourses about "What Is and what should be done about it." There is room for maneuver in the negotiations over objective reality and truth. Ideology gives a framework for inquiry, debate, and conflict. Ideology lays down the grid of truth conditions. It does not just describe What Is; it tells us how to go about determining What Is. Within a given ideological framework the ideology allows only those critiques that do not attack its premises, because questions and criticisms cannot be formulated outside the grid of its truth conditions. Ideology is the gatekeeper for objective reality.

Ideology, Law, and the State

Juristic law is not scientific law. Scientific law comprises observed regularities. The law of gravity consists of such regularities and so do regularities of human behavior and social relations. That most people stop at red lights is not the law; the normative requirement in the traffic code is the juristic law.

The law also consists of texts. In the case of nonliterate societies, the texts are oral, maintained by memory and often performative. Literate societies maintain the law in written texts. Both kinds of legal texts express, formally, normative aspects of ideology. As ideologies change through time, the texts of laws may change, or the texts may stay the same but receive different interpretations. The Second Amendment to the U.S. Constitution is an example. When written, the controversy was about ensuring the states' ability to keep militias (Bellesiles 2000; Bogus 2000). In more contemporary times, it has become tied to interpersonal violence. Whether texts are oral or written, the legal expression of ideology is made of signs, as is ideology as a whole. "*Without signs, there is no ideology*" (Vološinov 1973:9). Ideological, and therefore legal, signs partake of the ongoing social semiotic, and consequently they express meaning. The signs are material, whether performative or written. That is, they have a physical, observable form. They are not *mere* ideas, not Platonic forms.

Ideological signs' meanings include a sense and a referent. The referent is the object for which they stand. The sense is what social valences are attached to the sign. Gottlob Frege (1892), who elucidated the distinction, used the example of the planet Venus as the referent, which people know as the morning star and evening star. Consider Willie Horton, the referent; the sense of the referent made a major contribution to the presidential election victory of George Bush I over Michael Dukakis in 1988. The sense of an ideological sign and its form are always inextricably bound together, separable only in the abstract (Vološinov 1973:22). The sense of Willie Horton that made the sign so important was the television advertisements linking him with Dukakis. Horton was a convict temporarily released under Massachusetts' furlough program, and while on furlough he committed armed robbery and rape. The form of the sign—the television campaign advertisements—cannot be separated from the sense. Without the advertisement, Horton and his activities would have remained unknown except to those immediately involved. The same is true, though perhaps not as spectacularly, for all ideological signs. The social valence of the sign is bound with a particular historical time, events, situations, and so on. Change those, and the sense changes. This fungibility of ideological signs also makes them refracting and distorting media. Ruling elites strive to impart an eternal character to such signs, to extinguish or occlude the social value of struggles indexed by the sign, and to make the sign uniaccentual (Vološinov 1973:23).

> In actual fact, each living ideological sign has two faces, like Janus . . . This *inner dialectic quality* of the sign comes out fully in the open only in times of social crises or revolutionary changes. In the ordinary conditions of life, the contradiction embedded in every ideological sign cannot emerge fully because the ideological sign in an established, dominant ideology is always somewhat reactionary . . . so accentuating yesterday's truth as to make it appear today's. (Vološinov 1973:23–24)

William Chambliss's 1964 study of vagrancy law exemplifies the process. By tracing a law prohibiting nonemployment, Chambliss revealed the social struggles played out over six centuries. Certain themes kept repeating despite vast historical changes. What appeared to be a relatively stable law—certain definitional and penal aspects varied according to historical circumstance—became, on analysis, a story of class struggle over how to get the poor to work. With James Q. Wilson's (1996) call to recriminalize vagrancy, the old ideology is made new again.

The law, in its totality, is a sign that stands for force. It is in this sense that law and the state co-emerge. As the state claims a monopoly on violence, so it claims a monopoly on coining the law. At the same time, the state normalizes the law. Less necessary in absolutist governments where force, violence, and law exhibit quotidian links, forgetfulness of the force behind law reaches its apotheosis in liberal democracies. It is in law's "representativity that originary violence is consigned to oblivion. This amnesic loss of consciousness does not happen by accident . . . The parliaments live in forgetfulness of the violence from which they were born" (Derrida 1992:47). Derrida was commenting on Walter Benjamin's 1921 essay "Critique of Violence." Benjamin singled out police violence.

> Its power is formless, like its nowhere tangible, all-pervasive, ghostly presence in the life of civilized states . . . their spirit is less devastating where they represent, in absolute monarch, the power of a ruler in which legislative and executive supremacy are united, than in democracies where their existence, elevated by no such relation, bears witness to the greatest conceivable degeneration of violence . . . All violence as a means is either law making or law preserving. If it lays claim to neither of these predicates, it forfeits all validity. (287)

> . . .

> For the function of violence in lawmaking is twofold, in the sense that lawmaking pursues as its end, with violence as the means, *what* is to be established as law, but at the moment of instatement does not dismiss violence; rather, at this very moment of lawmaking, it specifically establishes as law not an end unalloyed by violence but one necessarily and intimately bound to it, under the title of power. Lawmaking is power making, and, to that extent, an immediate manifestation of violence. (295)

Eerily, Egon Bittner (1967) made a similar point about police as the armed force of the state. It is eerie because each was writing in the context of a failed revolution, Benjamin of 1919 and Bittner of 1968, in which state police forces crushed rebellions against state power. Benjamin's point is broader than Bittner's. What Bittner had in mind was the local cop-on-the-beat kind of policing. Benjamin addressed the police power of the state, as in that asserted by the U.S. Supreme Court in the *Slaughter-House Cases*, 83 U.S. 36 (1872):

> This is called the police power; and it is declared by Chief Justice Shaw that it is much easier to perceive and realize the existence and sources of it than to mark its boundaries, or prescribe limits to its exercise.

This power is, and must be from its very nature, incapable of any very exact definition or limitation. Upon it depends the security of social order, the life and health of the citizen, the comfort of an existence in a thickly populated community, the enjoyment of private and social life, and the beneficial use of property. "It extends," says another eminent judge, "to the protection of the lives, limbs, health, comfort, and quiet of all persons, and the protection of all property within the State; . . . and persons and property are subjected to all kinds of restraints and burdens in order to secure the general comfort, health, and prosperity of the State. Of the perfect right of the legislature to do this no question ever was, or, upon acknowledged general principles, ever can be made, so far as natural persons are concerned". (49–50, footnotes omitted)

Benjamin went on to contrast mythical violence of Greek gods with divine violence of Yahweh and that of the state. Mythical violence is a "mere manifestation of the gods . . . a manifestation of their existence" (Benjamin 1921:294). The mythical gods demanded sacrifice and punished challenges to their power. Divine violence predicates equality before the law. Divine law claims justice. Benjamin, however, questioned the logic of such justice. He cited Anatole France; the full passage makes the point even more sharply than the well-known fragment Benjamin used.

We in France are soldiers and we are citizens. Our citizenship is another occasion for pride. For the poor it consists in supporting and maintaining the rich in their power and their idleness. At this task they must labor in the face of the majestic equality of the laws, which forbid rich and poor alike to sleep under bridges, to beg in the streets, and to steal their bread. This equality is one of the benefits of the Revolution. (France 1930:80 [Chapter 7])

The law of the state is just another name for divine violence. "Divine violence, which is the sign and seal but never the means of sacred execution, may be called sovereign violence" (Benjamin 1921:300). The connection with divine violence is constitutional law, which Benjamin equated with the power to set boundaries, physical boundaries marking off the territory of the state's governance. "Where frontiers are decided the adversary is not merely annihilated; indeed he is accorded rights . . . And these are, in a demonically ambiguous way, 'equal rights' " (295). The boundaries and the establishment of territorial governance are the *nomos*, discussed by Carl Schmitt (1950) and Robert Cover (1982).

Getting *Nomos* into *Nous* Via *Soma*

Effective state hegemony does not use persuasive argument to inculcate ideology and obedience to law. Its motto is "bend the body; the heart and mind will follow." Penal systems, criminal justice systems, and all systems of law respond to changes of the state and its social environs. The state always disciplines. That is its primary function and its main modus operandi. Styles of punishment and law change, and so do the theoretical discourses that purport to explain but in fact rationalize.

State symbolic violence uses the forms of law and regulation to inscribe its demands on the bodies of citizens, much as "the apparatus" used knives to inscribe the crimes committed by miscreants in Kafka's "Penal Colony" (1919). Air travelers and other citizens of the English-speaking hegemonic states do not *decide* to comply with the current absurdities. These include allowing no nonpassengers beyond the checkpoint, the Gestapo-like demand for papers to travel within the United States, virtually having to strip just to get through the checkpoints, and so on. The travelers do not evaluate and judge through some public or even private discourse. Their submission comes from lifetimes of training. In day cares, nursery schools, and kindergartens, children's bodies get used to queuing in lines. Put Americans, Britons, Canadians, or Australians in front of a gate, and they will form a line without a word said. Compliance is a physical act; all the rest is later rationalization. Drivers attending to their cell phones or switching CDs catch a traffic signal turn red out of the corner of their eyes. They slam on the brakes, *without thinking*. When we learn another language or play a musical instrument we strive for fluency or accomplishment by training our bodies to perform automatically. We strive to respond to signs of language or musical notation without thinking, automatically, or as Freud would have it, preconsciously. So the state strives to train the populace.

The intellectualization of bodily conformity finds cognitive schema ready to be filled. Socialization consists first of training, but also mental categories molded by a succession of state apparatuses—families, schools, factories, offices, and so forth. Moreover, these mental appurtenances reflect the prevailing social structures. Pierre Bourdieu (2000:178) put it thus:

> For the problem is that, for the most part, the established order is not a problem; outside crisis situations, the question of the legitimacy of the State does not arise. The State does not necessarily need to give orders and to exert physical coercion, or disciplinary constraint, to produce an ordered

social world, so long as it is able to produce incorporated cognitive structures attuned to the objective [social] structures and so secure doxic submission to the established order.

Laws are the explicit linguistic signs of implicit obedience. Written laws are part of a dialectical process including agents of the state and the apparatuses where they work that inscribe obedience. The red traffic signal that causes inattentive drivers to brake suddenly has volumes of traffic rules behind it. Modern legal codes legitimize state apparatuses and depend on them to enforce the laws, and both rely on habits of obedience from a populace who rationalize their submission by an invented logic of the law. It is a process of *Aufhebung* in which each element depends on the other to continually construct the edifice of the state.

The processes flit between conscious and unconscious, between voluntary and coerced, a point made by Richard T. Ford by reference to learning the tango. Relying on ideas from Judith Butler's *Gender Trouble*, Ford describes a female tango student who finds "it easier to conform to the female role than to attack the Tango's structure ... Over time conformity will become 'second nature.'" Eventually, she forgets any urge to resist the relative passivity of the female's tango role; "At that point the status will also have become her identity" (Ford 1999:857). The status, of course, is gender, in which the tango is another building block in the apparent natural and biologically authorized category. Ford goes on to compare gender statuses to jurisdictional statuses, the legal statuses conferred by jurisdictional boundaries, such as citizenship.

Of course there are degrees of citizenship, as bearers of marginalized statuses continually rediscover. The status of citizenship coincides with the modern state in Europe in the seventeenth century and modern legal systems. These modernist inventions had everything to do with property. Hobbes's Leviathan was a three-dimensional space ordered vertically with the sovereign at the top and horizontally covering a territory. Spatiality of law and state play an important role in the creation of political subjects whose legal status is propertied, both in the sense of linkage to real property and as a property of the legal person. Legal and political space has three dimensions with respect to the "legitimation, origins, and workings of property": the frontier, the survey, and the grid (Blomley 2003:123). Frontiers divide the realm of law from the extralegal, a wilderness where savagery reigns. Surveys, and the maps that record them, emerged with European colonization in the sixteenth century. In England surveys and maps ruled Enclosure, that theft of the commons by the gentry extending over three centuries, which established a three-tiered class system and provided the population of landless laborers who eventually supplied the machinery of industrial capitalism (Tawney 1912). The grid is a modern version of nomos where law divides the land and certifies land use. In modern societies the grid lays out social relations in terms of property, "such as my 'right' to a parking spot on the street outside my house" (Blomley 2003:131). Jeremy Wauldron notes the intimate connection between property, class, and legal status.

> Everything that is done has to be done somewhere. No one is free to perform an action unless there is somewhere he is free to perform it. Since we are embodied beings, we always have a location. Moreover, though everyone has to be somewhere, a person cannot always choose any location he likes . . . and, physical inaccessibility aside, there are some places one is simply not allowed to be.
> One of the functions of property rules, particularly as far as land is concerned, is to provide a basis for determining who is allowed to be where. (Waldron 1991:296)

The same is true of time. Time too has a grid that deploys people and activities. Typically, time grids and space grids interlock so one is in a workplace during work time, for instance. Being in certain places at certain times makes one criminally suspect—a bank vault after closing time, for instance. The division of space-time by law is taken for granted as people depend on these divisions to orient themselves and define social role playing. Here, as in the tango dance movements, legal definitions are largely forgotten, but the differences in roles are inscribed on bodies as posture, demeanor, and movement that differ between, say the office, the cabaret, and home.

Originary Crime and Law: Sacrifice and the Camp

A story of sacrifice is at the root of Western crime and law. Cain's killing of Abel is the originary crime of breaking the law against fratricide. In contrast, the violations of Adam and Eve were not violations of law—that is, a general rule—but they violated a particular commandment addressed only to them. As the story goes, Cain envied Abel's ability to achieve atonement through animal sacrifice. Fratricide violated tribal custom, the kind of law Malinowski saw among the Trobriand Islanders. It was not a violation of codified law, since the law of Moses came later, propaedeutic to the founding of the State of Israel. As punishment, Cain had to carry the mark identifying him as the murderer of his brother and wander away from his land as a perpetual fugitive. Cain implored God to lessen the punishment because, as a fugitive, anyone could kill him with impunity, so God threatened a sevenfold penalty on any who would kill Cain.

Abraham's sacrifice of his second son, Isaac, ordered by God but stayed and then substituted with a ram, also precedes the giving of the law to Moses. Abraham seemed about to sacrifice his second son in the same manner as a burnt offering of lamb. The substitution then was double; first Isaac substituted for the usual lamb, then the ram substituted for Isaac.

These stories offer a foundation to Giorgio Agamben's insights into the place of law, crime, punishment, and the suspension of the rule of law in a state of siege or state of exception. The first thing to notice is that animal sacrifice precedes all. This occurred in a kinship-based social order usually associated with simple societies that typically rely on hunting, gardening, and herding for subsistence. René Girard (1972:4, 7–8), citing studies of the Dinka (Lienhardt 1961) and Ndembu (Turner 1968) in Africa, among others, explained the function of sacrifice as a primary way to displace destructive quarrels and violence. Regardless of the merit or comprehensiveness of Girard's functionalism, his interpretation has the advantage of drawing attention to remedies for internecine conflict and the danger for group integrity of vengeance and feud. Two possibilities present themselves. One is the Biblical solution: banishment with or without outlawry. The other involves compensation between kinship groups. The latter has a documented history in Europe among the ancient Greek and Roman law and the various Germanic and Nordic tribal peoples (Goebel 1937). Both solutions prevailed in Europe before modern states emerged. Compensation to avoid intragroup violence assuages the enmity of corporate groups. Such corporations are the main building blocks of nonstate societies. Here, instead of getting rid of the offending person, the corporate group is the injured party. To avoid revenge, the corporate group of the offender pays the injured corporation. Roman civil law used this approach, applying what today are considered criminal sanctions mainly to slaves who were nonpersons. Whether the solution is corporate compensation, exile, or sacrifice, the goal is avoidance of turmoil that threatens social solidarity.

Banishment or exile ejects the person who is the focus of potential violence or feud. This can offer sanctuary or social death. The latter usually entails imminent physical death. The possibility of sanctuary is what Cain received. He left the most dangerous place for him, as Abel's kin would likely have killed him in revenge. This Biblical story is complicated by the fact that Cain and Abel were of the same lineage and phratry, whereas most dangerous disputes occur between such kin groups. The notion of exile as sanctuary has been developed by Herman Bianchi (1994), who used the historical practice to build his argument for sanctuary as a general principle of justice. In contrast, banishment with outlawry exposes the exile to depredations of anyone and everyone. It designates the person as one who is outside the protections of law, hence outlawry. This version of banishment appears also in medieval Europe as infamy. In England one who was under the ban of infamy had established an irremediably bad reputation and so was barred from polite society (Goebel 1937).

This is the kind of figure Agamben analyzed in his *Homo Sacer*. The exile in this case is one who cannot partake of sacrifice, even as its victim, but who can be killed. Societies usually honor sacrificial victims, as in the case of soldiers who fight for their country. In contrast, the exile is set outside the law, and as Agamben pointed out, this is the same relation to the law enjoyed by the sovereign, one who is outside the law.

> It is in this sense that the paradox of sovereignty can take the form "There is nothing outside the law." *The originary relation of law to life is not application but Abandonment.* The matchless potentiality of *nomos, its originary "force of law"*, is that it holds life in its ban by abandoning it. (Agamben 1995:29)

Returning to Hobbes makes Agamben clearer. Hobbes's sovereign is the one who puts an end to the continual violence of the state of nature. The state of nature opposes civilization where law rules. The sovereign embodies the violence of the state of nature, which Hobbes elucidates by noting that the state of nature characterizes relations among sovereigns. So too, the exile is abandoned to the state of nature. The sovereign exercises violence; the banned one also is free to exercise violence, even as he is exposed to it. "[T]he sovereign is the one with respect to whom all men are potentially *homines sacri* [capable of being sacrificed], and *homo sacer* is the one with respect to whom all men act as sovereigns" (1995:84). Both the sovereign and the exile are liminal figures (Gennep 1909; Turner 1969) with respect to the law. They are both inside it and outside it. Agamben argued that understanding "the Hobbesian mythologeme in terms of *contract* instead of *ban* condemned democracy to impotence every time it had to confront the problem of sovereign power" (Agamben 1995:109). He brought the argument into the present by saying that life in the modern state puts everyone under the ban, because the essential structure of sovereign power, the power of the state, treats everyone as *homines sacri*. "*In the city, the banishment of sacred life is more internal* ... The banishment of sacred life is the sovereign *nomos* that conditions every rule, the originary spatialization that governs and makes possible every territorialization" (111).

The camp, as in the Nazi *Lager*, is the space where this interiorized state of nature was realized in the twentieth century. A historical debate concerns whether the Spanish created the first camps in Cuba in 1896 or the English in South Africa during the Boer War (Agamben 1995:166). In either case, they proliferated as the century wore on. In 2002 a famous camp returned to Cuba at Guantanamo, while the U.S. military continues to operate a number of camps in occupied territory in Afghanistan and Iraq. Such camps remain outside the law. Despite suggestive rulings by the U.S. Supreme Court (*Hamdan v. Rumsfeld* 2006; *Rasul v. Bush* 2004), the Military Commissions Act (2006) put the Guantanamo camp outside the law, subject to martial law—that is, as a state of exception. "The camp is thus the structure in which the state of exception—the possibility on which founds sovereign power—is realized *normally*" (Agamben 1995:170). The paradox repeats itself. An act of Congress, ostensibly the sovereign body in the United States, by law puts something and someones outside the law.

The law is the boundary, the liminal space, that defines when and where the sovereign declares a state of exception. It does not constrain state power, although it does express that power in discursive form. Crimes, which in simpler societies are acts threatening social stability, under the state are transgressions against sovereign rule—in effect, challenges to state power. Order is that which conforms to law. Disorder is not abolished by law but delimited by it. For instance, there are disorderly parts of cities that are constrained by sociospatial barriers. The most extreme, the defining case, is the camp, a site of disorder and lawlessness, a state of nature, decreed by law. When crime is just a particular form of lèse-majesté, where can justice dwell?

The Nature of Criminal Justice

Oh where is the noble face
of modesty, or the strength of virtue, now
that blasphemy is in power
and men have put justice
behind them, and there is no law but lawlessness
and none join in fear of the gods?
         (Euripides 405 BCE, ll. 1468–1473)

In 1968, on the eve of the world revolution that dismantled the liberal consensus (Wallerstein 2004), Herbert Packer (1968) described two models of criminal justice. He called them the crime control model and the due process model. The crime control model refers to a set of state apparatuses devoted to apprehending, prosecuting, and punishing lawbreakers. Its guiding rule is efficiency; it operates with a presumption of guilt. Alternatively, the due process model presumes innocence. It weighs on the side of individuals as against the state. While both models described the workings of criminal justice in the United States, Packer said there had been too much reliance on crime control, and he called for a shift in balance toward due process. Packer's was one of the last, brave articulations of the classical liberal tradition going back through the Enlightenment to classical Athenian thought.

The problem was that the classical, Enlightenment tradition of liberalism came up against an onslaught of a combination of realism and reaction. Nietzsche, as usual, expressed the problem posed by realism. "It is not he who does us harm but he who is contemptible who counts as bad" (Nietzsche 1878:45). The realism part reveals a criminal justice that provides a system for sorting out the contemptible. The reaction part emanated from the ruling class in America. They found challenges from hoi polloi threatening (Powell 1971), and so they constructed a moral crisis in which they used criminal justice to rein in the lower orders. As Dario Melossi (1993) observed,

> [T]hose "authorized" to identify and label social problems (Gusfield 1981; Spector and Kitsuse 1977; Becker 1963), whom I will call "moral elites," tend to act upon situations *perceived* as critical for the maintenance of . . . their own hegemony . . . Any situation perceived as upsetting the balance of power is, from the perspective of the elites, critical. (262)

> . . .

> [L]abor insubordination tends to be interpreted by moral elites as an aspect of the general moral malaise of society . . . Therefore, following social situations during which elites see their hegemony challenged, two things tend to happen almost simultaneously, apparently linked only in the murky atmosphere of a "public mood": people work harder for less money, and prisons fill beyond capacity. (266)

Both the realist and reactionary responses to liberal claims get at the root of the meaning of justice. Of course, justice is a perennial site of controversy and contemplation with a recorded history going back to antiquity. Two strains of thought about justice form the foundation for its conception in the West. One looks to classical Athens, the other to ancient Judaism.

Classical Greek thought recognized two sorts of justice. Themis represents one and Dike the other. Themis was a pre-Olympian Titan, born of Gaia and Uranus, earth and heavens. She embodied natural law and strove for harmony. Her Roman equivalent was Iustia, who often stands in front of American courthouses. Themis's character was split among her offspring. As the second wife of Zeus, she bore the Horae, who embodied the rightness of time unfolding in orderly procession, and the Fates (Hesiod ca. 700 BCE ll. 904–909). She also gave birth to Dike, the goddess of trial.

Dike has an ambiguous character, part justice and part force. The latter she inherited from her father, Zeus. Therefore, Dike includes equity but also test and tribulation. Dike's sister was Eunomia, the rule of law that brings harmonious civil life. How Dike, trial, came to represent justice in classical Athens starts with the story of another sacrifice—that of Iphigenia by her father Agamemnon so he could invade Troy. Upon his return from triumphantly defeating Troy, his wife, Clytemnestra, killed Agamemnon. Orestes, their son, avenged his father by killing his mother. Acquitted by earthly law, Orestes was, nonetheless, pursued by the Furies. The Furies, or Erinyes, were the three goddesses of vengeance: Tisiphone (avenger of murder), Megaera (the jealous), and Alecto (constant anger). They were also called the Daughters of the Night—the daughters of Uranus and Gaea. Without mercy, the Furies would punish all crime including the breaking of rules considering all aspects of society. They would strike the offenders with madness and never stopped following criminals. The worst of all crimes were patricide or matricide. They would also be the guardians of the law when the state had not yet intervened or did not exist, or when the crime was a crime of ethics and not actual law. Aeschylus's *Eumenides* is the story of the conversion of the Furies to the Eumenides by the intervention of Athena, the civilizing influence of the state. Concomitantly, Dike changed from an instrument of Zeus's power to the power of the state of Athens.

In classical Athens, Solonic law (594/3 BCE), with Cleisthenes' reforms (508/7 BCE), determined criminal justice (De Ste. Croix 2004). Outside of political crimes such as treason, Athenian law treated homicide as the most serious, and it could carry the death penalty. Intention of the accused determined the venue of the court, most of which were surrounding or at least in close proximity to the Agora—the central marketplace of Athens. Cases of involuntary homicide appeared in the Palladion, and the most serious penalty was temporary exile. Voluntary homicide cases came before the Delphinion, with a possible death penalty on conviction. The prosecutors were the relatives of the deceased. The major court remained the Aeropagus, but it usually heard only those cases that had significant social and political import. Professional lawyers—orators—pleaded for each side, the prosecution and defense. Juries paid by the state made the final decision (Freeman 1963; MacDowell 1963). Defendants acquitted of homicide in the court of the Aeropagus customarily went to the cave of the Furies to propitiate them with a purificatory offering (Freeman 1963:85).

Sacrilege was the only other category of crime that regularly had death as the punishment. In three dialogues (*Apology, Crito,* and *Phaedo*) Plato famously recounted the trial, conviction, and execution of Socrates for crimes against the gods. This was not, of course, his real crime, but rather his support for the tyranny of the Thirty that had overthrown Athenian democracy in 404 BCE, and his possible treachery with Sparta to install the oligarchic dictatorship (De Ste. Croix 1972, 2004:172; Stone 1988). Normally such a political crime would have led to ostracism, which was temporary and did not include loss of citizenship or property. At worst the penalty should have been permanent exile with loss of property. Granted, Socrates was age 70 at the time, so ostracism would have been permanent. In any case, Socrates refused to leave Athens, so the capital charge of sacrilege was the only way to dispose of him.

Crimes threatening civic solidarity embodied in the Athenian state were the most serious, and had the most severe penalties. Aeschylus, in his *Eumenides*, has the jury deadlock on Orestes' guilt of matricide. Athena herself casts the deciding vote acquitting him. Athena was not just the eponym for the city. The goddess symbolized the city-state; her presence was everywhere. Her intervention in the trial of Orestes can be read as state justice itself. While this deus ex machina transformed the tribal blood vengeance of the Furies, and created the Eumenides, the Furies were not destroyed, but relegated to a cave. Thus, there is recognition of the persistence of primitive retribution, even while it is submerged, out of sight and out of public discourse in the Agora. Recall further, that the story of Orestes' crime starts with Agamemnon's sacrifice of his daughter, Iphigenia, who in the end accedes to her own death to serve the interests of the state. *Classical criminal justice guards the integrity of the state.* That was its purpose and its function in practice.

Herman Bianchi (1994) proposed what he said was a new system of criminal justice, noting that the current systems in most countries are based on anomic justice. Bianchi connected Durkheim's anomie with Marx's alienation, noting that its literal meaning was "without nomos" (54). Bianchi proposed an alternative, based on the ancient Judaic concept of justice called Tsedeka, which he said better translates as righteousness. Tsedeka is a eunomic law built around an "incessant diligence to make people experience the genuine substantiation of truth, rights, and duties, and the eventual release from guilt" (22).

Judaic justice

Rabbinic discourse contrasts with Greek Agorian discourse. Judaic justice is not measured by the state, and the community of Jews, in whatever political organization, cannot be symbolized by a god. These contrasts go to the basic levels of epistemology and categories of knowledge and civic practice.

> The tendency to *gather* various meanings *into a one* is...characteristic of Greek thought in general: its movement towards the universal, the general, the univocal. The Rabbinic tendency, by contrast, is toward differentiation, metaphorical multiplicity, multiple meanings...Aristotle's theory of knowledge was at bottom representative, how the image is at the heart of Greek thought. (Handelmann 1982:33)

Keeping in mind the pivotal role of the goddess Athena, her ubiquitous representations in the center of civic life in Athens, and the important role of place in Athenian criminal justice, Susan Handelmann (1982) remarked on the difference from the present of the Hebrews. "The Greek *present* is defined by the place where the action takes place, and we are there as spectators and witnesses. The Hebrew present, however, is fluid, containing both past and future simultaneously" (37). In the Rabbinic tradition the Torah is the law and justice. Moreover, the Torah is the law of the universe. That is, there is no distinction between natural law as in the law of gravity and criminal law as that which forbids homicide. The final pertinent, basic difference is that the Torah preceded the creation of the world. First there was the law, which provided the blueprint, then God created according to its instructions: "He [God] looked into the Torah and created the world" (Handelmann 1982:38 citing *Ber. Rab.* 1:1). The Torah, the law of the universe, is only realized through human interpretation and application. Justice must follow the law, but as it is applied with human reason in social and historical context. Justice is realized through understanding and applying the law in its particularity. There is no preexisting, transcendent Justice. The story of Aknai's oven, in which R. Eliezer was disputing with the sages on whether the oven was ritually clean, makes this clear.

> On that day R. Eliezer brought forth every imaginable argument, but they did not accept them. He said "If the law agrees with me, let this carob tree prove it!" Thereupon the carob tree was torn a hundred cubits out of the ground. "No proof can be brought from a carob tree," they retorted. Whereupon the stream of water flowed backwards. "No proof can be brought from a stream of water," they rejoined...Again, he said to them, "If the law agrees with me, let it be proved from heaven!" Whereupon a Heavenly Voice cried out, "Why do you dispute with R. Eliezer, seeing that in all matters the law agrees with him." R. Joshua arose and exclaimed, "It is not in Heaven!" What did he mean by this? R. Jeremiah said that the Torah had already been given at Mt. Sinai; "we pay no attention to a Heavenly Voice, because Thou hast long since written in the Torah at Mt. Sinai. After the majority must one incline. (*Baba Metzia* 59a)

Instead of authority, instead of sacrifice to guard the state, Rabbinic justice realizes creation. It is a continual process, always ongoing. Instead of place and presence where jurors witness justice, the Rabbinic tradition of interpretation continually realizes justice. In this respect, it is not irrelevant that the Rabbinic tradition—indeed the recording of the Talmud, which was the oral law as opposed to the written law of the Torah—took place when there was no Jewish state, after the destruction of the Second Temple in 70 CE. Therefore, Judaic justice in the Rabbinic tradition cannot be the application of state power, as it is in the classical tradition. Rabbinic justice, like Rabbinic discourse, is quintessentially deconstructive. It challenges authority, demanding it account for itself. Crimes arise, not from being the wrong kind of person, in the wrong place and time—such a construction would be utterly alien to the Rabbinic tradition. Instead, crimes are those acts and practices that violate the law of the universe. The criminal is that which interrupts the duty of humanity to realize creation. Judaic justice resembles the Greek Themis more than Dike. Themis represents the harmonious functioning of the universe, and she is primordial, pre-Olympian, and pre-state. But Rabbinic justice goes further, as there is nothing prehistoric about it, no kind of autochthony. Rabbinic justice is and must be always already contemporary. To illustrate, there is a special law about informing. Anyone bearing witness against others to an alien authority—for example, the Roman state in antiquity, the Spanish state in the Middle Ages, or the Nazi state in modern time—is condemned to death (Steinsaltz 1976:173–174). The Rabbinic tradition of justice does not just deconstruct state authority; it challenges it.

5

"Liberation" Criminal Justice: Critical and Radical Theories

Whenever social scientists start breaking theories into two opposing categories, look out! Control and containment are just around the corner. Consider how "conflict versus consensus" defangs challenges to the received wisdom of sociology. Marxian thought in criminal justice now has to fit into either "instrumental" or "structural" approaches. These dichotomies should be seen for what they are—damage control. Concluding his 1987 book *Against Criminology*, Stanley Cohen cited Thorsten Sellin to the effect that as social scientists, criminologists cannot afford to allow nonscientists to fix the terms for studying crime. "But this is nothing like the problems when we 'scientists' try to fix these terms and boundaries ourselves" (Cohen 1987/1988:273). Understanding what liberation criminal justice could have been has to start before the control efforts were successful. Historically, that means going back to the cusp of the crisis from 1968 through 1972 and linking it to its beginnings in the postwar period.

Surveying the landscape of a postindustrial Britain, not dissimilar to the United States, Stuart Hall and Tony Jefferson commented on the new edition of their classic *Resistance Through Rituals*.

> Post-industrialization didn't "just happen": it was coercively imposed or driven through—in the old industrial communities, where workers fought for their jobs, communities, and "ways of life"; and in the inner cities and areas of social exclusion and racial disadvantage ... The restoration of private capital's prerogative to "manage" and the spread of privatization "shook out" many jobs and "shook up" those that remained ... The downside of the 1980s, then, was a conflict-ridden decade of induced social disorganization and cultural transformation, as a painful transition to a new, globalized economy and culture was ruthlessly imposed. (Hall and Jefferson 2006:xxvi)

Viewed from the early 1960s this outcome, 20 years hence, was not at all assured. In both Britain and the United States the public recognized inequality as the social and political problem of the day, even as it was on its way down to the lowest in the century. In the next few years, increasing segments of society demanded the promise of industrial productivity be put to use to realize the American and British promise of political democracy. Three questions follow. First, how did 1960s liberation come about? Second, what did liberation criminal justice liberate from? Third, how did critical and radical criminology create liberation criminal justice? The next chapter addresses the question of how liberation criminal justice failed.

Roots of the Sixties' Liberation

> The young militants know or sense that what is at stake is simply their life, the life of human beings which has become a plaything in the hands of politicians and managers and generals. The rebels want to take it out of these hands and make it worth living; they realize that this is still possible today, and the attainment of this goal necessitates a struggle which can no longer be contained by the rules and regulations of a pseudo-democracy in a Free Orwellian World. To them I dedicate this essay. (Marcuse 1969:x)

So ended his preface to an essay Herbert Marcuse wrote at the height of the rebellion of the 1960s. The young militants to whom he referred included political agitators among mainly young—maybe under 30 and probably under 40—Black Americans and members of a more vaguely defined New Left, predominantly White and largely from middle-income if not truly middle-class backgrounds. These young militants drew on several sources for intellectual inspiration and guidance, not the least of which was Marcuse himself. Nonetheless, the initial fire for the political struggle itself may have erupted within American criminal justice, specifically in the prisons.

The writings and personas of prisoners George Jackson (1970, 1972) and Eldridge Cleaver (1967, 1969) inspired Black militancy, especially the Black Panthers, and many non-Black youth of the New Left. Even before them came Caryl Chessman, one of the first to use writing to challenge prison authority and injustice in American criminal justice, and to bring left political attention to capital punishment and prisons (Cummins 1994; Hamm 2001). Eric Cummins (1994:62) asserted that Chessman's main contribution to the California Left was reverence for the outlaw. The "outlaw" should not be understood as defined by criminality, but as the image of those who live outside the law, outside authority structures, and outside of the class, gender, and racial system of conformity.

Although Cummins went on to treat the outlaw imagery's connection with leftist politics as misguided, he brought out another aspect worth exploring—the connection with the hard-boiled detective heroes of Dashiell Hammet and Raymond Chandler, who bore a more than passing resemblance to the gunfighter-cowboy heroes of western writers such as Louis L'Amour. By the postwar period, their stories came to cinema, first in the form of film noir and later in the 1950s by movies such as *Rebel Without a Cause*, *East of Eden*, *The Wild One*, and *On the Waterfront* (Cummins 1994:53). Such artifacts of popular culture bear on the liberation theme of sixties social and political movements because the young people who formed the leadership cadres and mass support grew up on the fiction, film, music, and other expressions of popular culture. Regarding film noir, for instance, George Lipsitz argued that it was not just a commercial trend or artistic cliché. "Film noir addressed the central political issue in U.S. society in the wake of World War II" (Lipsitz 1994:284). He explained that the genre emphasized a desire for community, fear of isolation, struggling for a decent life, and hostility to authority. Citing Alvin Gouldner's 1954 *Wildcat Strike*, he said film noir reproduced the sense of illegitimacy that lay behind wildcat strikes, which was a quotidian part of working-class life. Of course an essential element of detective noir and westerns of the 1940s and 1950s was the fight against corruption associated with wealth and power.

Coinciding with the popular culture's hostility to authority and resistance to corruption, the public relations apparatus of the business and political establishment promoted Cold War propaganda, its attendant anticommunism and concomitant Americanism. Cold War domestic political rhetoric and propaganda, lumped together by the slightly misleading rubric of McCarthyism, attacked radical unionists, many less-than-radical artistic figures, and a range of politicians as Communists and consequently incipient if not actual traitors to the United States. McCarthyism was the domestic arm of Truman's, and later Eisenhower's and Kennedy's Cold War strategy. The international version featured an arms buildup and nuclear stockpiling. Much of the initial impetus for these strategies arose from Truman's penchant for governing by "crisis politics" (Kofsky 1995:234 citing Freeland 1974). This entailed close cooperation with big business, especially those sectors connected with armaments, such as Chase National and National City banks, General Motors, and the DuPont and Rockefeller families. The Truman administration was top heavy with their representatives, including James Forrestal, Averell Harriman, Robert A. Lovett, and Stuart Symington. The war scare of 1948 and ensuing decades of the Cold

War rescued the ailing armaments and aviation industries, but of course laid the foundation for the military-industrial complex that Eisenhower lamented in his 1961 farewell speech.

While the 1950s seemed to represent a victory for big business, its struggle to attain ascendancy went back to the 1930s, when it resisted and later fought to roll back the New Deal. In these struggles, business tried to construct a vision of Americanism that emphasized social harmony, free enterprise, and individual rights (Fones-Wolf 1994:2). The keys to the success of the business program called for technically enlightened management, continually increasing industrial productivity, and celebration of consensual democracy based on the presumptive principles of the founding documents, the Declaration of Independence and Constitution. These last implied equality and equity for all Americans. The problem with such idealizations was an old one in the United States. Equality and equity only applied to certain status groups defined by race and gender. Moreover, equality of opportunity had been shrinking as early industrial capitalism turned into monopoly capitalism and finally the imperialist capitalism that emerged full-fledged after 1945.

A. Philip Randolph, leader of the Black International Brotherhood of Sleeping Car Porters, along with Bayard Rustin and A. J. Muste, threatened a march on Washington in 1941 to ensure fair employment in the war industries. They cancelled it after Roosevelt issued Executive Order 8802 for Fair Employment Practices. After the war, a similar threat forced Truman to desegregate the enlisted men in the military with Executive Order 9981. These milestones marked the beginning of what became known as the civil rights movement, culminating in major federal legislation in the 1964 Civil Rights Act and 1965 Voting Rights Act. Legislative, executive, and judicial successes did not, however, realize the promises of equity and equality so touted by big business propaganda. Nonetheless, the social and civil tactics associated with the movement—sit-ins, boycotts, mass demonstrations, and the like—mobilized not only many heretofore silent African Americans but many White Americans, especially among the youth. Experiences and successes in the 1950s and early 1960s laid the foundations for the sixties radicalism both ideologically and tactically. When those radicals found themselves confronted with increasing resistance to their demand for putting Americanism into practice, many turned to the ideas propounded by the prison writers. The civil rights movement was pivotal in two ways. It brought together Black and White agitators, and it provided grounding for radical thought and demands.

By 1965 Malcolm X represented a nexus among Black and White radicals and political agitation among prisoners. His later work and speeches brought a class consciousness to Black protest and helped the Black prison movement, energized in the early 1960s by the Nation of Islam, to come in line with radical workers' movements and White youth movements. To the prisoners, George Breitman's 1967 *Last Year of Malcolm X: The Evolution of a Revolutionary* created what Eric Cummins described as a "lightning strike" (Cummins 1994:97). Smuggled into prisons, the book presented an antiracialist, class-based ideology, later enunciated by Martin Luther King and, of course, the New Left.

San Quentin Prison in the Bay Area had a fertile field for radical and liberation ideas, actors, and actions surrounding it. Home to some of the leading radical prisoners, it could draw on the radical and antiracist traditions of Harry Bridges' dockworkers' and maritime unions of the 1930s and 1940s. By the mid-1960s, the Bay Area was a focus for countercultural groups and movements: the University of California at Berkeley, Ken Kesey's Merry Pranksters in the Haight, and by 1967, the Summer of Love in San Francisco. Oakland was the birthplace of the Black Panthers under the leadership of Huey Newton and Bobby Seale, and the Panthers soon found common ground with a spectrum of radical movements throughout the country.

Liberation criminology owes much of its foundation to the political, social, and intellectual ferment of the 1960s, and especially the prisoners' movement of the period. Prison writers, international radical intellectuals, and American agitators, not university researchers, broke open the sclerotic discourse of criminal justice in the United States, along with many other hegemonic discourses. How they shaped the discourses in criminal justice and which ones reacted against it, is the story that follows.

Political Radicals

Bobby Seale and Huey Newton organized the Black Panthers in Oakland in fall 1966. In recounting its history, Seale said they self-consciously directed their organizing toward "lumpen proletarian Afro-Americans [in] putting together the ideology of the Black Panther Party" (Seale 1970:ix). He went on to note that by doing so, they contradicted the Marxian dictum that the lumpen proletariat was not revolutionary and often served as the shock troops of reaction. Two clarifications are in order. First, whatever the Panthers thought their target audience may have been, the Panther leadership did not qualify as lumpen. Seale and Newton met in college. Many others came from working-class and a few from professional-class backgrounds. Second, the working class Marx saw in mid-nineteenth-century Europe probably more closely resembled the denizens of mid-twentieth-century American ghettos than the latter did the lumpen proletariat. There were, of course, lumpen Afro-Americans who lived in the neighborhoods where the Panthers organized, but they played the role described by Marx and Engels. In Chicago, for instance, the Blackstone Rangers street gang successfully foiled Panther organizing in the Woodlawn neighborhood. Seale's assertion rose more from the kinds of radical theories to which the Panthers and other radicals had turned. Prominent among them were the anticolonialist and Third World analysts who argued that the most oppressed peoples could make revolution. Their theories appeared well supported, as one only needed to regard the Vietnamese, Cuban, and Chinese revolutions, all of recent origin in the 1960s.

The writings of Amilcar Cabral, Frantz Fanon, Che Guevara, Ho Chi Minh, Mao Zedong, and Vo Nguyen Giap played an important role in forging the thought of sixties radicals. They also drew on leftist, Marxian, and radical critiques of James Boggs, W. E. B. DuBois, C. L. R. James, and Robert F. Williams among others. These mingled with the more traditional European Marxist thinkers and Frankfurt School critical theory, largely through Herbert Marcuse's works (1964, 1965, 1966, 1969, and 1972). Not all the radical agitators and organizers read all these authors. Some probably never read any of them, but typically some did, and they passed on the ideas to those who were not so well read. The point is that sixties radical politics had an impressive intellectual base of Marxian (in the broadest sense), antiracist, and anticolonialist theory and rhetoric. At the same time, the sixties radicals in the United States believed in the ideals of the American Revolution and the viability of democratic institutions (Aronowitz 1986:xi).

The political agitation began with the civil rights movement, then the anti-Vietnam War movement, and soon involved the feminist movement and later the gay movement. Criminal justice issues always came up, since the first-line defense of the status quo historically relied on cops, courts, and prisons. At the twentieth century's midpoint, this was nowhere more obvious than in the South, the old Confederacy. Jim Crow laws passed during the Bourbon restoration at the end of the nineteenth century not only maintained segregation, but Southern criminal justice used both formal and informal means to sustain what Michael Omi and Howard Winant (1994:66) called a racial dictatorship. At first, the civil rights movement used adjudication to mitigate and then modify the established White supremacist regime. In the early years, direct confrontation would have been too dangerous, so the NAACP Legal Defense Fund and other organizations sponsored legal challenges in federal courts. By 1955 the Montgomery, Alabama, bus boycott marked the move toward mass, direct action and increasing reliance on civil disobedience—in other words, law-breaking. Right at the beginning of the mass movement for civil rights, protesters put the question to any presumptive, intrinsic connection between law and justice. Within a few years, the movement began attracting increasing numbers of Northern youth, both Black and White, to take part in sit-ins and freedom rides, which challenged the criminal justice system. The freedom rides were arguably not illegal because of the 1960 U.S. Supreme Court decision in *Boynton v. Virginia*, which struck down segregation laws in interstate transportation. Nonetheless, the freedom riders quickly learned the difference between Supreme Court judgments and American criminal justice. In 1961 Police Chief Eugene "Bull" Connor gained international fame for leading police and Ku Klux Klan volunteers in assaulting and then arresting the freedom riders in Birmingham, Alabama. The publicity attracted more freedom riders and more civil rights workers and protesters to the movement in the South (Arsenault 2006).

By the mid-1960s, the pace began to pick up. The civil rights movement of the South led to passage of the 1964 Civil Rights Act and 1965 Voting Rights Act. The White supremacist political leadership continued massive resistance to implementation by official and unofficial terror. Mass movements and increasing federal enforcement under Attorneys General Nicholas Katzenbach and then Ramsey Clark gradually wore down the resistance. When the movement turned north, it met similar resistance. The issues differed; Northern segregation was not decreed by law as in the South. Northern racism was de facto not de jure, although it often gained support from public policies such as redlining. Economic inequality, large racially defined urban ghettos, and exclusion from political power combined to make the Southern tactics less effective. One result was the urban uprisings of the middle 1960s, typically triggered by provocative tactics from the still almost exclusively White police forces. Harlem in 1964 was followed by Watts in 1965. Newark and Detroit in 1967 were the bloodiest. Many northern cities found themselves occupied by military detachments during these years.

Strikes, sit-ins, and building seizures on university campuses also broke out, usually around a combination of antiwar protests and demands regarding racial equality. Latinos, led initially by agricultural workers but soon including city dwellers, added an additional ethnic dimension to the liberation movements. The National Organization for Women (NOW) was formed in 1966, signaling an increasingly radical feminist movement. These movements used mass protests and various kinds of public demonstrations as important parts of their tactics. Taken together, they challenged the prevailing public order to a degree unseen since the labor militancy of the 1930s. The iconic clash took place around the Democratic National Convention in Chicago during the last part of August 1968. Called a police riot in the Walker Report (1968), the scene soon shifted to the courtroom of federal judge Julius Hoffman in the trial of the Chicago Eight. With Black Panther leader Bobby Seale bound and gagged in his defendant's chair the message became clear. American criminal justice did not tolerate liberation movements.

What's Liberating About Critical and Radical Theories?

Liberation criminal justice thought coincided with much else that claimed a liberation theme associated with the period in history known as "the sixties." In fact, the liberation theme stretched into the first part of the 1970s, and arguably back to at least before the Second World War. Nonetheless, "the sixties" captures a cultural moment, which is comprehensible even if not technically accurate. Contrasting radical criminology with what he called "left realism," Cohen commented as follows:

> What is gained by giving up the romantic and visionary excesses of the 1960s is lost by forgetting the truisms of the new criminology of that decade: that rules are created in ongoing collective struggles; that "crime" is only one of many possible responses to conflict, rule breaking, and trouble; that the criminal law model (police, courts, prisons) has hopelessly failed as a guarantee of protection and social justice for the weak; that crime control bureaucracies and professionals become self-serving and self-fulfilling. These are truths that have not been refuted. Abolitionists might take these truths too literally by trying to translate them into a concrete program of social policy. Realists, however, convert too literally victims' conceptions of their problems into the language of crime. This is to reify the very label that (still) has to be questioned and to legitimate the very system that needs to be weakened. We gain political realism but we lose visionary edge and theoretical integrity. (Cohen 1987:271)

A big part of what is liberating about radical theorizing is questioning the prevailing categories and assumptions. A theorist need not be especially radical to raise such questions. To illustrate, Leroy Gould's work on property crime raised basic questions. In contrast, that of Lawrence Cohen and Marcus Felson, known as routine activities theory, did not (Cohen and Felson 1979; Cohen, Felson, and Land 1980). Gould (1971:98) observed that crime is not simply an act that violates a law, but a complex phenomenon involving a number of individuals and institutions and minimally involving processes of criminalization, control, and criminality. He went on to argue that property crime rates are misleading, as they use population as a base whereas they more usefully should be based on property.

The rate of theft, for instance, is better calculated according to how much there is to steal, rather than how many people can be stolen from.

Cohen and Felson not only take for granted the validity of the Uniform Crime Reports' measures of property crime, they go to some lengths to justify them in comparison to the National Crime Victimization measures. In addition, they base their theory on two assumptions: thieves prefer less-guarded property and closely related people make better guards than those distantly connected to property owners (Cohen, Felson, and Land 1980:98). Granted, the two assumptions serve utilitarian, operational functions, but Cohen and Felson use them without questioning their enormous theoretical baggage. For instance, they do not problematize the concept of theft, which is unforgivable after Jerome Hall's (1935) landmark study. Hall focused on the Carrier's case, 13 Edw. IV, f. 9, pl. 5 (Star Ch. and Exch. Ch. 1473), which transformed the English law of theft from a situation implicitly involving trespass to one in which a servant could steal from his master even when the master had given over the stolen property to the servant. That is, the Carrier's case began to establish theft in a mercantile economy.

Merely by way of illustration of the unquestioning theorizing of Cohen and Felson, consider shoplifting. Today, it is one of the most common property crimes, so common in fact that its total occurrence remains almost impossible to calculate. Now consider how it turned into a crime; by the invention of self-service merchandising. The advent of department stores and supermarkets meant that customers obtained their own merchandise. What then makes shoplifting a crime instead of a simple cost offset to the merchant who initially reduced costs by employing fewer clerks to wait on customers? As Gould pointed out, crime involves many complexities—the concept of property, ownership, the state of economic relations, and so on. Only once those have been specified does it make sense to talk of criminalizing certain kinds of interactions, and only after criminalization has been explored can one justify talk of "offenders," which is the term preferred by Cohen and Felson. In order to display their technical brilliance, Cohen and Felson reified the labels that should be questioned and legitimated the system that needs challenging, to use Stanley Cohen's words.

Critical and radical theorizing in criminology promised liberation from reifications. It offered ways to challenge systems of social control that ultimately depend on physical force backed by the power of the state. The social policy programs, to which Cohen referred, were the kind articulated by the Black Panthers, one of the most radical organizations of the 1960s and 1970s, and one identified by J. Edgar Hoover as Public Enemy Number One (Hilliard 2007). Their proposals involved ways to eventually eliminate prisons or at least humanize treatment within them; to decriminalize so-called victimless crimes such as illicit drug use, prostitution, and the like; and to reconfigure law enforcement so as to make police truly answerable to the public. Their proposals and similar proposals of other radical political organizations hardly seem revolutionary, and in fact they were not. Their importance lies less in their specific programs and more in their emergence from a radical analysis and rejection of prevailing assumptions.

Juvenile justice

In 1968 Aaron Cicourel published a study of juvenile justice with the express intent of exploring methodology and theory for sociology. In his concluding remarks he said, "The study challenges the conventional view which assumes 'delinquents' are 'natural social types distributed in some ordered fashion and produced by a set of abstract 'pressures' from social structures'" (Cicourel 1968:336). He found that delinquents were constructions mainly of authorities—police, probation officials, juvenile court personnel, and occasionally other officials. Official accounts depended to a large extent on local politics, both of the broader electoral kind and the internecine and bureaucratic type found in all organizations in modern societies. Furthermore, the delinquency of particular juveniles depended on the class and status of their family of origin. On this last point, Cicourel observed interactions and official and unofficial discourses.

> Within the same community, differences in law-enforcement personnel perspectives on juveniles, who are in "defiance of authority" or possess "bad attitude," can lead to accelerated incarceration away from home ... Middle-income families, because of their fear of stigma imputed to incarceration, mobilize resources to avoid this problem. (331)

Much of Cicourel's critique aimed against the easy acceptance of official statistics and the prevalent inclination to find delinquency associated with disadvantaged people and neighborhoods. The latter, of course, is a holdover from the Chicago School's social disorganization theory (Shaw and McKay 1942). Shaw and McKay are not the only theorists he criticized. He also referred to Albert K. Cohen (1955), Walter B. Miller (1958), Richard Cloward and Lloyd Ohlin (1960), Gresham Sykes and David Matza (1957), and Matza (1964), among others. That is, he criticized the major theoretical positions about juvenile delinquency dominant at the time. All of them, from Cicourel's point of view, assumed too much, especially when it came to the official versions of delinquency propounded by the very apparatuses designed to control it.

Cicourel's theory of delinquency, which some have mischaracterized as a type of labeling theory, explains a good deal about empirical findings in juvenile delinquency. For instance, it explains the preponderance of impoverished minorities identified as delinquent not by what the juveniles do, but by how they and their social origins fit with official assumptions about delinquency. It helps explain the age distribution of delinquency. Specifically, the older people become, the less likely they are to be construed as "defiant," unless, of course, their delinquent careers continue into adult criminality. In that case, findings of delinquency continue, but with a continual updating to adult standards. Moreover, Cicourel's theory meets the objections of Peter Kraska (2006), who lamented the paucity of criminal justice theory, which focuses on the systems and organization of criminal, as opposed to criminological, theory with its focus on crime and criminality. In sum, Cicourel's approach has much to recommend it, but those who search through citation guides, works cited, and references sections of contemporary publications, or for that matter discussions of criminal justice theory, would find few mentions of it. In contrast, Travis Hirschi's 1969 *Causes of Delinquency* remains a mainstay in the literature.

There are two problems with Cicourel's theory for post-1970s criminal justice. First it uses a framework not favored by the abstracted empiricism regnant in the discipline. Second, and related to the first, his theory leads to questioning and possibly undermining the systems, organizations, and ultimately the raison d'être of academic criminal justice. Cicourel used the phenomenology of Alfred Schutz (1932, 1962) derived partly from the philosophy of Edmund Husserl. The part of social phenomenology that can give it a liberating effect insists on questioning and minutely examining the received wisdom of social objects—that is, social phenomenology is a sharp tool for slicing apart reifications.

Critical Theory

Liberation criminological theory owes much to the critical theory of the Frankfurt School. Few Frankfurt School theorists directly addressed criminal justice, but their perspective and philosophical methodology allows for radical analyses. The best-known and only truly comprehensive attempt by Frankfurt School representatives remains Rusche and Kirchheimer's 1939 *Punishment and Social Structure*. Two aspects of their analysis have proven resilient. First, they contextualized penality historically. The main thesis of the book, that variations in regimes of punishment correlate with variations in the political economy, has suffered simplistic vulgarizations by later researchers. The second aspect, the relevance of class conflict to criminal justice, has had wider application.

Combining phenomenological insights and methodology with the American pragmatism and transactional analysis of George Herbert Mead permitted students of social deviance such as Edwin Lemert (1951, 1967, Lemert and Rosberg 1948) and Howard Becker (1963) to develop what some, often disparagingly, called labeling theory. As Becker pointed out in 1973 by adding a chapter to his 1963 *The Outsiders*, the labeling perspective was never meant as a theory. Becker, in despair at correcting the continual misunderstanding, wrote that from then on, he would call it "an interactionist theory of deviance" (181). Both he and Lemert often invoked social stratification to explain patterns of deviance. Briefly, they argued that those who labeled were the powerful, and those who got labeled were the weak. In modern society the powerful and weak are defined by class and status.

On the dictum that comedy captures contemporary society better than tragedy, consider William Chambliss's study of deterrence (1966), which focused on campus parking. Nonacademics often believe that the professoriat devote their cogitating moments to profound mysteries of their chosen field of study. The cognoscenti realize that parking more often occupies their minds. The main thrust of Chambliss's article focused on the proper scientific methodology in studying the deterrent effect of punishment, but along the way, he described something perhaps even more significant. He began by noting that an influx of students to the campus in the early 1950s resulted in insufficient parking space. First, the university restricted student parking to a few peripheral lots. Then the faculty council introduced fines for parking violations: one dollar for faculty, but for students, one dollar for the first offense, three for the second, and five for the third. Students with more than three violations had their driving rights revoked, and if they received four or more tickets, they faced disciplinary action by the dean. Although the faculty received one-dollar citations, collection was voluntary and they faced no additional punishments. The system prevailed from 1951 until 1956. Presumably, parking violations by students and faculty bore the same character—that is, student illicit parking was neither more nor less heinous than that of faculty. Within the relatively restricted milieu of the campus, the faculty criminalized students for the same infractions as those perpetrated by faculty, whom they did not criminalize.

A bit of speculative imagination leads to the following scenario. As parking and enforcement became more of an issue, student offenders began to organize various rackets—counterfeit parking permits, for instance. Criminologists began to study the student offenders, noting their home backgrounds, associations with other delinquents, perhaps certain psychological characteristics such as excitability and defiant attitudes. Soon, an entire subfield of criminology arose. The more politically inclined faculty lobbied for administrative positions with a "get tough on parking violators" policy, and so on. Going out on a limb, one could say that overall, the faculty probably came from a higher-class background than the students. The university in question was a state institution. The student influx came from the expansion of educational opportunities facilitated by the postwar GI Bill. Established faculty entered their careers when academics tended to come from a class where remuneration was not the most important criteria, because they were economically comfortable. Needless to say, the status of faculty was higher than that of the students. Obviously too, the faculty on that particular campus controlled administrative minutiae. Parallels to the American criminal justice system should be apparent.

Now consider another scenario. Take President George W. Bush and Vice President Richard Cheney. Arguably both have perpetrated a series of crimes leading to extensive loss of life and destruction of property. In their youth, both had minor criminal citations associated with inebriation and motor vehicles, which taken together present dangers to themselves and others. Cheney came from a middle-income family. His father worked as a soil conservation engineer with the U.S. Department of Agriculture. Bush came from an upper-class background. A review of their careers reveals that they never desisted from criminal behavior. Nonetheless, they do not fit the assumptions about crime, criminality, or criminalization embedded in American criminal justice. Neither, in their youth, appeared as defiant or threatening to authority, although both clearly exhibited such behavior in their public offices. That they were not criminalized should come as no surprise. Critical theory allows, indeed invites, analysis of why this should be so.

As Cicourel pointed out, their youthful contretemps mobilized family resources to ensure no serious involvement with the criminal justice system. They learned good manners, so their interactions with authorities tended not to antagonize control agents or lead them to display a defiant attitude. The image of Richard B. Cheney as vice president is consistent with a high-level business executive. High-level business executives carry, as part of their persona, a presumption of conformity and law-abiding behavior, regardless of the reality of their deeds. Thus, even if they were not well-known public figures, law enforcement personnel would be unlikely to target them for scrutiny. Class and status, including their obvious racial and ethnic characteristics, immediately frame interactions with norm enforcers. What critical theory opened were the kinds of questions about American criminal justice that problematized why people like George W. Bush and Richard B. Cheney were not criminalized and why members of minority categories from lower-class backgrounds living in impoverished ghettos are criminalized, and to an astonishing degree. Without belaboring the data, a Black male, born as of 2006, stands a one in three chance of going to prison in his lifetime.

Liberating from Liberal Criminal Justice

Radical questioning of reifications and legitimized systems typically involves a paradigm shift of the kind Thomas Kuhn (1970) described for natural sciences. The paradigm from which radical analyses liberated criminal justice thinking bore all the trappings of the systems paradigm so popular in the postwar intellectual zeitgeist. Two efforts embody the systems paradigm: the President's Commission on Law Enforcement and Administration of Justice (1967a, 1967b, 1967c, 1967d) and the American Bar Foundation survey of 1955–1959. According to Samuel Walker (1992:47), the Bar Foundation survey set the standard for the 1967 President's Commission, and the survey's approach "dominates teaching and research [citations omitted] and has shaped most of the reform efforts over the past 25 years." Although the systems paradigm survived, its liberal orientation disappeared during the 1970s. It disappeared partly because of the success of radical movements and radical questioning regarding almost all areas of social life, which peaked in the late 1960s and early 1970s. The other force that destroyed the liberal consensus of the postwar era came from the reaction against the radical movements.

Samuel Walker began his review of the systems paradigm by quoting Frank Remington, a codirector of the Bar Foundation survey. "To a large extent, the administration of criminal justice can be characterized as a series of important decisions from the time a crime is committed until the offender is finally released from supervision" (Walker 1992:47). Remington's statement exudes reifications and assumed legitimacy. First, it assumes the administration of criminal justice is a thing that is observable, a reification. Second, it assumes the legitimacy of two categories—"crime" and "offender." Third, its perspective is that of the apparatuses of social control—police, courts, and corrections. Finally, the image of justice it projects is the assembly line, which Herbert Packer (1968) identified with the crime control model of criminal justice. Of course the assembly line still dominated the organization of industrial production and, to a large extent, implicit models of social organizations of all types.

Walker (1992:52) went on to note that the Bar Foundation's findings took their shape from its methodology, the direct observation of criminal justice agencies in action. The survey leadership, Frank Remington and Lloyd Ohlin, were academics, as were most of the research and analytic staff members. Many had served in various kinds of administrative and advisory posts in the very systems they studied. As Leon Trotsky so trenchantly said, "in times of alarm, the priests of 'conciliatory justice' are usually found sitting on the inside of four walls waiting to see which side will win. [But] the serious and critical reader will not want a treacherous impartiality, which offers him a cup of conciliation with the well-settled poison of reactionary hate at the bottom" (1932:v). The Bar Foundation conducted its survey before the times of alarm had begun to shake the walls of criminal justice. The late 1950s contained only premonitions of what was to come. The 1967 President's Commission, on the other hand, was a response to the alarm created by reactionary interests worried about the civil rights movement, the extension of constitutional protections to individuals under the Warren Supreme Court, and the ghetto uprisings beginning in 1964. Part of the reaction and part of what became received wisdom and unquestioned fact was the rise in crime rates, created by measuring police reaction to individuals of lower classes and statuses.

The main product of the President's Commission was the final report, *The Challenge of Crime in a Free Society* (1967a) and its addenda task force reports (1967b, 1967c, 1967d). A year later, the National Advisory Commission on Civil Disorders (1968) found racism, especially among police, as a major cause of the ghetto uprisings. The 1967 President's Commission also found rampant racism. In addition, the President's Commission found complexity in the criminal justice system, exacerbated by the complexity of tasks faced by police and the inevitable discretionary character of policing and other justice tasks contributed to discriminatory justice. It also found that many criminal justice decisions failed to follow legal norms. Finally it stressed that each of the agencies operating in the various aspects of criminal justice—law enforcement, the judicature, and corrections—affected the others in systemic ways (Walker 1992:66).

The President's Commission proposed recommendations that in some ways seemed counterintuitive but in fact should have been expected, given knowledge of government and academic bureaucracies. Basically, they recommended more of the same. This meant enhancing the trend toward professionalization of police, added technology and better record keeping, streamlined court processing, rationalization of sentencing—all with continued monitoring and advice from academic experts and supported by federal funding. This program kept in line with much of the Johnson presidency's pattern of policies. It placed a heavy reliance on technical expertise and top-down hierarchical administration of federal programs, which in turn supported existing local efforts. Ideals of increasing equality and access to opportunity also characterized the Johnson approach, not just in criminal justice but in health, education, and welfare. It was a liberal program in the sense of carrying on the reforms of the New Deal, and in the sense of helping to realize the liberal consensus that had dominated American politics and social policies since the New Deal. The trouble it presented to liberation movements was that the liberal consensus was the establishment against which they were rebelling.

Federal money, some parceled out through the Law Enforcement Assistance Administration and some through block grants to localities, began to move American criminal justice in the direction outlined by the President's Commission. Much of the money went to train and equip local police for crowd control. Some aided in the professionalization of police, although it also supported lawsuits in federal courts that changed police departments from White enclaves to include increasing numbers of minorities and women. Certain kinds of misdemeanor offenses, such as drunkenness, were decriminalized, thereby giving some relief to court dockets. Regular criminal defense for indigent defendants became institutionalized at state and federal levels throughout the country. The most instructive changes occurred in corrections.

Correctional Reform

One of the codirectors of the President's Commission, Lloyd Ohlin, edited a volume on correctional reform, *Prisoners in America* (1973), that served as background reading for a session of the American Assembly at Columbia University. The Assembly session found that rehabilitation had failed (Nelson 1973). In his introduction, Ohlin referred to a report by the American Friends Service Committee on corrections in the United States entitled *Struggle for Justice* (1971). In a sense, because it was unintended, *Prisoners in America* was the liberal establishment's response to *Struggle for Justice*. The former contains chapters written by academics on various aspects of corrections—juvenile justice, jails, community corrections, prisons, diversion programs, and research programs. In contrast, *Struggle for Justice* is a collective work in which not only academics but political agitators and prisoners themselves participated. They began by citing two recent riots, one at Holmesburg Prison in Pennsylvania and the other at the Tombs in New York City. They quote a description of Holmesburg: "a cruel, degrading and disgusting place, likely to bring out the worst in man . . . a place ruled . . . by 'cold-blooded terror'" (AFSC 1971:1). Of the Tombs, they refer to a list of grievances by the prisoners challenging conditions and court procedures, emphasizing inadequate food, filthy cells, brutality, lack of medical care, and insufficient legal representation. The report went on to characterize American penality as mainly unwarranted, completely unequal, discriminatory and arbitrary, and failing in one of its stated goals—rehabilitation. This last point is the principle point of agreement between the findings of the American Assembly and those of the American Friends. Secondarily, they paralleled each other on the issue of discrimination and arbitrary sentencing, although they started from entirely different, if not opposing, premises. A telling differentiator are their respective references and suggestions for further reading. While both cite renowned academic works like Herbert Packer's *The Limits of the Criminal Sanction*, the American Friends also cited Eldridge Cleaver, George Jackson, and Malcolm X.

Struggle for Justice represents liberation criminology. It questioned the basic social structures of inequality in the United States and pointed out that criminal justice has long served to maintain that inequality. It questioned the legitimacy of punishment for any purpose, finally concluding that the very best that could be said for it was that it was a necessary evil, with stress on the evil. In examining the nature of legal prohibition, it identified three prerequisites to passing a criminal law. First, there must be a compelling social need, recognizing at the same time that widespread nonconformity with cultural norms is a strength rather than a weakness in a democratic society. Second, prohibitive laws must be a last resort in that there is no other feasible way of obtaining compliance with absolutely necessary norms. Third, there must be a substantial basis for thinking that punishment is better than doing nothing. Going back to Chambliss's study of parking regulation, it should be clear that the system of violations and punishments failed each of these prerequisites. So, upon reflection, would vice regulation. On the other hand, criminalizing violations of worker safety, product safety, toxic emissions, and similar white-collar activities seldom treated as crimes would pass all of them. The book concluded by saying, "A major emphasis of this study has been to cut back the inevitably coercive criminal law and to avoid using the criminal justice system to solve social problems." This viewpoint is one with which all liberation criminal justice perspectives could agree.

Later Developments in Liberation Criminology

Lewis Lapham began an essay prompted by the recent police killing of a civilian, Sean Bell, that occurred in New York City on November 25,

2006, by quoting from John Milton, to wit: "There is no art that hath bin more cranker'd in her principles, more soyl'd, and slubber'd with aphorisming pedantry then the art of policie" (Lapham 2008:8). His Milton quotation allowed him to compare American criminal justice and its judicature in particular to Milton's condemnation of the English Star Chamber of the seventeenth century and the royal taking of forests and common grazing as trial by fiat. In the incident, five plainclothes policemen who had been staking out a strip club in Queens fired 50 shots at Sean Bell, a 23-year-old Black man who was sitting unarmed in a car with two companions. On April 25, 2008, New York State Supreme Court Justice Arthur J. Cooperman, in a bench trial, found the three defendant policemen before his court "not guilty" of any of the homicide and aggravated assault charges. Hardly any similar incidents ever make it as far as a criminal trial, and of those rare cases, defendant police seem perennially not guilty. Critiques written in the 1970s and after often revert to the continuation of abusive use of power by police as part of their empirical support for analyzing criminal justice as an instrument of social policy aimed at controlling the masses.

Several important innovations in criminal justice theory appeared in the 1970s, and more have developed since then. Those that fall into the liberation category probably owe their origins to the social changes of the late 1960s and early 1970s. Theoretical thinking, taking time to incubate, tended to be formalized only afterwards.

Surveying the various liberation criminologies published after 1970 is easier if they are sorted into categories. The danger of such typologies is the tendency to think of them as Weberian ideal types instead of rubrics for their respective main emphases. With that caveat in mind, they fall into the following: Marxian, racial feminist, transactional, and non-Marxist social conflict types of theories. Current, so-called postmodern theories usually identify postmodernist trends in criminal justice, but they also rely on one or more of the foregoing typical emphases for their analysis.

Representatives of Marxian kinds of approaches include Richard Quinney, Steven Spitzer, and Austin T. Turk. Not meant as an exhaustive list, these three share an emphasis on examining criminal justice as a set of apparatuses and practices that function as weapons in class struggles. Quinney summed up the central thrust of Marxian criminology (again keep in mind that the following is illustrative rather than exhaustively representative):

A new form of crime control was being established in capitalist society [beginning in the late 1960s]. Not only was the war on crime intensified by legislation, presidential commissions, and policy research by liberal academicians, but the capitalist state was now instituting a new system of domestic control ... [A]ll levels of government were involved in planning and implementing an apparatus to secure the existing capitalist order. (Quinney 1980:10)

Whereas Marxist critiques emphasized class, racial and feminist critiques at least as forcefully emphasized status, race/ethnicity and gender respectively. Sometimes combining a class and status analysis, feminist critical theory pointed to the role of criminal justice in supporting patriarchy. That patriarchy and capitalism co-occur in all modern societies points to criminalization of women's shoplifting, prostitution, and other involvement in vice. Women bear the brunt of those patterns of criminalization because of their role in production, consumption, and, most importantly, reproduction of labor power (Balkan, Berger, and Schmidt 1980; Schwendinger and Schwendinger 1983).

Critical race theory, sometimes combined with a class analysis, has enormous empirical fodder for its incisive analyses. Black Americans, Latinos and Latinas, and Native Americans are persistently overrepresented as victims of crime and in every part of the criminal justice apparatus. These minorities, who often live in racial and ethnic ghettos, are at much higher risks from violence including homicide and rape. They are the victims of theft of all kinds, not just from their fellow ghetto denizens but systematically through white-collar crime. They are arrested more, jailed more, convicted more, and imprisoned more than Whites or some other ethnic/racial groups such as those with Asian ancestry.

To name just one analyst, Katherine Beckett (1997) explored the origins of the racialization of American criminal justice as part of right-wing politics of the 1960s and beyond. She showed that the civil rights movement gained early identification in the South as crime and criminal conspiracy. National politicians such as Barry Goldwater in 1964, followed by Richard Nixon in 1968 and thereafter, used underlying racism in American culture to further their political campaigns and as part of a broad strategy of social and political control. Another theoretical perspective views the criminal justice system as one of the historic apparatuses for maintaining status boundaries and hierarchy. For instance, David Barlow and Melissa Barlow (2000), in their history of policing, emphasize the foundational character of police as mainly slave patrols, and not just in the South.

A non-Marxist but still social conflict perspective on criminal justice is found in the theoretical work of Donald Black (1976, 1998), who saw law in general, not just the criminal part of it, as a force in social inequality. He famously hypothesized that the more unequal a society, the more law it will have and employ to maintain hierarchical relations. Law in this case should be understood to include more than just statutes and regulations. Black meant law to cover policing, adjudication, and penality as well as much of what occurs in regulatory and civil realms.

The preceding brief review of some of the post-1970 critical criminology merely highlights and illustrates the rich production of analytic and theoretical work after the rebellious years of the late 1960s and early 1970s. The ideas did not go away, but they were swept out of strategic positions from which they could influence policy. How and why that happened is the subject of the next two chapters.

6

The Rule of Law and the Ruling Class

The failed world revolution of 1968 may have signaled the beginning of the end for the global hegemony of what Wallerstein (2004) called centrist liberalism, but that was not the first time liberalism came under attack. Famously, the reactionary right, spearheaded by the National Socialists, successfully defeated Weimar liberalism in Germany by the early 1930s. They replaced the Weimar Republic with the Third Reich. In 1940, the year the Third Reich arguably reached its apex, Otto Kirchheimer, the Frankfurt School legal theorist, wrote an article on criminal law in Nazi Germany. Kirchheimer said that in the immediate aftermath of the fall of the Weimar Republic, there arose an authoritarian ideology that mingled with elements of the old classical criminal theory. Their amalgamation immediately led to harsher punishments and weakened the status of defendants.

In the early period when the Nazis consolidated power, the main national socialist contribution, according to Kirchheimer, was the "volitional character of penal law [which] completely shifted emphasis from the objective characteristics of the criminal act to its subjective elements." Furthermore, the Nazi legal theory demanded "greater self-control from the individual ... The most important practical consequence of this more or less deliberately vague theory was a disappearance of the distinction usually separating criminal attempt and consummated act" (Kirchheimer 1940:172). He went on to note that as the Nazis consolidated power and increasingly deployed their peculiar brand of populism, the Aryan *Volksgemeinschaft*, this volitional criminology ran into complications from the Nazi racialist ideology, and the two strains of thought could never be fully reconciled (Wetzell 2000). Some other consequences of Nazi criminal law perspicuously included an increasing harshness in juvenile justice. Under the new Nazi approach, juveniles between 16 and 18 could be waived into adult court if their offenses or the circumstances of the offenses were especially heinous. Additionally, the Nazi criminal justice system undermined the independence of defense attorneys, threatening them with charges of criminal collaboration for defending their clients. Perhaps most relevant was Kirchheimer's discussion of the importance of images of criminals. "The war parasite, the precociously dangerous criminal youth, and the brutal criminal, as they appear in the war decrees, are criminal types for which the pictorial impression (*Bildtechnik*) prevails over precise legal definition (*Merkmalstechnik*)" (Kirchheimer 1940:183)—shades of Willie Horton.

For those who monitor policy and administrative practices in the criminal justice systems of the United States, the post-Weimar program in Germany bears an uncanny resemblance. The following are all too familiar in the United States of the last three decades: (1) rolling back or skirting gains made under the Warren Court to protect defendants' rights; (2) increasingly longer prison sentences and reduction or elimination of parole; (3) legislation that lowers the age of juvenile culpability and increases the ease of waivers to adult courts; (4) crime by association under such laws as RICO (Racketeer Influenced and Corrupt Organizations Act); (5) asset forfeiture laws allowing seizure of wealth of those suspected but not necessarily even accused of a crime; and (6) most recently, terrorism laws that make thinking about terrorism a crime and expose defense attorneys to prosecution, for example Lynne Stewart, who was sentenced to 28 months in prison for making public statements about her imprisoned client Omar Abdel-Rahman. Finally, of course, imagery replaced legal precision to create a public sentiment in favor of retributive justice and incapacitation as normal policies. The parallels are not incidental. The authoritarian bent in American criminal justice in theories, policies, and practices has arisen since the 1970s for the same kinds of reasons it arose in post-Weimar Germany. Moreover, and especially relevant for this argument, the theoretical orientation of authoritarian German criminal justice and American criminal justice share the same ideological frameworks and conceptual foundations.

Of course, twenty-first-century America is not 1930s Germany. The United States is much larger—the world's third-largest country in population with over 300 million inhabitants whose origins are truly global, and who add to an increasingly diverse and ever-expanding culture. The United States was one of the first states based on classical liberal political principles, while Germany had come to them only neoterically. While Germany was crushed diplomatically, economically, and politically by the First World War, U.S. hegemony in the world has been increasing since that time. Nonetheless, some of the other differences support rather than detract from useful comparisons, even analogies. Take the issue of racism, for example. As Kirchheimer pointed out, the rationalistic authoritarianism of the early Nazi state became entangled with the emerging *Völkisch* racial state. In contrast, the United States has always been a racial state, and arguably a prime function of its criminal justice system over the centuries has been to police the boundaries of racial status groups. The argument does not, however, rest on an always-suspect historical just-so narrative. Comparing the two, Nazi Germany and contemporary America, brings out basic, structural characteristics and similarities, which have predictable effects on criminal justice systems and theories about them.

The main structural factors pushing the criminal justice system toward authoritarianism are the assault on liberalism and a crisis of capitalism. Again, the particulars differ between post-WWI Germany and postmodern, twenty-first-century America, but they have similar influences and effects. In both cases, a leftist, revolutionary force pushed against a liberal bourgeois state. With remarkable regularity, capitalist ruling classes, when threatened by mass movements, always turn to the right and authoritarianism, rather than accommodating leftist demands. Marx's *Eighteenth Brumaire* (1852/1869) is the classic analysis. In Germany, the liberals turned to the Junker-dominated army and the reactionary paramilitary bands to put down the Spartacist revolt and assassinate its leaders, Rosa Luxemburg and Karl Liebknecht. Repeatedly during the Weimar period, whenever the liberal bourgeoisie perceived a challenge from the left, they allied themselves with the right and used the armed organizations associated with state power to quell disruptions. Each time, the ruling class moved further right, closer to the haute bourgeoisie and landed gentry. By the time of the 1932 presidential election, Hitler was the moderate candidate who lost to the conservative Hindenburg.

The potentially revolutionary movements of mid-twentieth-century America culminated in the great confrontations and failed revolution of 1968, as discussed in more detail in the previous chapter. Just as in Weimar Germany, the liberal, bourgeois ruling class kept moving to the right, aligning themselves more closely with their class allies, the conservatives. Just as in 1920s Germany, not only did capitalists face a political challenge, but the capitalist economic system veered toward a crisis. In the early twentieth century, the crisis eventuated in the world depression of the 1930s. In the late twentieth and early twenty-first centuries, the crisis is even more threatening as the falling rate of profit in world capitalism approaches its asymptotic nadir. Dario Melossi (1993, 2000, 2003, and 2004) has argued that when elites perceive challenges to their hegemony, two things happen simultaneously: "people work harder for less money, and prisons fill beyond capacity" (1993:266). Furthermore, the elites promulgate images of

moral crisis as public relations gambits to shape mass opinion and acquiescence toward, as Melossi so aptly put it, revanchist criminology (2000)
and mass internment (2004).

Neither 1920s Germany nor postmodern America had a shortage of
authoritarian criminal justice theories. The supply will probably never dry
up. At times they fall out of favor and retire to the academic and policy
margins, only to reemerge when needed, often dressed in more up-to-date
fashions. That is what began to happen in 1968. The first was cobbled
together by the neoliberal economist Gary Becker. Also in 1968 James Q.
Wilson made his first book-length foray into criminal justice issues with
Varieties of Police Behavior. Then, a Berkeley sociology student, Travis
Hirschi (1969), disguised his warmed-over psychologism as social bond
theory. Had not a reactionary program emanating from Wall Street and
Washington DC intervened, these theoretical essays might have remained
minor turbulences in the mainstream of criminology. Becker's theory owes
its origins to the liberal economists of the eighteenth century. The likes
of Adam Smith and David Ricardo had managed to idealize reciprocal
activities of people that had been occurring since time immemorial while
neglecting the real substance of how things get produced, distributed, and
consumed. Hirschi's social bond theory gestures toward Durkheim and his
concepts of social solidarity, but in fact it finds its roots in seventeenth-
century psychology, what H. B. Gibson (1970) called Hobbesian. So, the
ideas were not new. Becker, Wilson, and Hirschi merely dressed them in
mid-twentieth-century American vernacular, embroidered with popular
images of contemporary social life.

A Tale of Two Universities: Chicago and Harvard

The stories always start in Hyde Park at the University of Chicago, but
then they end up on the east coast as part of the Cambridge–Wall
Street–Washington axis. This trajectory even applies to Travis Hirschi's
ideas, despite his absence from Chicago as either student or faculty mem-
ber. Conceptual incubation takes place at the University of Chicago, then
hatches into policy at Harvard, whence it turns into laws in Washington
and practices on Wall Street. After that they multiply and colonize America
and the world.

Hyde Park turned into the hotbed of neoconservatism gradually in the
1950s. It centered in two departments, economics and political science. In
economics Milton Friedman was the dominant figure. He espoused a libertarian political economic philosophy that had much in common with
the thought of Friedrich Hayek. William Scheuerman (1997) linked Hayek
with the thought of Nazi jurist Carl Schmitt. The main idea they held in

common was that the welfare state and state intervention were revolutionary and destructive of the political structure, which depends on the domination by those with property and education (183). In the 1970s Friedman got to use his economic theories by redesigning the economy of Chile under Augusto Pinochet, the fascist military dictator. In many ways, Friedman's Chile became the model for neoliberalism in Latin America—reliance on first-world investors, payoffs to comprador elites in the home country, all backed up by a police state. The critical aspect of the neoliberal economic perspective is its antiwelfarism, not its misleading rhetoric about limited state intervention. Neoliberalism needs plenty of state intervention so long as its aim is to control the masses and refrain from regulating the profit centers.

Gary Becker's Rational Choice criminology springs from the same ground. It unabashedly claims to account for criminal activity as thoroughly volitional.

> The approach taken here follows the economists' usual analysis of choice and assumes that a person commits an offense if the expected utility to him exceeds the utility he could get by using his time and other resources at other activities. Some persons become "criminals," therefore, not because their basic motivation differs from that of other persons, but because their benefits and costs differ. (Becker 1968:176)

Becker's understanding of criminality bears all the earmarks of neoliberalism. It is highly abstract, using an imaginary economic person as its central unit of analysis. It offers a mathematical model that purports to account for and predict crime, but in fact it has never done so. It appeals to the classical liberal assumption of human rationality, without realizing that classical liberalism was thoroughly grounded in class consciousness and class analysis because the aristocracy of the ancien régime denied human status to commoners. Classical liberalism asserted the rationality of all persons as part of its argument in favor of equality and a rational political system. Neoliberalism ignores its roots in those respects.

While there are differences between neoliberalism and neoconservatism, they come down to variations of tactics to ensure ruling-class control. Therefore, Becker's Rational Choice criminology may be neoliberal rather than neoconservative, but scholars in criminal justice have used it in neoconservative ways (Cornish and Clark 1986). Just as Milton Friedman used neoliberal economics to support the fascist regime in Chile, Rational Choice theory rationalized revanchist criminology and mass internment (Melossi 2000, 2004).

James Q. Wilson's criminology does not lack class analysis, even if he rarely made it explicit. Its whole import is to ensure that the lower classes know their place, as he said in the eponymous article for Broken Windows theory (Wilson and Kelling 1982). At the time of the article, Wilson was already at Harvard, but he started his academic career at Chicago in political science. There too was Leo Strauss, the father of what came to be called neoconservatism. Strauss's brand of reactionary political philosophy came to Wilson mainly through his mentor Edward Banfield, a great friend of Strauss. One of its main tenets, as with the neoliberals on the economics faculty, was antiwelfarism. Consider Wilson's identification of the problem his theory and policy solves:

> Everyday in most big cities and many small ones, we experience the problem. Homeless people asleep on a grate; beggars soliciting funds by the bus stop; graffiti on the bridge abutment; teenagers hanging out in front of the deli; loud music coming from an open window. How should conduct in public spaces be regulated and by whom? (Wilson 1996:xiv)

When Edward Banfield moved to Harvard, he brought his protégé there to join him. Ensconced in an endowed chair in the Harvard political science department, Wilson, supported by a number of right-wing think tanks and foundations such as the Manhattan Institute, could wield enormous influence on public policy. He became well known with his 1975 book *Thinking About Crime*, which mainly consisted of articles he had published in trade magazines, especially the one administered by the elder neoconservative Irving Kristol. Malcolm Feeley claimed the book soon "became the bible of the new criminology" (2003:120). It also attracted policy advocates and criminal justice practitioners. Always benefiting, not only from his position at Harvard but also from support by neoconservative money and organizations, his Broken Windows became arguably the single most influential statement of policy since the end of the Second World War.

Tracing the genealogy of Travis Hirschi's social bond, and later his Self-Control theory with collaborator Michael Gottfredson, is more circuitous than tracing the ideas of Becker and Wilson. Hirschi himself was never at Chicago or Harvard, but he built his ideas on a distorted kind of social theory prominent in the Chicago School of sociology. Chicago sociology was beholden to two main European theorists and one that was local. The founder of the Chicago School, Albion Small, and some of its most prominent early faculty such as Robert Park and W. I. Thomas, had attended lectures by Georg Simmel and Emile Durkheim. At the same time, the early twentieth century, George Herbert Mead was propounding what later became symbolic interactionism.

Hirschi initially put together the Durkheimian idea of the importance of social bonds with Mead's idea that social interaction was formative for the self. Others did the same, including an early Chicago criminologist,

Edwin Sutherland. Unlike Sutherland, Hirschi turned the concepts into a brand of psychologism. Durkheim focused on social bonds, notably in his book on suicide (1896). There, Durkheim argued for a sociological understanding of suicide and explained variations in rates of suicide by differences in social bonds in societies and subcultures. Mead, of course, stressed the importance of symbolic communication in primary groups. In Hirschi's hands in Berkeley, these very sociological approaches became a stripped-down version of the psychology of delinquents. What may have assisted in the distortion was Hirschi's reliance on the work of Eleanor and Sheldon Glueck. They were at Harvard Law School and were known for their psychobiological explanation of delinquency. Their best-known publication was the 1950 *Unraveling Juvenile Delinquency*, where they claimed to offer a multifactor approach. In fact, it reiterated a medical model of delinquency inherited from their mentor, William Healy, MD (1869–1963). Criticized for what Jon Snodgrass (1972:321) called "methodological irregularities and statistical prestidigitation," they found what they had already decided they would find, namely that delinquency and crime came from aberrations internal to delinquents and criminals. Hirschi emulated their theoretical conclusion and methodology in both his "social bond" and "general" theories of crime.

Two common threads run through these genealogies. First, they locate criminality inside individuals. Second, they assume a distinction between criminals and noncriminals. In the case of Becker's Rational Choice, his claim that anyone could be a criminal does not obviate the observation. If Rational Choice determined criminality, then criminality should be more or less evenly distributed in the U.S. population. It is not. Criminality occurs disproportionately among those in the lower economic rungs and among racial and ethnic minorities. Behavior that violates the law might be evenly distributed, but criminality, the designation of behavior as criminal and identification of criminal actors, has a decided racial and class bias. Therefore, using Becker's model for policy ensures the promulgation of a criminal class. Volitional theories in criminal justice always disguise class theories—a criminal versus a noncriminal class. These criminal class theories are not innocent of other kinds of stratification theories, because the criminal class always derives from the lower classes and marginalized status groups, usually based on race or ethnicity. In this way, criminal justice theories become instruments of class warfare.

The Ruling-Class Backlash

Lewis F. Powell (1907–1998) created a pivotal document in the class war. On August 23, 1971, he sent a confidential memorandum, "Attack on the

American Free Enterprise System," to Eugene B. Sydnor Jr., the chair of the Education Committee, U.S. Chamber of Commerce. Powell himself was a strategically placed corporate lawyer in the Richmond, Virginia, law firm of Hunton, Williams, Gay, Powell, and Gibson, now known as Hunton & Williams. In the memo, he decried the attack on America's ruling class, which he called "business leaders," by "Communists, New Leftists and other revolutionaries." Some of those he named were the attorney William Kunstler, Yale professor Charles Reich, and Ralph Nader. One noted academic he approved of and quoted was Milton Friedman. Powell laid out a multiple-point program for the ruling class to defend itself. The first order in the program identified higher education. He called for establishing a "staff of scholars" supported by corporate interests, a "staff of speakers" and "speaker's bureau," "evaluation of textbooks," and "balancing of faculties." Next he said that ruling-class interests should be represented in the mass media, scholarly journals, books, advertising, and political activism. Viewed in retrospect and by its effects, the ruling class adopted his program. Powell's memo and program initiated a flow of enormous resources to the promotion of ideas, policies, and political ventures already under way (O'Connor 2008). Powell, himself, apparently decided to join the fray shortly after he wrote his memo. Because of his lucrative law practice, he had turned down Richard Nixon's 1969 request that he serve on the U.S. Supreme Court. In 1971 he accepted, and Nixon nominated him and William Rehnquist on the same day.

Volitional criminal justice theories increasingly garnered support through money and influence in the 1970s. Another arena converged with the purely ideological, that of the political economy. Various politicians had been working against the leftist movements of the 1960s, but Richard Nixon put them together into a winning strategy in 1968. There are two kinds of explanations for the reactionary shift in American political opinion. The first speaks vaguely of some sort of mood change among Americans. The other, not so willing to accept magical explanations for observed phenomena, attributes the shift to deliberate efforts that bore fruit, because of shifts in structural factors of the political economy along with concerted efforts backed by elements of the ruling class (Schulman 2001; Schulman and Zelizer 2008).

The material basis for the backlash

Understanding the backlash of the 1970s needs an understanding of the post – Second World War world economy. In 1945 the United States held most of the world's capital, in the form of money and intact capital goods, machinery and the like. While it had a large internal market, American finance capital sought new investments in the rest of the world, but for that to be successful, other countries had to acquire capital. Three strategies emerged. The first was the Bretton Woods economic agreement that made the dollar the main reserve currency and pegged its value at $35 per ounce of gold. Second, the Marshall Plan and others injected capital to rebuild Europe and Japan, thereby making them viable customers for U.S. capital investment and U.S.-produced goods. Both strategies were eminently successful. Germany and Japan became economic powerhouses during the 1960s. A third strategy turned out to be less successful. The United States took over the neocolonialist empires of the European powers and Japan. The Vietnam War was a testament to the partial failure of this third prong of the world economic strategy. Even so, the monetary strategy and the rebuilding strategy meant that by the mid-1960s there was increasing pressure on the dollar—there were not enough dollars to keep the world economy going—and European and Japanese manufactures began to compete with American products. The competition was relatively successful, as the manufacturing sector of those areas was new because it had been completely rebuilt after the devastation of the war. New industry meant more efficient industry, hence lower production costs.

Adding to the economic squeeze on American capital was the success of U.S. organized labor. Following massive strikes in 1946, U.S. industrialists took a new tack in dealing with unions. First, they got federal legislation that curbed unions' propensity to make radical demands and enforce them with economic weapons—strikes, boycotts, and so forth. Taft-Hartley in 1947 was followed up by the Landrum Griffin Act of 1958. Federal courts opted for labor peace, as seen in the Steelworkers Trilogy (1960). By the mid-1950s two things had gelled. Organized labor leaders became politically conservative, and heavily unionized manufacturing sectors such as auto and steel had high wage and benefit packages. Consequently, between 1968 and 1973 the degree of equality in income and wealth in the United States reached historic highs (Piketty and Saez 2004). The working class had made demonstrable economic gains. High wages plus growing competition from overseas competitors prompted the leaders of those core manufacturing industries to look for ways to lower wages. It was those interests that formed the liberal wing of the ruling class, backing the early civil rights movement and later the gender equality movement, supporting many of the Great Society programs, and so on. The liberals were especially willing to go along with these programs, as most of the burden was borne by the extractive and agricultural industries of the South and West, whose leadership formed the conservative wing of the ruling class.

Two events disrupted the pattern. The first was a culmination of the long-term trend of increasing pressure on the dollar. Because there were not enough dollars to keep the growing world economy going, Nixon finally took the U.S. currency off the gold standard in 1971, letting it float with respect to other currencies. In effect, Nixon devalued the dollar while still keeping its reserve currency status as the currency of last resort in world financial transactions. The second was a serendipitous event, the Yom Kippur War of 1973 and the subsequent Arab oil embargo. The governments of the oil-producing countries of the Middle East greatly reduced oil shipments to the United States in retaliation for backing Israel and to try to gain control of oil production from the international oil companies. By early 1974 a new deal was cut. The OPEC countries' governments gained controlling interest in the oil-producing companies on their soil, the transnational oil companies retained monopoly control of refining and distribution, and most importantly for the present story, the petrodollar was born. All oil traded anywhere in the world had to be traded in dollars. In a sense, the oil standard replaced the gold standard. One implication was that the United States could print dollars as long as there was a seller's market in oil. It also meant that dollars became not just the reserve currency but the capital currency for the world. The beginnings of the recent globalization stem from these two economic events of the early 1970s.

When dollars became the main form of capital investment in the world, a new solution came to the ruling class in America. Instead of trying to lower wages by increasing the size of the labor force through civil rights and similar strategies, manufacturing industries could just ship their factories overseas. The era of deindustrialization was born. Politically defanged unions became even more conservative as union bosses held onto a shrinking workforce. There was no real effort to unionize low-wage service sector workers. Industrial cities became rust belts. Specialized manufacturing using light industry and cybernetic controls moved to the suburbs along with increasing numbers of finance-related industries. Deindustrialization and urban sprawl left the central cities with an abandoned working class that was largely non-White. The Democratic Party, which had long relied on developers and construction for their money base turned away from central cities to gain political power elsewhere, thus abandoning the interests of those remaining urban dwellers. With the removal of economic controls on those urban populations—once workers do not have jobs they cannot so easily be controlled through credit schemes like home ownership—the main way to control them increasingly turned to force, the criminal justice system. Also, with a new solution to the falling rate of profit (Duménil and Lévy 2002)—globalization and overseas capital development—the ruling class could once again close ranks to control the masses, resorting to the already established method of using race to divide and rule. Such movements of material relations show up in political discourses. By the late 1970s *liberal* had become a pejorative term as the ruling class no longer had a use for it. In addition to the transformation of capitalism, and in conjunction with it, the standards of American racism underwent a test.

The racial backlash

Michael Omi and Howard Winant (1994) said the racial backlash began in the 1970s, perhaps with roots in the later 1960s. They especially noted Nixon's 1968 Southern strategy to make electoral gains in the formerly Democratic South. They also noted the success of George Wallace's campaign to attract White blue-collar working-class voters in the North. They attributed much of the success of these appeals to an underlying, simmering White racism and economic dislocations in the country and the world (Omi and Winant 1994:114–115). Several years after publication of their book, Katherine Beckett (1997) made a more detailed study of the backlash, with the express intent to link it to new criminal justice policies. Beckett outlined the historical progression. The early 1960s showed the relative success of the civil rights movement in the form of federal legislation such as the 1964 Civil Rights Act and the 1965 Voting Rights Act, the administrative efforts of the Johnson administration to ensure fair employment practices, various lawsuits to further desegregation, and so forth. Southern segregationists first responded with massive resistance. Public officials and private businesses just refused to recognize court orders and federal laws. By the mid-1960s the strategy clearly had failed, and so they turned to another. They linked Black agitation and resistance against oppression to crime, and eventually to expanding government programs designed to end poverty—Lyndon Baines Johnson's War on Poverty and the Great Society. This linkage and rhetoric that went with it resonated with White working-class people in the North who were beginning to experience most immediately the economic squeeze brought on by the Vietnam War, but also the declining rate of profit in U.S. manufacturing industries. Moreover, as Beckett pointed out, once the civil rights movement went North, demanding equality in housing, education, and jobs, politicians like Nixon successfully articulated an underlying racism to fuel a reaction against those making demands—civil rights demonstrators, anti-war demonstrators, and in even more complex ways, those who challenged previously stable cultural practices with the sex, drugs, and rock 'n' roll revolution of the late 1960s. Racialist politics put the fears of the White working class together to blame a concatenation of "Blacks, Communists, Crime, Hippies, and Welfare" on the Democratic control of government. "[F]ormer Democrats indicate that many of these voters switched their allegiance to the Republican party largely as a result of their perception that the Democrats have granted minorities 'special privileges'" (Beckett 1997:86). The campaign succeeded even as the real economic and political situation continued to worsen for the American working class, beginning in the 1970s and accelerating to the present (Sugrue and Skrentny 2008).

Backlashes Converge on Criminal Justice

The April 2007 "Harper's Index" contained a comparison between 1953 and 2007. The percentage of U.S. adults confined either in mental institutions or in prisons was about the same—0.67 percent in 1953 and 0.68 percent in 2007. In 1953, however, three-fourths of those confined were in mental institutions, while in 2007, 97 percent of the confined were in prisons. The United States changed from a welfare society to a security society in the last part of the twentieth century. Michel Foucault described contemporary, developed societies as "carceral" in his 1975 *Discipline and Punish*, but the transformation of the United States had already begun when he published the book in French. Foucault put great stress on what he called pastoral control through social welfare, mental health, and similar social institutions that use persuasion more than force.

In the twenty-first century, David Garland (2001) described a "culture of control," and Jonathan Simon (2007) wrote of "governing through crime." In his review of Garland's book, Malcolm Feeley said that "What took place in the United States in the 1970s was a rejection of a soft welfare state" (2003:117). He traced the seeds of the rejection of welfare in favor of security to the President's Commission on Law Enforcement and the Administration of Justice, who eventually produced their report in 1967, *The Challenge of Crime in a Free Society*. As Feeley himself noted, the bulk of the report and the majority of those on the Commission represented the standard of liberal, welfare criminal justice policy. Nonetheless, Alfred Blumstein from the Institute for Defense Analysis brought a different perspective, heavily indebted to a systems perspective and Pentagon-like approach to operations control (Walker 1992). Feeley went on to observe that it was Blumstein and his group on the Commission's Task Force on Science and Technology that influenced criminal justice policy. "What was begun by this small band of whiz kids was later institutionalized at RAND in Santa Monica and elsewhere. A new systems-analysis of crime was created. Members of this group landed positions in LEAA" (Feeley 2003:119).

Although the Law Enforcement Assistance Administration (LEAA) orchestrated a wide range of programs, it began its 14-year life (1968–1982) with a heavy emphasis on crowd control. A great proportion of the federal money administered by the agency outfitted and trained police to deal with protests and riots that had been occurring in American cities beginning in the mid-1960s. It is safe to say that the strategy aimed at quelling social unrest and rebellion through police power, as designed by Pentagon analysts. It marked a shift toward a militarized and militant policing (Kraska 1999).

Robert Martinson's 1974 "What Works?" signaled a milestone in penology. It appeared in the neoconservative magazine *The Pubic Interest*. It is debatable whether this article actually spurred a shift from a policy of rehabilitation to incapacitation, or whether it merely signified the transformation. In either case, the change occurred. A retrospective glance at U.S. incarceration rates over the last one hundred years provides an easy way to measure its effects. The incarceration rate hovered around 100 per 100,000 population for three-fourths of the twentieth century, until about 1975. It was a little high compared to other developed countries, but not out of line. Then, it began to rise geometrically to the 2006 rate of 751. More people have been going to prison and staying longer. Moreover, more people are controlled by criminal justice authorities—7.2 million, including those on probation or parole, out of a population of about 300 million, 230 million of them adults (Bureau of Justice Statistics 2007; Pew Center on the States 2008; U.S. Census Bureau 2008). What makes these numbers so trenchant is that they are demonstrably unrelated to measured crime.

Measuring crime in the United States remains an unfulfilled promise. Nonetheless, the Uniform Crime Reports (UCR) and the National Crime Victimization Survey (NCVS) typically serve as surrogates. The UCR goes back to 1930, when the FBI began collected data on reported crimes from police agencies around the country. The NCVS has collected self-reported victimization since 1973, although pilot studies preceded it. Generally, the UCR has shown an increase since its inception, except for some dramatic declines beginning in the 1990s. Since the UCR measures police activity (Pepinsky 2000), not crime, increased numbers of police and more diligence means higher UCR crime rates.

Early measures of victimization began with a pilot study in Washington DC in 1965. It was then applied to three cities, and the National Opinion Research Council made a national study. The most publicized finding was the "dark figure" of crime. Victimization studies revealed that most victims did not report the crime to the police. In effect, that meant an untapped reservoir of crime for the police to find. The harder they looked, the more crime they would report (Mosher, Miethe, and Phillips 2002:54–56). The record of NCVS since 1973 shows a steady decrease in property crime, with violent crime fluctuating around a plateau until the early 1990s and then declining steeply. Moreover, extrapolating from the pilot studies used by the President's Crime Commission, victim- ization by all crime shows a decrease since the mid-1960s (President's Commission 1967a and 1967b; Bureau of Justice Statistics 2007). The polit- ical genius of Richard Nixon largely explains the discrepancy between the NCVS-measured crime decline, at least since 1973, and the skyrocketing incarceration rate since 1975.

The war on drugs

When Nixon ran on a law and order platform in 1968 and 1972, he faced a problem. Although the situation has changed by the increasing federal- ization of crime (American Bar Association 1997), back then, states had the primary responsibility for crime control. Federal enforcement of drug laws went back to the Harrison Narcotics Act of 1914. In addition, Harry Anslinger's Bureau of Narcotics had long enforced and prosecuted drug laws selectively, singling out minorities more often than not (Cockburn and St. Clair 1998; Valentine 2004). Drug enforcement and targeting polit- ical radicals went hand in hand. By the twenty-first century, a majority of federal prisoners were serving time for drug violations, and drug law enforcement provided a generous new source of prisoners at all levels of the penal system (Mauer 2006).

The war on drugs beginning with Nixon's presidency represented the Panzer assault in the war-on-crime blitzkrieg. Both domestically and inter- nationally the drug war has served the interests of the U.S. control appara- tus. In both the domestic and world arenas, the drug war has depended on determined public relations campaigns (Beckett and Sasson 2004). Inter- nationally, Sweden has joined the United States in prosecuting the war. "Sweden gives legitimation and the US gives power." Consequently, about half of Sweden and Norway's prisoners are locked up on drug related con- victions (Christie 2004:39). The drug war serves as a shining example of the effects of moving from a welfare society to a control society. Before Nixon's drug war, the U.S. drug policy inclined toward dealing with drug addiction as a public health problem. Additionally, movements to legalize long- banned drugs like marijuana emerged from the White, middle-income drug culture of the late 1960s. Declaring war on drugs—actually, of course, on segments of the population who used them—became the greatest contribution to new criminalization, and the new confinement.

The war on youth

Juvenile justice reveals a similar trajectory and similar characteristics—movement from welfare to control and politically motivated criminalization. With patterned fluctuations, almost like Kondratieff cycles in economics, the swings between welfare and control in juvenile justice act as bellwethers for the political economy. While everyone knows youth has been going to hell in a handbasket at least since Aristotle's time, Thomas Bernard (1992) reviewed the ebb and flow of punitive versus habilitative strategies in the Anglo-American system of justice. By the late 1990s the punitive was reaching new heights. In 1996, William Bennett, John DiIulio, and John P. Walters warned America that not only were youth going to hell in a handbasket, but they posed a mortal threat to everyone because of their propensity to violence. They predicted a massive, 62 percent increase in juvenile homicides because the country was beset with a generation of youthful "superpredators." In fact, juvenile homicide had peaked three years earlier and has shown a steady and steep decrease since (OJJDP 2006). Their book, heavily supported by right-wing foundation money and influence, produced the desired results. States passed new laws making it easier, in some cases mandatory, to try juveniles as adults and sentence them accordingly (Allard and Young 2002). Those included, in 2005, over 2200 juveniles serving life without parole (Amnesty and HRW 2005). Not surprisingly, the majority are minorities.

The changes in juvenile policy illustrate issues of political economy. When Sheldon and Eleanor Glueck's major book came out in 1950, a juvenile delinquency hysteria had begun to grip public attention. Within a few years, Hollywood depicted the crisis in three classic movies: *The Wild One* (1953), *Blackboard Jungle* (1955), and *Rebel Without a Cause* (1955). The last derived its title from a 1944 book by Robert Mitchell Lindner, a popularizer of psychoanalysis. He warned that so-called psychopathic youth hated their fathers and transferred that hate to society at large. Lindner especially feared that such youths made easy recruits for future Storm Troopers. Interestingly, the Gluecks wrote an introduction to Lindner's book. It is interesting because although they took a psychological approach to juvenile delinquency, it was hardly psychoanalytic. Compare, for instance, their psychobiology to the writings of August Aichhorn (1925, 1965) whose *Wayward Youth* had an introduction by Sigmund Freud. Aichhorn recognized the very personal constellation of relationships that affect youths. He saw that conflicts in important relationships often lie behind what authorities label as delinquent behavior. Psychoanalysis may find generalized patterns associated with neurosis, but it always examines the concrete situatedness of particular individuals. It is not a nomothetic trait psychology. In contrast, the Gluecks' brand of psychology consists of describing certain traits that they link to, and by implication use to predict, delinquency: hedonistic, distrustful, aggressive, socially assertive, physically active, plain spoken, and so on. Marvin Wolfgang (1967) compared them to those exhibited by the Renaissance man who defied authority or by American captains of industry. The problem with delinquents, as far as the Gluecks and later Travis Hirschi were concerned, is that they are youths who do not conform.

In 1950 the issue of conformity loomed large. Popular images of nonconformity had an ambiguous quality. There were the beats, Marlon Brando – type tough guys as in *The Wild One* and *On the Waterfront* (1954), and Communists. Communists, needless to say, were especially dangerous. Not only did schools teach children to hide under their desks in case of a Soviet nuclear attack, but the Red Scare found Communists everywhere. Fears about juvenile delinquents and Communists probably sprang from similar roots in postwar America, but the preferred policy toward juvenile justice largely turned toward welfare rather than prison. The difference between, say, 1955 and 1975 had less to do with the fear and more to do with relations of production. In 1955 the United States approached its apex of industrialization, union membership reached its all-time high, and in the next 15 years members of the working class would close the economic gap with the bourgeoisie more than at any time in America's history. For most people, things were looking up. The view in 1975 came from the opposite perspective. The United States had begun to deindustrialize, union membership had been declining, and the economy had entered a period of stagflation set off by the Arab oil embargo. The gap between the working class and the elite began to widen again, to reach historic highs in the twenty-first century. For the working class in 1975, things were beginning to get worse. The ruling class was reasserting control, and welfare would be taken off the table. The rollback of gains made since the 1930s depended on ending the liberal consensus, but unlike the end of the Weimar Republic, it was no coup d'état.

The End of Liberalism

Conservatives fought against the New Deal of the 1930s from the beginning. Well into the 1960s, the conservative political agenda included a rollback of social support and wealth-leveling measures associated with the New Deal legacy and revived under Lyndon Johnson's Great Society. Until the late 1960s, criminal justice in the United States was part of that liberal tradition. Regulation rather than control in policing, rehabilitation in penal policy, extension of civil rights, and welfare instead of punishment for juveniles remained the touchstones of criminal justice policies. The President's Crime Commission report of 1967 and the Kerner Commission (National Advisory Commission 1968) report on urban rebellions reflected these orientations. Unlike the conservatives in Weimar Germany, American conservatives had no hereditary aristocracy with whom to ally themselves. The United States began without the encrustations of the European ancien régime. The United States was the paradigm of classical liberalism. Its political systems and apparatuses of state were almost tailor-made for modern mass societies and a capitalist economy. American conservatives were not about to give up those apparatuses that had done so much to ensure the success of its ruling elite. Therefore, despite a commitment to rollback and reassertions of authority, there would be no coup d'état. Rebellious radicals of the 1960s also had no program for getting rid of the republic. To a large extent, their demand for racial equality, and ending the Vietnam War with the concomitant imperialism and militarism, represented their vision of American republican values. Nonetheless, the radicals rejected the hypocrisy of New Deal and Great Society liberalism. The alliance between left and right against the American liberal consensus brought it down, but by dismantling it rather than toppling it.

In law and the politics of criminal justice, the dismantling of liberalism therefore had to abide by certain rules and procedures. In policing, there was no sudden *Gleichschaltung* as in the Nazi creation of Himmler's apparatus, which subordinated all police agencies to central control. Consequently, a more controlling form of policing followed stages: first training in riot control, then improved record keeping, then deployment of military-style weapons, then technologically advanced surveillance, and so on. Only recently has there been Nazilike centralization with the formation of the U.S. Department of Homeland Security. Modern policing depends on a level of consensus and legitimacy. The ideology of modern policing rationalizes the ultimate service of police to domination by the elite class with policing's claim that "from its very beginnings the police function sprang from the body of the people and that its integral identity with the community has never changed ... the police are armed 'with prestige rather than power thus obliging them to rely on popular support'" (Robinson and Scaglion 1987:148 quoting Critchley 1967). The ideology of policing to maintain a politicized law and order has had to tack in shifting political winds rather than sail a straight course (Hinds 2006). The popularity and deployment of so-called community policing reflects this dialectic.

Similar patterns are found in the other parts of criminal justice in the United States. The U.S. Supreme Court, led by chief justices Burger

(1969–1986), Rehnquist (1986–2005), and most recently Roberts, has gradually limited the constitutional guarantees to defendants that the Warren Court (1953–1969) had done so much to extend. The federalization of crime decried by the American Bar Association in 1997 likewise followed a gradual, step-by-step process. All the various criminal justice apparatuses contributed over a period of three decades to the new, perhaps postmodern, penal system (Feeley and Simon 1992; Hallsworth 2002). Ideology played a pivotal role in the transformation, as the Powell memo (1971) made an important contribution to the strategy. Moreover, academic theoretical work underpinned the more popular public relations tactics. Those theoretical ideas had roots going back to Weimar Germany.

7

Roots of Reaction

The reaction of the U.S. ruling class to the ferment of the 1960s partially relied on an intellectual foundation. It was not an unthinking, emotion-laden response, even when its public manifestations took populist form. The first wave of American neoconservative intellectuals came to prominence in the late 1960s and early 1970s, when the reaction was taking its form. Mainly born in the 1920s and 1930s, they include figures such as Irving Kristol, Norman Podhoretz, Nathan Glazer, Daniel Patrick Moynihan, Jeanne Kirkpatrick, Daniel Bell, and Gertrude Himmelfarb. Some had a left-liberal or Trotskyist past, which was fashionable in their youth during the 1930s and 1940s. The neoconservatives rejected the Communism of their youth and the politics of the new left in the 1960s. Kristol (1995:6) cited the thought and work of Leo Strauss as basic to the neoconservative philosophy. Strauss is pivotal to neoconservatives because he taught many of the second generation, including significant advisers and administrators in the Reagan and Bush regimes such as Douglas Feith, Richard Perle, and Paul Wolfowitz. Another intellectual figure contributing to neoconservative philosophy but without direct influence on American politics was Carl Schmitt (Stern 2006:72), the leading Nazi jurist. The ruling-class reactionary program Lewis Powell outlined in his 1971 memorandum depended on neoconservative ideology, despite the fact that most members of the ruling class themselves held traditional conservative or liberal political ideas and values.

Carl Schmitt (1888–1985) and Leo Strauss (1899–1973) shared Weimar intellectual roots. Eleven years senior, Schmitt served in the German army in WWI after finishing his studies in law and gaining his habilitation. He taught at low-prestige universities during the Weimar period when he began publishing political tracts. He joined the Nazi party in 1933 and promptly gained promotion to the University of Berlin. Strauss came of age in the Weimar years. As a young political philosopher he critiqued

Schmitt's 1927 book *The Concept of the Political*, and then corresponded with Schmitt about the critique and their political ideas (Meier 1988:91ff.). Schmitt went on to become the leading jurist in the Nazi government. Detained after the war, he was never prosecuted, but the government banned him from holding an academic position. In 1932 Strauss left Germany to do research in Paris and did not return because of the Nazi accession to power in 1933. Leo Strauss eventually went to the University of Chicago where he was a professor of political science (1949–1969) publishing and teaching on classical political philosophy.

Schmitt and Strauss espoused antiliberal, antidemocratic, and morally absolutist views. Both wrote obscurantively with copious hints at esoteric truths. In their works, one finds the ideological underpinnings of the reaction of the 1970s. Strauss's influence in criminal justice is traceable most directly through James Q. Wilson, a graduate student at the University of Chicago whose mentor was Edward Banfield, a close friend of Leo Strauss. Schmitt was not influential outside Germany, especially after the Second World War, although his work has recently resurged as leftist intellectuals such as Giorgio Agamben have used certain of his concepts to critique the new imperialism of the twenty-first century. The importance of Schmitt and Strauss occurs at the level of ideas, which lend themselves to authoritarianism.

Reactions Against Liberal Democracy

Both men grew up in the intellectual milieu of the Weimar period. Both found the times abhorrent. Both found Weimar culture offensive to their religion and morality, and they connected the culture to the politics. The culture, especially Berlin of the 1920s, was transgressive, challenging the traditional *bürgerlich* values and lifestyles, not unlike the counterculture of late-1960s America. Licentiousness replaced bourgeois German reserve, and from the Schmitt-Strauss perspective, the cultural transformation could be laid at the doorstep of the Weimar constitution and the politics of the republic. Their principal political enemy was not, oddly enough, socialism, even the revolutionary socialism of the communists. The real problem, as they saw it, was the Western, liberal, democratic political tradition. They traced the roots of Germany's fall to the Enlightenment and the secular liberalism first ushered in by Thomas Hobbes, then realized in the English Glorious Revolution of 1688. Therein lay the Serpent in the Garden for Schmitt and Strauss.

Religion underlies the politics of both Strauss and Schmitt. Schmitt came from a petit bourgeois Catholic backwater, Plettenberg, Westphalia.

Strauss's parents were religiously conservative, observant Jews who ran a farm supply store in Kirchhain, Hesse. Religion and a conservative, small-town way of life marked both men. Their intellectual trajectories allowed them to translate their upbringing into abstract political theory. This comes through clearly in Strauss's critique of Schmitt's *The Concept of the Political*. Strauss, while generally approving of Schmitt's argument, said that Schmitt had not fully escaped the liberal bias. The problem, according to Strauss, was that Schmitt argued for the respect of all antagonists; those who fight each other do not follow the liberal value of toleration for the sake of peaceful society, as Hobbes would have it. But that is where Schmitt showed his liberal bias, because "he [Schmitt] who affirms the political as such respects and tolerates all '*serious*' convictions, that is, all decisions oriented to the real possibility of *war*" (Strauss 1932a:117). Strauss saw that stance as still reflecting a liberal bias, because Schmitt was arguing for the political as bedrock. For Strauss, after antiquity and since Hobbes, the political can only take a liberal form. The political, therefore, cannot offer the ultimate critique of liberalism. "The critique introduced by Schmitt against liberalism can therefore be completed only if one succeeds in gaining a horizon beyond liberalism" (119). That horizon for Strauss, and eventually for Schmitt too, relied on religion, even though it did not spring from religion. The distinction is important. For Strauss and Schmitt religion was a tool for social control. The political philosopher does not base his politics on religion, but recognizes the necessity of religion to govern and maintain the state.

To enunciate their arguments, both Schmitt and Strauss reverted to the critique of Hobbes. For Hobbes, civil war was the greatest calamity. That is why Hobbes favored the *Leviathan* (1651), the overwhelming power of the sovereign ensconced before the controls of the state apparatus. It is only through absolute control of force that civil society does not fracture, eventually leading back to the state of nature and the war of all against all. Civil war had to be avoided at all costs, because humans would revert to animalistic dangerousness. Schmitt and Strauss agreed that humans were dangerous. It is a major premise of their thought. But they argued that the Hobbesian solution evades the evil and dangerous character of humanity by attributing the danger to an animal-like nature. There is, however, nothing morally evil about the behavior of animals; they are essentially innocent. Not so with humans. Humans are both dangerous and evil. It is human evil, immoral evil that needs the strength of religion to control it.

> The ultimate foundation of the Right [*Recht*] is the principle of the natural evil of man; because man is by nature evil, he therefore needs *dominion*. But dominion can be established, that is, men can only be unified, only in a

unity *against*—against other men. The *tendency* to separate (and therewith
the grouping of humanity into friends and enemies) is given with human
nature; it is in this sense destiny, period. But the political thus understood is
not the constitutive principle of the state, of "order," but only the condition
of the state. (Strauss 1932b: 125)

Only the true philosophers can transcend the moral judgment in a sort
of perverted Nietzschean way. They are the overmen (Übermenschen). All
others need controls. This same theme runs in the thought of the authoritarian criminal justice thinkers, James Q. Wilson and Travis Hirschi chief
among them, and for similar reasons.

Although Schmitt and Strauss held antidemocratic views, they saw
liberalism as the main problem. In fact each made the point repeatedly in
his work that liberalism and democracy arose from historical circumstance,
not conceptual affinity. Their emphasis on the antagonistic nature of
democracy and liberalism was part of their critique of the Enlightenment
and its progeny, modernity. The problem with the Enlightenment was that
it renounced authority as the basis for political life and morality. The root
problem with liberalism is that it forgets the dangerousness of human
beings; Strauss again: "If it is true that the final self-awareness of liberalism
is the philosophy of culture ... liberalism, sheltered by and engrossed in a
world of culture, forgets the foundation of culture, that is, human nature
in its dangerousness and endangeredness" (1932a:101). In short, liberalism is flabby and weak because it is permissive. It allows, even celebrates,
individuals doing as they will. Once the Enlightenment loosed the bonds of
authority, it led, in Germany at least, inevitably to the weakness and license
of the Weimar Republic.

In contrast, the problem with democracy lies not with popular decision making—that is, the problem is not populism but the pretense of
equality. Schmitt made this clear in an early Weimar work, his 1923 *The
Crisis of Parliamentary Democracy*. There, he argued that democracy is
bound to the nation. In democracy the citizens are equal because of their
racial, linguistic, cultural, and religious homogeneity, but that does not
mean all humans are equal simply because of their humanity, or as the
Enlightenment philosophers had it, because of their innate ability to reason. Equality, for Schmitt, is tied to membership in the group, which
in turn is defined by those opposed to the group, the enemy. Moreover,
Schmitt went on to argue, liberalism is no friend of equality. As Marx
pointed out—and for this Schmitt admired Marx—liberalism was tied to
capitalism and imperialism, which trumpeted liberalism only to ensure the
extremes of wealth and poverty (Drury 1997:85). Schmitt's main objec-
tion to liberalism, by which he meant classical Western liberalism, not

American liberalism associated with programs like the New Deal and Great Society, was its indecisiveness. "The essence of liberalism is negotiation, a cautious half measure, in the hope that the definitive dispute, the decisive bloody battle, can be transformed into a parliamentary debate and permit the decision to be suspended forever in everlasting discussion" (Schmitt 1922/1934:63). As the next chapter makes plain, this point by Schmitt is the focus of Jürgen Habermas's attack in several of his books. Habermas has argued that discussion is the main aim of politics. Schmitt grounded politics in decision; Strauss completely agreed with Schmitt on this point.

The parliamentrianism of Weimar lent itself to these kinds of Schmittian attacks. Weimar had multiple parties, and for most of its existence none could claim a majority. Ruling parties, therefore, needed coalitions. Especially in the last years of the republic, maneuver almost completely replaced debate, so that President Hindenburg increasingly ruled the country by decree while the most militant political actors fought out their differences with guns and clubs on the streets rather than in the halls of deliberation in the Reichstag (Abraham 1986; Peukert 1987). In contrast, neoconservatives did not castigate twentieth-century American liberalism for political indecisiveness. Their criticism aimed more at its ineffectuality and moral, not political, vacillation. Nonetheless, Strauss sided with Schmitt in his denunciation of universalism. To both men, the Enlightenment's universalism was its greatest failing, leading inevitably to a deracinated kind of humanity.

Fortunately for him, Leo Strauss did not have to face the German cure for Enlightenment liberalism, as he went to Paris for research on Hobbes before Hindenburg named Hitler chancellor. From Paris Strauss went to Cambridge University in England, then New York, finally ending up at the University of Chicago Political Science Department in 1949, where he stayed until 1969. Moving through those countries most associated with the Enlightenment, liberalism, and universalism seemed congenial to Strauss, despite his intellectual convictions to the contrary.

Strauss at Chicago: His Mentoring Years

Irving Kristol, the éminence grise and frequent publisher of many first- and some second-generation neoconservatives, admired Leo Strauss, though not as a teacher, because he was never his student. Kristol admired his thought and writings, because Strauss taught him to view history backward. "[H]e turned one's intellectual universe upside down. Suddenly one realized one had been looking at the history of Western political thought through the wrong end of the telescope" (Kristol 1995:7). The wrong end is the view of antiquity from the standpoint of modernity. What Strauss offered was a view of modernity from the standpoint of the ancients, the classical expositors of philosophy and political ideas, the ancient Greeks. Strauss's ideas are radically reactionary, because he did not just offer such a viewpoint; he favored it. He used the classics to diagnose the modern malaise.

In her laudable exegesis of Strauss, Shadia Drury claimed that "It is important for one who would understand Strauss to study all of his work as a unity and not as isolated texts" (1988:x). I will not make the attempt here. First, Drury has already done the job. Second, she devoted an entire book to the project, whereas this is but one part of a work on a different topic. Finally, my expertise lies in other quarters than that of Drury, and I rely on her for a framework for my arguments. With that in mind, the most important of Strauss's ideas appear in a lecture he gave sometime in 1958 at Hilllel House at the University of Chicago. At the time of Drury's book, the lecture was not published in an accessible format. The lecture was entitled "Freud on Moses and Monotheism," now available in a collection of Strauss's works on Judaism (Green 1997). The year 1958 was the mid-point of Strauss's career at the University of Chicago. According to Drury (1988:8), who referred to Allan Bloom (1974), Strauss had already developed his esoteric style of philosophizing. That is, Strauss used various techniques to disguise his most profound meanings while offering up an exoteric text for the nonphilosophers, the masses, hoi polloi. Even so, a close reading of this single lecture can reveal his disguised message.

Strauss criticized Freud's book *Moses and Monotheism*, but he aimed his most severe criticism elsewhere. Strauss attacked Freud's intellectual project and Freud's relationship to Judaism, although not at Freud *as* a Jew: "I believe one can say that Freud was a good Jew without qualifications in this sense [concern with the truth of Jewish tradition]. The question is whether he was a good thinker on this august theme" (Strauss 1958:288). Strauss identified the problem with Freud's thought, not because of highly questionable assumptions, sources, and reasoning found in the *Moses and Monotheism* book. As David Bakan (1958:249) noted Strauss himself as saying, if a great author commits schoolboy errors, we should search for a deeper meaning behind the apparent blunders. There is no doubt that Strauss thought Freud a great author. Therefore, although Strauss criticized Freud for all the aforementioned mistakes, that was not Strauss's main criticism. Strauss then proceeded with his exposition by referring to his own studies of what he called "one of the greatest Jewish works of the Middle Ages, Yehuda Halevi's *Kuzari*," which Strauss opined that Freud did nor know, although he had no reason to assert Freud's ignorance. In passing, Strauss said that "The use of the term philosopher at this time meant automatically not a Jew" (Strauss 1958:288). Later in the lecture, toward the end, Strauss said, "Freud's book completely lacks a philosophic basis" (305). What, then, makes Freud, and this book in particular, unphilosophical? The answer lies in the following passage from the lecture. I quote at length, because the subsequent unpacking of it reveals the core of Strauss's political ideas and the roots of neoconservatism.

> The act of Freud is an act of self-denial, but also an act which looks like an act of treason against the national interest. The justification is that it is done for the sake of truth. The question arises, is truth a part of the national interest? Does the true national interest necessarily lead to truth? Does this apply to the Jewish people in particular or to all peoples? At any rate, Freud seems to make a suggestion of the utmost importance—that truth is more important than society. Truth means knowing the truth as distinguished, in the first place, from proclaiming the truth. Freud, however, tacitly identifies knowing the truth and proclaiming the truth. *This is justifiable only if the truth is essentially salutary* [emphasis added]. This would be the case if knowledge of the truth and only knowledge of the truth makes us good men and good citizens. But if truth is essentially edifying, as I believe it is, one should not begin with "To deny." Moreover, if this is so, knowledge of the truth, quest for the truth, and communication of the truth, would be *the* key to the understanding of man, to the analysis of man, to the analysis of the soul, to psychoanalysis. (288–289)

Moses and Monotheism is divided into three parts. Freud published the first two parts in the psychoanalytic journal of the arts, *Imago*, in 1937. The third part is the longest and contains the important philosophical arguments about belief, religion, and the human nature. Freud wrote two prefaces for the book. He wrote the first sometime before March 12–14, 1938, the Nazi invasion and *Anschluss* of Austria. In it, Freud said that although he wrote the essay, part 3, he would not publish it. Among other observations, Freud commented that he thought his researches led him to conclude that religion is but a neurosis of mankind, with the implication that it might be cured by psychoanalysis. He wrote the second preface in London, where he had to flee after the Nazi invasion. It was there that he decided to publish part 3. A main reason for not publishing in Vienna before the invasion was that Freud feared for the fate of the psychoanalytic movement, which until then had enjoyed the protection of the Austrian Catholic church. That is, he believed the book was too critical of religion, even more than his 1927 *Future of an Illusion*, which straightforwardly argued that religion is a neurosis. I believe that what Freud feared about his *Moses and Monotheism* was what Strauss saw in it that led him to dismiss it as unphilosophical. What did Strauss see, and what did Freud fear others would see?

The year before Strauss's lecture, he wrote a short book review of Jacob L. Talmon's *The Nature of Jewish History: Its Universal Significance* (1957). Strauss said that the Jewish tradition was one of two great parts of Western civilization. The other part was Greek philosophy. The Jewish contribution was right acting—that is, ethical behavior. What Freud threatened was removal of moral constraints. Freud's psychoanalysis, if carried out pervasively, would put all people, even and especially the common folk, beyond good and evil, beyond fear and trembling. These two phrases are meant to refer to Nietzsche's 1886 book by that name and Kierkegaard's 1843 work, respectively (cf. Drury 1988:48, 52). Strauss's interpretation of those nineteenth-century writers, whether or not he was correct, was that the true philosopher stood beyond morality because truth was beyond morality. Nonetheless, the social fabric, the commonweal, could not hold were those truths published. Moreover, most people, except the true philosophers, could not stand to live knowing such truths. They would suffer a sickness unto death, to borrow another of Kierkegaard's titles, a despair that only faith can lift.

The problem such a state of affairs would pose awaited Strauss's finale to his lecture. There, he drew attention to the supposed perennial opposition between science and religion, or between Athens (science) and Jerusalem (religion) as he put it metaphorically in many of his writings. He reminded the audience that science cannot justify itself. The truths science offers are but one set of truths, and science does not and cannot offer a standpoint beyond itself that would allow one to choose the scientific method versus faith. Science, therefore, must be grounded in a nonrational, not irrational, choice. "This being compelled to choose would be *the* fundamental phenomenon behind which we cannot go . . . " At that point, Strauss appears to shift track. He stated that "Freud's book completely lacks a philosophic basis" (Strauss 1958:305). Since he had just said that science lacks a scientific basis, which in Strauss's usage is the same as philosophic (Drury 1988), Strauss could only mean that Freud's book is thoroughly scientific even though it does contain numerous fatal flaws that would banish it from any modern scientific journal.

This is the point at which Strauss returned to his worry about Freud and psychoanalysis. If Freud were to be successful in his psychoanalytic project, if he replaced mankind's neurosis (i.e., religion) with self-knowledge, conscious choice, and therefore intelligently considered living, "there cannot be tragic conflict. For example, such a conflict as between loyalty to the city and loyalty to one's convictions cannot be a tragic conflict. All men can become cogs in a big machine" (Strauss 1958:305). Strauss ended his lecture with a lengthy quote from Nietzsche's *Thus Spake Zarathustra* (1883–1885). The quoted passage has Zarathustra saying to the multitude that they can exceed themselves, they have each one within the potential to be an overman (*Übermensch*), to go beyond the multitude, to stop conforming. Of course, that is what Freud advocated.

Freud made two critical errors in his *Moses and Monotheism* as far as Strauss was concerned. The first was in publishing it. Had he kept it to himself, or transmitted it only orally, Freud's insights in and of themselves would have remained scientific and philosophical. Strauss himself followed the practice of transmitting what he thought were the most profound understandings orally to his students, and differently to different students (Drury 1997). According to Strauss, Moses Maimonides advocated this strategy, adjuring the wise to convey the great secrets orally and not publish them. David Bakan, a colleague of Strauss at the University of Chicago, albeit in the psychology department rather than political science, argued that Freud also followed this rule.

> We believe that Freud often wrote with obscurity ... to hide the deeper portions of his thought, and that these deeper portions were Kabbalistic in their source and content ... The Kabbalistic tradition has it that the secret teachings are to be transmitted orally one person at a time ... This is indeed what Freud was doing in the actual practice of psychoanalysis, and ... *is still maintained in the education of the modern psychoanalyst ... (in the training analysis).* (Bakan 1958:35)

To deceive without flat-out lying was very much a part of the Straussian method (Drury 1988). That it was part of Freud's is not supported by Bakan's argument. Nonetheless, it is likely Strauss would have approved of Freud's ideas, if he had made them known only to the select few, the overmen. This represents Strauss's adherence to the concept of the noble lie. "[T]here is no more noteworthy difference between the typical premodern philosopher ... and the typical modern philosopher than that of their attitudes toward 'noble (or just) lies' ... Every decent modern reader is bound to be shocked by the mere suggestion that a great man might have deliberately deceived the large majority of his readers ... these imitators of the resourceful Odysseus [premodern philosophers] were perhaps merely more sincere than we when they called 'lying nobly' what we would call 'considering one's social responsibilities' " (Strauss 1952:35–36).

If psychoanalysis is about anything, it is about undoing lies. Strauss saw lies as necessary, much as the saint Zarathustra first encountered when he set out to bring his message to the people. " 'Give them nothing!' said the saint. 'Rather take part of their load and help them to bear it—that will be best for them'" (Nietzsche 1883:123). The only truths worth telling, according to Strauss, were salutary truths, which might include lies if they were noble lies. Strauss used that term as a derivative from Plato, but changed the meaning by abstracting it from context. Plato's noble lies were exemplary stories, myths, which showed truths through fiction. They were not lies with the intention to deceive. "You don't know, I replied, that all gods and men hate, if it is possible to say it, what is truly false? . . . Everyone refuses to be willingly deceived in the most authoritative part of himself and about the most determinative things; he especially fears to have false-hood there beyond all else" (Plato ca. 370 BCE:67, BkII, 382a). Strauss's noble lies were deliberate deceptions meant to lift the burden from the masses.

The other error by Freud from Strauss's viewpoint was his treason, as Strauss described it. Why would Freud's story of Moses and monotheism constitute treason, and against whom? The treason was against the Jews as a nation, a people. Strauss said that Freud was trying to solve the problem of Jewish survival despite hostility from surrounding peoples throughout almost all their history (Strauss 1958:301). The answer was their binding through the Jewish religious tradition. It kept them together as a people. But in Freud's story of Moses and monotheism, the religion came about because the Jews killed Moses, the original, quintessential lawgiver. Thereby, Jews became the original god-killers, long before Jesus arrived on the scene. As Bakan described in the preface to the 1965 edition of his book, one Jewish scholar, Chaim Bloch, was aghast when he read it, telling Freud, "Anti-Semites accuse us of killing the founder of Christianity. Now a Jew adds that we also killed the founder of Judaism. You are digging a trap for the Jewish people" (Bakan 1958/1965:xix).

Beyond the god-killing accusations, however, lies a deeper form of treason. By killing off Moses, or claiming that the Jews killed him, Freud showed that God was dead and the people had killed him, just as Zarathustra had set out to show the people. Moses was the cultural superego, the lawgiver, who established the basis for not only Jewish theology, which is of secondary importance in the Judaic religion, but also of the law, the Torah and Talmud, the guide for right living. Freud's psycho-analysis tamed the superego, bringing it under control of the ego, and so Freud tamed Moses in his book. Moses was no longer the terrible figure coming down from Mt. Sinai to tell everyone how to live; psychoanalysis puts control within every individual's grasp. Psychoanalysis offers *universal* liberation. That was the main treason for Strauss. The very thing that had allowed Jews to survive through the millennia, Freud had debunked. That is why Strauss went to such pains to criticize Freud for his dedication to science as the ultimate problem solver. "He [Freud] seems to live in the perspective of the infinite progress of science . . . The scientific explanation of the genesis of religion, and therefore of religion itself, cannot be truer than science in general" (Strauss 1958:304–305). Science is the ultimate universalizer. Its laws are meant to be, indeed must be, universal. Freud's treason consists in his replacement of the Torah with universal, individual choice. He removed the mystery of religion so the masses would no longer be in awe of the law's authority. It is a treason, from Strauss's view, that undermines everything that has allowed Jewish survival in particular even as it undermines the cohesive force for all nations.

The role of law is crucial in understanding this part of Strauss's argument. In the rabbinic tradition, the law, the Torah, is not just a set of ethical guidelines; it is the blueprint for the universe. As Susan Handelman pointed out, in the early Jewish commentaries, the Midrash, the law came before creation: "He looked into the Torah and created the world (*Ber. Rab.* 1:1) . . . The Torah is not seen as speculation *about* the world, but part of its very essence" (1982:38). By taming the authority of Moses, Freud made each person a lawgiver, a law interpreter. That is exactly what Strauss found abhorrent about liberalism—its universalism and what he saw as its encouragement of license. It is much safer and more salutary to maintain the comfortable hypocrisy of small-town bourgeois values and lifestyle of Sinclair Lewis's *Babbitt* (1922) and *Main Street* (1920).

Before Strauss fully developed his dissembling esotericism, he revealed his basic political ideas in a series of lectures soon after arriving at the University of Chicago. Expanding the lectures delivered under the auspices of the Walgreen Foundation in October 1949, he published *Natural Right and History* in 1953. He espoused a natural right perspective on law and politics. Strauss opposed relativism of either the historical (Troeltsch 1922/1934) or cultural variety. "If there is no standard higher than the ideal of our society, we are utterly unable to take a critical distance from that ideal" (Strauss 1953:3). In this context, Strauss's antirelativism resonated with Carl Schmitt's so-called right of resistance, which I elucidate below. He also opposed modern versions of natural right mainly associated with the Enlightenment, especially figures such as Rousseau. Strauss's natural right doctrine was classical, by which he meant chiefly Platonic-Socratic.

Using the Socratic method of answering political and ethical questions with reasoning about ontology, Strauss's politics assumed a teleological definition of humanity. He said that since humans are social animals, realizing their full humanity only in and through society, the best society and best laws must be those best promoting human realization. "Natural right in its classic form is connected with a teleological view of the universe. All natural beings have a natural end, a natural destiny, which determines what kind of operation is good for them" (Strauss 1953:7). He said the classics keep a distinction between nature and law as social convention along with a distinction between genuine virtue and vulgar—that is political—virtue (121). To understand the nature of a things, in this case, human beings, Socrates via Strauss said that we must understand the greater whole of which the thing is a part: "everything that is 'something' 'is'; the whole must be '*beyond being*' [emphasis added]" (122). In this view, there is some ideal, a nonmaterial thing, that determines the nature of material things, such as a soul (127) that determines human character. Knowing the nonmaterial thing is crucial for true knowledge: "all understanding presupposes a fundamental awareness of the whole" (125). He reasoned further that because a defining characteristic of humanity is reason, "Therefore, the proper work of man consists in living thoughtfully, in understanding, and in thoughtful action ... The good life is the perfection of man's nature [127] ... [and] Because man is by nature social, the perfection of his nature includes the social virtue par excellence, justice; *justice and right are natural* [emphasis added]" (129).

Strauss then claimed that only small, closed societies such as the classical polis can ensure that perfection. Open societies operate on a lower level, although they may contain strivings toward perfection. Small closed societies are those where everyone can know everyone else and where laws constrain the lower impulses, by which he meant physiologically based drives such as sex, hunger, and the other appetites. Society must provide the coercive constraint through its laws (132–133). Basic to the good society is the way of life particular to it, the *politeia*, which "meant the way of life of a society rather than its constitution" (136). Thus, the basic part of the American political system is not derived from the Constitution, but from the American way of life, whatever that might be or according to whomsoever's definition. For Strauss, those who provide the definition are the natural rulers, those who are wise. But, he said, the rule of the wise is unlikely, and therefore, "The political problem consists in reconciling the requirement for wisdom with the requirement for consent ... But whereas, from the point of view of egalitarian natural right [Enlightenment natural right], consent takes precedence over wisdom, from the point of view of classic natural right, wisdom takes precedence over consent" (141).

To sum up Strauss, behind every system of laws is a way of life. A good way of life expresses an absolute, ideal morality constraining physical desires. Only the small, homogeneous society can offer the necessary controls, which in the end promote true freedom—that is, freedom from physical desires and impulses. Nonetheless, modern mass societies are unlikely to institute the kind of government required of the good society, rule by the wise, so the modern political problem must modify rule by the masses so it can approach rule by the wise. That will be possible only by the noble lie, deceiving the masses into wanting what is good for them. The kind of American small town idealized in Norman Rockwell's *Saturday Evening Post* covers and satirized by Sinclair Lewis and H. L. Mencken, among others, fits perfectly with a modern version of Strauss's idea of the good society.

Schmitt in Weimar and Nazi Germany

Carl Schmitt saw the same problem as Strauss: how to reconcile moral and wise rule with modern, mass societies. His published contributions began directly after the overthrow of the Hohenzollern *Kaiserreich* following WWI, November 9, 1918. The Social Democratic Party (SPD) leaders under Friedrich Ebert and Phillip Scheidemann proclaimed a republic and called for a constituent assembly under their auspices. The revolutionary Spartacists led by Karl Liebknecht and Rosa Luxemburg, finding the plan less than open and democratic, led an armed revolt. Ebert and company turned to right-wing paramilitary bands to help put down the rebellion and assassinated Luxemburg and Liebknecht, who were shot while under arrest on January 15, 1919. A monarchist counterrevolt led to the assassination of Kurt Eisner, but little else. By April, Bavaria declared itself a soviet republic, but the socialist government in Berlin overthrew it and executed or imprisoned its leaders. On July 31, 1919, the constituent assembly adopted what became known as the Weimar Constitution. It was in this context that Carl Schmitt first published *Political Romanticism*, later adding a new preface and his 1920 essay "*Politische Theorie und Romantik*," (Oakes 1986:xxxii).

The reader looks in vain for any mention of these momentous events, even by indirect reference. Instead, the tract purports to discuss German Romantic political thought. Possibly even more surprising is Schmitt's definition of Romanticism. Ernst Troeltsch (1922/1934) called German Romanticism a counterrevolution against the Enlightenment and French Revolution, rejecting universalistic science and political egalitarianism in favor of an "'organic' ideal of a group-mind (*Gemeingeist*)—an ideal half aesthetic and half religious, but instinct throughout with a spirit of antibourgeois idealism" (Troeltsch 1922/1934:203–204). This group-mind then becomes realized in a society's basic norms, and "It placed leadership in the hands of great men, from who the spirit of the Whole essentially radiated. . . . '*Recht* [norm, right, law] is *Volksrecht*: *Volksrecht* is the product of a *Volksgeist*: the *Volksgeist* is an embodiment and 'objectification' of the Eternal Mind" (Troeltsch 1922:213). Troeltsch's definition and usage corresponds with that of most historians of ideas. Furthermore, it comes close to Schmitt's own approach to politics. Perhaps for that reason, Schmitt eschewed Troeltsch's definition. He argued that political romanticism could be either revolutionary or counterrevolutionary. It was not the ideas that set political romanticism apart, according to Schmitt, but its style, a certain approach to living, a lifestyle.

The characteristics of Schmitt's version of political romanticism bear an uncanny resemblance to those scornfully attributed to the revolutionary generation of the 1960s and 1970s. "[T]he romantic attempts to define everything in terms of himself and avoids every definition of himself in terms of something else" (Schmitt 1919/1925:7).

> This, therefore is the core of all political romanticism: The state is a work of art. The state of historical-political reality is the occasion for the work of art produced by the creative achievement of the romantic subject. It is the occasion for poetry and the novel, or even for a mere romantic mood. (125)

According to Schmitt, the hallmark of political romanticism is aestheticizing politics. Its purpose is to allow the romantic a kind of aesthetic experience. It has no allegiance to any set of political or intellectual principles outside of a narcissistic self-absorption and self-celebration. "The point around which the circle of the romantic play of forms turns is always occasional. Therefore, the romantic quasi argument can justify every state of affairs" (145). Moreover, political romantics prefer discussion and critique to political action. Their politics consists of café life. "[T]he romantic, in the organic passivity that belongs to his occasionalist structure, wants to be productive without becoming active" (159). Schmitt's paradigmatic political romantics were Adam Müller and Friedrich Schlegel. Those whom he wanted to distance from his criticism were the Catholic Church, Louis Bonald, Edmund Burke, and Joseph de Maistre. What attracted Schmitt to Bonald (1754–1840), de Maistre (1753–1821), and Burke (1729–1797) was their support for monarchy and a Catholic background. They had many differences. Burke especially differed from the two French figures Bonald and de Maistre. Burke maintained right-wing Whiggish politics, and he argued from a more pragmatic rather than theological position. Also, he was an Anglican following his father's conversion from Catholicism. Nonetheless, their similarities converge on an authoritarian paternalism supported by an overarching morality. While historians do not necessarily place Burke in the camp of Romantics, Bonald and de Maistre virtually define it for early nineteenth-century politics. Schmitt wanted to indict a figure he himself invented, the political romantic, while at the same time espousing monarchical or at least authoritarian restoration, moral absolutism, and what has been identified as decisionism. The last is one of the consistent cornerstones of Schmitt's writings.

Schmitt's decisionism brings together his moral absolutism and his predilection for authoritarian rule. Briefly, decisionism states that a unified political will must use the state, it laws and coercive apparatuses, to ensure the well-being of society, because liberal democracy cannot be counted on as it relies on procedural rectitude rather than substantive right. Although Schmitt's Weimar-period writings all support the centrality of decisionism, his *Legality and Legitimacy*, published in 1932 on the eve of the Nazi takeover, expresses the ideas most explicitly and clearly. The decisionism Schmitt recommended at the time supported President Hindenburg's rule by decree allowed under Article 48 of the Weimar constitution. The first Weimar president, Ebert, had used it extensively, mainly against the Spartacists and Communist Party (KPD) in the early republic. Ironically, Schmitt urged its use against the Communists and the Nazis, the National Socialists. It is ironic because the ideas of decisionism underpin the ideology of the *Führerprinzip*. The Führer principle was central to Nazi rule, but because Schmitt advocated its use against the National Socialist Party (NSDAP), the Nazis, he fell into disfavor after 1936. Most importantly for the time at which Schmitt published *Legality and Legitimacy*, his decisionism called for a suspension of liberal parliamentarism. It was, as John P. McCormick put it, a blueprint for fascism (2004:xlii).

Cutting through Schmitt's meandering, pedantic style reveals a simplistic argument that depends on logical inconsistencies and assertions of fact that are not just false but empirically unsupportable. Schmitt argued in *Legality and Legitimacy* (1932) and in *The Crisis of Parliamentary Democracy* (1923/1926) that modern, mass societies have made parliamentarism untenable. There are two reasons. First, parliamentary systems devolve into party systems where the "parliament had become an 'antechamber' for concealed interests and that its members were no longer as the *Reichsverfassung* [imperial constitution] declared them, 'representatives of the entire people ... bound only to their consciences and not to any instructions" (Kennedy 1985:xxvii–xxviii). That is, parliamentary representatives depended on demagoguery mediated by political parties. The parties orchestrated popular opinion using a variety of techniques; not the least were new communication media such as radio. The representatives then became party hacks instead of independent representatives. What is noteworthy in this line of argument is that it does not posit an essential conflict between representatives carrying out the will of the electorate versus voting their consciences. Instead it sees political parties as the villain in the piece, because each represents special interests, which are often concealed from public view. It was a concern voiced in the early American republic, and of course it has a currency in contemporary American politics where the two great political parties are often accused of merely representing hidden special interests rather than the will of their constituents. Schmitt identified parliamentarism with liberalism, not democracy.

The other criticism Schmitt leveled against parliamentarism was that it elevated discussion to the role of ruling the nation. It was this point in particular that led Schmitt to argue that liberal parliamentarism was in fact antidemocratic. Citing Harold Laski (1921) to the effect that parliaments are governments by discussion, Schmitt claimed that "the development of modern mass democracy has made public discussion an empty formality" (Schmitt 1923/1926:49). As government by discussion, parliamentary government lacked legitimacy. The problem was that the German Weimar Republic had been born of revolution rather than some sort of organic, historical development of the nation—that is, the German *Volk*. This harkening back to historical organicism revealed Schmitt's fundamental romanticism, and it was linked to one of his pet theories of legitimacy. According to him, there was a primal right to resistance predating any written constitution. The right to resistance was the right to resist a tyrant for abuse of state power. Legitimacy under a democratic system depends on the will of the people, but that will was no longer represented in parliament. The reason was that parliamentarism meant that majorities could outlaw minorities, thereby exercising the tyrannical abuse that legitimated the right to resistance (Schmitt 1932:29–30). Moreover, the republic faced a crisis in that antiparliamentary parties such as the National Socialists and the Communists sought parliamentary control in order to destroy the parliament. As constituted under Weimar, the Reichstag failed legitimacy on two counts: it was (potentially) tyrannical and it was feckless in the face of challenges from the left and right.

Schmitt saw a way out of the dilemma. The first relied on provisions in the Weimar constitution that allowed for legislation through plebiscite in Articles 73, 74, and 76. Citing Rousseau, whom Schmitt had elsewhere excoriated for romantic liberalism (Schmitt 1919/1925), he said that "the [parliamentary] representative must fall silent when the represented speak, the democratic consequence is that the popular assembly must always recede, if opposed by the people it represents" (1932:61). The problem was that the plebiscite transforms the parliament into an intermediary organ instead of a legislature, but it does not change the rest of the legislative apparatus. That is, laws passed by the Reichstag would still be laws. He concluded that the plebiscite and parliament were, therefore, two different and contradictory types of state (61–63). How to resolve the conflict, Schmitt asked.

The answer lay in the presidency and particularly the president's decree powers under Article 48 of the constitution. Because the president's decrees have been "tolerated" by the Reichstag (69), they have the force of law. Effectively, they become statute. Moreover, since the presidency also embodies the executive part of the government, "the distinction between statute and statutory application, legislative and executive, is neither legally nor factually an obstacle" (71). The constitution even allows the president to set aside fundamental rights by his decree power. It is at this point that Schmitt's argument takes on the character of legerdemain. He noted that the parliamentary system in particular eliminated the right of resistance as "All parties that are not partners of the pluralist system [the majority, ruling coalition] will be denied an equal chance" (88). In other words, the very weakness of the Weimar Reichstag, resulting from a party system without a true majority party, made the Reichstag into a tyranny. He went on to say that the presidency resolves the problem, because "the President, who serves as the counterbalance to parliament, find[s] support in the legitimacy of the popular, plebiscitary election" (88–89). The president is more powerful than the Reichstag because he combines legislative and executive functions. He counterbalances parliamentary tyranny, and he represents all the people by plebiscite, because he is elected by direct popular vote rather than party-mediated indirect election. Therefore, the president is the democratic part of the government, and he is able to take care of emergencies, like the threats from Nazis and Communists, by direct decree. That is Schmitt's argument in favor of decisionism. It is more democratic and more effective. Of course, Schmitt distorted a few facts and left out others in addition to torturing logic.

Schmitt's main worry after the dissolution of imperial Germany was a proletarian revolution. He shared this worry with fellow conservatives, of course, but also with liberals and the right wing of the socialist party represented by the Ebert government. To that end, Ebert and his socialists secretly collaborated with Field Marshall Hindenburg. Later Ebert said, "We allied ourselves in order to fight Bolshevism . . . Our aim on 10 November [1918] was to introduce as soon as possible an orderly government supported by the army and the National Assembly . . . the parties of the right had completely vanished" (Neumann 1944:11). Once in power Ebert's socialists showed their working-class mettle by executing and imprisoning leftist revolutionaries such as those involved in the Bavarian Soviet Republic of 1919, while extending amnesty or leveling light sentences against right-wing putschists such as those in the Kapp putsch of 1920 or Hitler's of 1923 (20–23). Throughout the Weimar period, and especially in its last years, 1930–1933, the government used and tolerated right-wing paramilitary bands such as the *Frei Korps, Stahlhelm*, and most notably the Nazi Brownshirts, the *Sturm Abteilung* or SA. Later Nazi propaganda to the contrary, the Weimar government was in a partnership with the army from its very beginning. Also throughout the Weimar period Ebert repeatedly used the rule by decree to circumvent parliamentary government. Ebert and his colleague Gustav Noske, who made the alliance with the *Frei Korps*, had "the stench of treachery that clung to them" (Haffner 2000:25). Parliamentarism increasingly became a diversionary spectacle, while the real work of government was done in the executive functions. The ineffectuality of democratic rule opened the door to armed resistance against the state. Since the reactionary forces had years of government support behind them, leftist resisters such as Communists were fighting a losing battle. "The Communists had been sheep in wolves' clothing" (98).

During the Weimar years, Schmitt may have been "the theorist for the resentments of a generation" (Kennedy 1985:xiii), but he soon became a March violet—the pejorative for those Germans who joined the Nazi Party after it had secured power. Despite repeated protestations that he was just a scholar, Schmitt's history reveals a pusillanimous opportunist who, behind his abstract and pedantic styling, always tried to be ready to leap on either side of a fence while ever maintaining deniability for his own decisions. When it looked like his academic career might be in danger he joined the party while he watched friends and colleagues being removed from office. In 1933 he revised his *Concept of the Political* to fit better with the Nazi agenda. He criticized friends and former students who emigrated, thereby earning their enmity, which eventually precipitated his fall from favor among the Nazi leaders. His writings became increasingly anti-Semitic to curry favor with Nazis when he thought they might suspect his loyalty. In October 1936 he gave an address at the Conference on Judaism in Jurisprudent, calling Jews "sterile intellectual parasites who had nothing to offer Germans ... To those in the audience who remembered his friendship with Moritz Julius Bonn and the dedication of his *Verfassungslehre* to Fritz Eisler [both Jews], Schmitt must have appeared more like the opportunistic romantics he had criticized in his 1919 book than a loyal servant of the Third Reich" (Bendersky 1983:235–236). Once the Red Army occupied Berlin, Schmitt told them that he "drank the Nazi bacillus, but it had not affected me" (264). Detained at Nuremberg and under interrogation, Schmitt retreated into academic obscurantism passed off as scholarly opinions (199–273).

Schmitt's Postwar Influence

His main work and probably most influential after the war was his 1950 *Nomos of the Earth*. Its ideas go back to the Nazi era after Schmitt's fall from grace in 1936. In 1938 he had returned to Hobbes. In his Introduction to

his 1996 translation, George Schwab argued that Schmitt had been criti-
cizing the Nazi indirectly. Nonetheless, it reads more like a continuation
of Schmitt trying to regain favor as it contains more anti-Semitism along
with a celebration of absolutism: "the Jews stand by and watch how the
people of the world kill one another. This ritual slaughter is for them lawful
and 'kosher' and they therefore eat the flesh of the slaughtered peoples and
are sustained by it" (Schmitt 1938:100). Schmitt opposed the sea power,
Leviathan, to the land power, Behemoth. He thought Germany would not
accept Hobbes's political theory because the Third Reich came close to an
ideal of the land power (Balakrishnan 2000:218–219). The next year, 1939,
Schmitt followed his Hobbes book with a still-untranslated essay on the
concept of *Grossraum*. This concept was a form of geopolitical thought in
which Germany should establish hegemony in *Mitteleuropa* to oppose the
Anglo-American leviathan and the Soviet Union (Bendersky 1983:255).
Where Schmitt differed from the leading lights of Nazi thought was his
retention of rationality in political theory. Schmitt spoke of *Grossraum*
as opposed to *Lebensraum*, and he always wrote in terms of state power
from a rationalist perspective, similar to Weber's rational authority. Nazi
intellectuals criticized Schmitt on both counts, noting that the Nazi state
and its Führer were thoroughly *Volkish*—that is, an autochthonous and
prerational communality.

The next step during the war, Schmitt began writing what he would later publish as
his *Nomos* book. It was Schmitt's first postwar publication. "*The* Nomos
of the Earth is in part a coded animosity in response to the victory of
the United States and its orchestration of the extra-judicial sovereignty of
the Allied Powers as demonstrated by the Nuremburg trials" (Aravamuda
2005:234). He began his argument philologically. He argued that the
root meaning of *nomos* was not law, but marking out and appropriation of land. He claimed the ancient Greeks took the word from Egypt
where it meant something akin to urban zoning, the marking of districts
(Schmitt 1950:75). Schmitt associated land appropriation with an originary power of nomads settling a particular place. He also likened it to a
wall. "because like a wall, it, too, is based on sacred orientations" (70);
"land-appropriation, both externally and internally, points clearly to the
constitution of a radical title" (81).

The next step in Schmitt's argument was his assertion that the golden
age of European international law and politics, from the sixteenth to the
twentieth century, "was determined by a particular course of events: conquest of a new world" (Schmitt 1950:101). He went to some lengths to
claim a right by power for the conquest, conveniently neglecting to say
that it was accompanied by genocide of the native inhabitants abetted by
enslavement from another victim of European imperialism, Africa. He said

that the conquest of the Western Hemisphere promoted regulated warfare among European states on the continent. Opposed to the rational regulation of continental states with definite boundaries, lay the sea. "The *sea* remained outside of any specific state spatial order: it was neither state or colonial territory nor occupiable space. It was free of any type of spatial sovereignty" (172). Next, he denigrated the Leviathan.

> England thereby [after the Treaty of Utrecht, 1713] became the representative of the universal maritime sphere of a Eurocentric global order . . . To this extent, there was a continental, but not a maritime equilibrium. What is to be kept in mind is the great balance of land and sea that the *nomos* of the Europe-dominated earth sustained. "There is no maritime equilibrium. The ocean, this communal possession of all nations, is the prey of a single nation" (Laurent Basile Hautefeuille, *Histoire des origins, des progress et des variations du droit maritime international* (1858), second edition (Paris: Guillaumin et cie, 1869). (173)

A great advantage to the European nomos of the earth was limited warfare. "The essence of such wars was a regulated contest of forces gauged by witnesses in a bracketed space" (187). That is, European imperialism ensured that continental wars would not be total wars, as they were in the colonies. The neocolonialism formalized in the Congo Conference of 1885 marked the beginning of the end for the golden age of European nomos. Schmitt made a point of noting that the United States did not ratify the Congo Treaty. This set the stage, in Schmitt's view, for the end of European nomos, which resulted first in the First World War and realized fully in the Second World War—30 years of total war in Europe. The United States became the new Leviathan, but without participation in the European nomos. That was, according to Schmitt, the great tragedy of the extinction of the *Jus Publicum Europaeum*, the subtitle of Schmitt's book reflecting his romanticizing of the old order, before WWI.

Schmitt followed his *Nomos of the Earth* by two lectures in 1962, which he then published as *Theory of the Partisan* (1975). In it Schmitt lauded the guerilla leaders of various wars of liberation and nationalism such as represented by Che Guevara and Ho Chi Minh. This peculiar stance brings out Schmitt's attractiveness to both the Leftist, postmoderns and the neoconservative new right. Partisans, guerrilla revolutionaries, represented the telluric and autochthonous, the power inhering in the nomos of the earth. That they fought against the new world hegemonic imperial power, the United States, made them especially appealing to Schmitt. "Schmittian arguments became a powerful weapon to criticize the new world order or the new Empire from the Left" (Müller 2003:229). Moreover, leftists despaired at what they saw as deterioration of the rule of law, which Schmitt had examined in his decisionism from the Weimar period. The postmodern left, exemplified by such as Michael Hardt and Antonio Negri, owed their intellectual heritage to the destruction of liberal hegemony begun by the worldwide revolts of 1968.

Because the isolated space and time of war in the limited conflict between sovereign states has declined, war seems to have seeped back and flooded the entire social field. *The state of exception has become permanent and general*; the exception has become the rule, pervading both foreign relations and homeland" (Hardt and Negri 2004:7). They based their analysis in part in what they saw as Schmitt's insight that all serious conflict arose not from politics, but the more basic friend-enemy distinction. Furthermore, Schmitt's attack on liberalism suited the postmodern leftists and the neoconservatives. The latter could argue from similar Schmittian premises to support what has become officially designated as the Global War on Terror, a war not of states but of peoples and even a religious war of medieval resonance. Much of this Janus-faced allure comes from Schmitt's argument that serious political conflicts cannot be resolved by law, thus paving the way to resolution by armed conflict. Moreover, Schmitt's antiuniversalism and antiliberalism opposes global human rights laws in which individual rights protect people against states (Scheuerman 2006:116–117). As William Scheuerman (2006) pointed out, arguments by the Bush White House and the memoranda of Alberto Gonzales and Jay Bybee on the legality of torture based in the absolute power of the commander-in-chief echo Schmitt's decisionism and his postwar writing on law and the state. Jan-Werner Müller summarized Schmitt's current influence as coming from a combination of Schmitt's own fuzzy thinking and misinterpretations by both the Left and Right.

> Schmitt asked too much from politics in terms of meaning, and yet he asked too little in terms of morality. Rather than living with the tension between the autonomous demand of power on the one hand, and moral justification on the other, Schmitt dissolved the tension by opting for a politics cleansed of morality...Conservatives who see Schmitt as a kind of "Hobbes of the twentieth century"... miss the point no less than Schmitt's admirers on the left who believe that an emphasis on conflict will lead to a more democratic politics. (Müller 2003:249)

Neither Carl Schmitt nor Leo Strauss is cited as a forebear of neoconservative writings by its main exponents in the field of criminal justice.

Whether this obtains out of ignorance or deceptive design, I cannot say. Nonetheless, their ideas form its foundation: antiliberalism, antiuniversalism, a petit bourgeois morality divorced from politics, and a deep suspicion of the ability of ordinary people to make collective decisions and run their own lives.

8

Theories in Other Places: Europeans and Others

Habermas

Jürgen Habermas has argued against neoconservatism in both its German and American versions. His attack has included contemporaries, but his aim focuses on Carl Schmitt. The battleground is the rule of law, authority, and collective decision making in modern mass societies.

The generational background of both men helps reveal their orientations. Schmitt was born in 1888, and the First World War and Weimar defined his generation. Habermas was born in 1929 and spent his childhood under the Third Reich. He reached conscious awareness of the world in the immediate aftermath of WWII—his was the Nuremberg generation—when Germans had to face the issue of universal moral norms and that nemesis to Schmitt, individual responsibility under international criminal law. In diametric opposition to Schmitt, Habermas supported parliamentarism and its rule by discussion. In fact, Habermas's main contribution to social and political philosophy was the theory of communicative action. Habermas is radically democratic, and he supports liberalism's main tenet of individual freedom.

Habermas's disagreement with Schmitt and critique of Weber has significance for criminal justice theory, because Habermas continually raised the vexatious issue of the grounds for valid law. Without valid laws, there can be no crime, something pointed out by every introductory textbook in criminal justice—*nullum crimen sine lege*. Both Habermas and Schmitt contended with Weber, Weimar, and Nuremberg, which make the validity and rule of law unavoidable questions. In his book on Weber and Habermas, John P. McCormick (2007) made two pertinent observations about Habermas. First, he noted that Habermas's career has been largely one of critiquing, correcting, and extending Weber's project (16). Second, "Habermas's work has always been stalked by this [Weimar's] collapse and the subsequent turn of events in Germany and Europe" (16–17). The turn of events, of course, was the rise and fall of the Third Reich, a criminal state; Nuremberg; and the reconstitution of Germany and Europe.

> Habermas's argument begins with Max Weber. Weber, it should be remembered, was one of the architects of the Weimar constitution and the main supporter of the infamous Article 48, which allowed rule by presidential decree. A project of Weber was the conciliation of two kinds of moral authority. One comes from Kant, a quintessentially Enlightenment proposition of autonomous ethics revolving around individual choices and responsibility. The other is that of a general moral order, imposed on individuals as an objective force, a world spirit, as developed by Hegel. The question posed by these two alternatives is whether morality should be conceived as something individuals do, or whether it is something to which individuals respond. If the latter, one expects to find a transcendental moral authority realized in an institution such as the church or the state. In this view, morality is realized and enforced through law. This was Schmitt's position. If the Kantian version were the case, classical bourgeois democracy comes closest to realizing it in society. What Weber saw was that either led to an untenable philosophy. Habermas interpreted Weber to propound "a specifically German view of government by law, a view quite compatible with the elitism of political parties" (1992:73). Schmitt, in contrast, found political parties to lie at the root of the problem of Weimar liberal democracy, a suspicion he shared with Weber, hence Article 48.

Habermas eschewed the authoritarianism inherent in the Weber-Schmitt solution to social control in modern mass polities, but he could not philosophically justify the Kantian, transcendental morality. He solved the conundrum by his theory of communicative action. Drawing on speech act theory and the pragmatic semiotics of Charles Sanders Peirce, the logic of inference from Gottlob Frege, the analytic philosophy of Bertrand Russell and George Edward Moore, and Edmund Husserl's phenomenology, Habermas formulated a theory of law and order that arose from communicative activities of human sociation. Valid laws, in this scheme, arise from two sources—facts and norms. Facts are those things about which people can make assertability claims. When someone asserts a valid fact—some state of affairs about the world—a communicative community of competent interpreters evaluates its validity value, in effect its truth value. Habermas uses this perspective to replace Kant's morality with agreement: "For Peirce, the reference to an *unlimited* communication community serves to replace the eternal moment ... that transcends the boundaries of social space and historical time . . . the learning processes of the unlimited communication community build the bridges that span all local and temporal distances" (1992:15).

Norms too share in the test of assertability. In this sense, norms are directions for behavior that relate to values. Values are intersubjectively shared preferences. Norms are deontological; values are teleological. Norms should not contradict each other, at least within the same communicative community. Values, on the other hand, compete for priority from case to case (255).

> Norms and values therefore differ, first in their references to obligatory rule-following versus teleological action; second, in the binary versus graduated coding of their validity claims; third, in their absolute versus relative bindingness; and fourth, in the coherence criteria that systems of norms and systems of values must respectively satisfy. (255)

By distinguishing between norms and values, Habermas was able to undermine Schmitt's argument that democracy is not compatible with the rule of law. Schmitt worried that laws that the majority could change at any time inevitably produced chaos and then tyranny. Habermas's democracy continually debates applicable values and sets norms (laws) that have limited contingency. That is, they are changeable, but with a degree refractoriness that stabilizes social interaction. Thereby chaos is avoided.

Moreover, tyranny does not ensue because "the core of modern law consists of private rights that mark out the legitimate scope of individual liberties and are thus tailored to the strategic pursuit of private interests" (27). The logic of rights, in turn, does not entail atomized, estranged individuals. On the contrary, rights presuppose collaboration among mutually cognizant subjects who intersubjectively recognize the legal order from which actionable rights are derived. Rights, then, are validity claims, whereupon those who claim a right are calling in a debt from their communicative community to enforce their claim. "In this sense 'subjective' rights emerge co-originally with 'objective' law" 89). Habermas recognized the coercive force of law but said that democracy and individual rights set limits, and in fact, democratic rights necessarily characterize law in modern, mass societies. "The substance of human rights then resides in the formal conditions for the legal institutionalization of those discursive processes of opinion-and will-formation in which the sovereignty of the people assumes a binding character" (104).

Habermas tried to defend against the fascist descent to barbarism by recuperating a Kantian, enlightened reason, but his project did not shed

Kant's idealism. Throughout Habermas's discussion of his theory of communicative action in *The Philosophical Discourse of Modernity* (1985), especially the last two lectures, he reverts to valorizing logos with explicit reference to the discourse of the classical Athenian agora. What appealed to Habermas was the regulated venue by law, by grammar, by logic, by space, and time of his imagined democratic classical setting. With all the rules set in place, Habermas's agora provided the ideal marketplace of ideas. Habermas defended his theory against all the French deconstructionists, their forebears Nietzsche and Heidegger, and even Hegel and Marx. He accused them all of subjectivism, something of which they are all least likely to be guilty, and interpreted Nietzsche (wrongly, I think) and Heidegger (correctly) as fostering an antirationalism that must end in fascism. As evidence of the idealized and circumscribed nature of Habermas's concept of democratic communicative action, he used court cases as an example of settling disputes through understanding and agreement. As Bent Flyvbjerg has pointed out, "court cases are typically settled by power, not by mutual understanding and agreement" (2000:13). Think of the kind of court cases that absorb federal courts in civil litigation, Microsoft versus IBM or Sun Microsystems for instance. Alternatively, think of the typical criminal case, the United States versus some inner-city drug dealer. In his effort to avoid the fascist abyss of populist irrationalism, Habermas had to pretend not to notice the way the law really works. His antagonist interlocutors, the deconstructionists, went in the opposite direction.

Foucault

David Garland observed that "In the 1970s and 1980s, the Marx- and Foucault-inspired focus of the field was on class control and disciplinary domination" (2006:420). The field to which he referred was, presumably, criminology or maybe penology. It certainly could not have been criminal justice, judging from what the leading journals were publishing. In some areas of study, Michel Foucault's (1975) most directly pertinent book, *Discipline and Punish*, had an enormous impact with its English translation in 1977. Understanding why that was so, and why criminal justice disciplinaries largely ignored it, reveals much about the field. Before using Foucault in that way, the book needs context within Foucault's own projects and within European intellectual endeavors. Born in 1926, Foucault's intellectual milieu in his young adulthood was defined by French communism, existentialism, and structuralism. His initial project focused on the history of institutional ideas, "epistemes," that constituted the rationale for institutional practices. He published his major doctoral thesis, *Folie et déraison: Histoire de la folie à l'âge classique* (Madness and Insanity: History of Madness in the Classical Age) in 1961. It was translated as *Madness and Civilization* in an abridged version in 1965. *Discipline and Punish* marked a transition from his project on discursive practices to practices of power.

What ties his projects together also connects him with a line of European thought associated with Habermas's background, namely his Frankfurt School mentors, especially Adorno and Horkheimer. In his critique of the Enlightenment, Foucault tried to show that reason did not necessarily result in freedom and democracy. Just as often, maybe unavoidably and always, enlightened reason merely produced different forms of control. The truth of that perspective relies on his demonstration that power, in the form of social control, always involved particular forms of knowledge—hence the power-knowledge connection. There is an echo of Max Weber's iron cage of rationalized capitalism in *Discipline and Punish*, but its most immediate foundation is Rusche and Kirchheimer's *Punishment and Social Structure* (1939). Associated with the Frankfurt School, Georg Rusche and Otto Kirchheimer argued that the character of penal regimes coincided with social structures of particular societies, in particular times, with particular relations of production. In other words, kinds of punishment go along with kinds of political economy, not kinds of crime.

Foucault marked the beginning of the modernist penal regime at January 22, 1840, when the Mettray juvenile institution made its debut. He placed it at that point because Mettray "concentrated all the coercive technologies of behaviour... 'cloister, prison, school, regiment'" (1975:293). The prison and penitentiary system marked modern penality, but more importantly, they served as models for a disciplinary technique that pervaded the entire social body in six ways, which Foucault laid out in the last chapter. First, the penal system, or criminal justice system in American parlance, established a continuity of norm, deviations, and punishment so as to constitute a hierarchical carceral system. Second, the carceral system allows recruitment of delinquents by organizing disciplinary careers—the creation of a criminal class. Third, it naturalizes and legitimizes the power to punish by an apparent freedom from excess and violence. Note here that it is power that is legitimized by way of appearance. Fourth, through its connection with adjudication under law, the carceral system legitimizes judging of normality in other disciplinary regimes: "We are in the society of the teacher-judge, the doctor-judge, the educator-judge, the 'social-worker'-judge" (304). Fifth, the carceral models "examinatory" justice, which is further realized and elaborated in the human sciences. Foucault posited the human sciences as part of and emerging from modernist forms of social control: "The carceral network constituted one of the armatures of this power-knowledge that has made the human sciences historically possible" (305). Sixth, because the carceral system is so bound up with a wide network of other institutions, practices, and discourses, it possesses great inertia. It is an elemental part of the social structure, which is built into vast varieties of social relations.

Foucault summarized by identifying the political problem. First he identified what it is not—rehabilitation or incapacitation; the relative authority of judges, psychiatrists, or sociologists versus administrators; or even whether there ought to be prisons. Instead, he said the current (1975) political problem was the "steep rise in the use of these mechanisms of normalization and the wide-ranging powers which, through the proliferation of new disciplines, they bring with them" (306).

Recall that the mid-1970s in the United States showed two effects of exactly what Foucault elucidated: the geometric rise in incarceration rate, unprecedented in American history, and the establishment of criminal justice as an academic discipline, not just a community college program for police. These contemporary developments provide strong clues for why criminal justice as a discipline assiduously avoided Foucault and the implications of *Discipline and Punish*. Had his analysis found its way into the academic and research practices of criminal justice, it would have undermined the entire project by bringing into question the discipline's dependence on the carceral disciplinary regime. It also is no wonder that Habermas took issue with Foucault's projects, because they show that laws and rules follow practices of power instead of defining, limiting, and regulating them. Foucault deconstructed regimes of control, but Derrida deconstructed the very way we conceive them and the laws they entail.

Derrida

In his early work—*Of Grammatology, Speech and Phenomena*, and *Writing and Difference*—all published in 1967, Derrida famously aimed his polemic against Western rationality itself, Logos, and the culture from which it arose, the Platonic Greeks, especially the Athenian agora. He derided what he considered the propaganda that writing was just a secondary re-presentation of speech. He argued that writing preceded speech and that to think otherwise entailed a faith-based, mystical metaphysics. When followed through to its conclusion, Derrida's deconstruction project would undermine the basic assumptions of not only the legal system but also the distinctions needed to identify crime, among many other things, of course. What were his grounds for maintaining these positions, and what makes them something more than outlandish posturing?

First, although he expended little effort in this regard, there is some archaeological basis for saying that writing, at least making material marks, preceded speech. For instance, Neanderthals, who preceded physically modern humans in Europe, North Africa, and the Middle East, arguably did not speak, but they did employ a variety of material marks and signs using colors, shaped artifacts, and the like as burial goods. Nonetheless, prehistory does not provide the most important basis for Derrida's argument. Instead, his attack on speech as the origin of logical thought rests on the idea of presence. Until the late nineteenth century and the advent of the telephone, people who would converse had to be in each other's presence. This is a precondition of Agorian discourse. The Greeks who wanted to argue, reason, and decide as part of their civil privileges and duties had to be physically present to each other in the agora or similar locales. Yet presence has broader implications. Presence is a necessary component of what Samuel C. Wheeler calls "magic language." "This is the language of *nous* [mind or thought], a language that is . . . self-interpreting. The magic language is the language in which we know what we mean our thoughts, and form intentions . . . There is no question of interpreting sentences in the magic language, since the magic language is what interpretation is interpretation into" (2000:3).

There are two ways to understand Derrida. One follows his own arguments, which are philosophical. Since, however, readers more familiar with the Anglo-American traditions of analytic philosophy have difficulty following Derrida's line of thought, another path to grasping his meaning relies more on history. Beginning with the historical interpretation makes his reasoning clearer. In the period of early imperial states—Egypt, Babylon, Assyria, and so on—and the heroic age of Greece, discourse relied upon a mode of representation that Eric Havelock (1983) called Mythos. Havelock distinguished Mythos from Logos. Under a regime of Mythos, cultural traditions and socialization into them were transmitted via myths that were performed. The pre-Homeric poets of ancient Greece carried and distributed traditions, norms, and the classical Greek worldview by performing the Iliad and Odyssey. Early Greek theater embedded the historical shift from Mythos to Logos as the number of main actors increased from one, who had originally been the poet, and the chorus gradually shrank in importance.

Ancient imperial states relied on a somewhat different method of presenting Mythos. The conqueror and king of Assyria Assurnasirpal

(884–860 BCE) imposed his rule over conquered territories by erecting stone monuments. Inscribed on them in cuneiform is the following:

> I built a pillar over against his city gate and I flayed all the chiefs who had revolted, and I covered the pillar with their skin. Some I walled up within the pillar, some I impaled upon the pillar on stakes. . . .
>
> Many captives from among them I burned with fire, and many I took as living captives. From some I cut off their noses, their ears and their fingers, of many I put out the eyes. I made one pillar of the living and another of heads. (Roux 1966:263)

The monuments bear bas-reliefs and inscriptions to inspire awe and fear. One art historian has argued that the cuneiform script not only represented its subject matter, but that contemporaries treated the inscriptions as being a part of what they represented. Therefore, the inscription of Assurnasirpal mutilating bodies was to be experienced as if he were actually there (Bahrani 2003). Presence, whether one stands before a conqueror's monument or attends the poetic performance of a culturally paradigmatic epic, affects the mind directly. When the Greeks adopted alphabetic writing and Homer recorded the epic poems, Mythos gradually gave way to Logos. Plato famously recorded the speech of the Athenian agora in his dialogues, thereby fixing Logos as the standard for rational discourse. The root meaning of Logos pertains to gathering and arranging, thus gathering in the agora in rule-governed arrangement, fixed by time, place, grammar, and social status of interlocutors, took on the dual meaning of spoken discourse and rational thought (Bowman 1954:67–68). The Platonic dialogues in both form and content became the new paradigm, what Derrida called the logocentric bias of Western culture.

Logocentric Greek discourse formed the basis for Christian discourse and reasoning, forming a Greco-Christian mode of thought, which has formed the basis for Western philosophy from Plato, through Augustine, Aquinas, Descartes, Kant, and so on. It is that mode of thought that Derrida deconstructed and opposed.

The historical antithesis of the Greco-Christian or patristic tradition is the Rabbinic tradition of Judaism. In that tradition the Torah, the law, is originary. It precedes the universe, as God was supposed to have consulted the Torah to create the universe. Susan Handelman (1983) brought out this viewpoint citing the Talmud: "The Torah preceded the world [*Shab.* 88b] (37), and the Midrash on the first verses of *Genesis*: "He [God] looked into the Torah and created the world [*Ber. Rab.* 1:1] (38). Moreover, the Judaic tradition against making graven images captures the notion that there was something fundamental in at least a part of Judaic discourse and worldview that rejected presence as a necessary precondition for knowledge.

Without relying on a mere play on words, the opposite of presence is absence. Derrida associated absence, which should not be taken to mean nonexistence, with written text. Readers of Torah view it in the absence of its author. Torah originates as written text and is originary for creation and knowledge of creation. Keep in mind that Torah is both the law of the universe in the sense of natural law and law in the sense of norms for conduct (e.g., Rabinowitz and Branover 1985). As the author of the Torah must always be absent to the reader, two of the basic precepts of Aristotelian logic lose their paramount status in Rabbinic thought and Derrida's philosophy—namely the identity principle and the distinction between being and not being.

The identity principle underlies the distinction between signified and signifier. Derrida related the two principles, noting that "the intelligible face of the sign remains turned toward the word and the face of God" (Derrida 1967a:13). In the Greco-Christian tradition, meaning depends on ontology. God, the first mover, is the eternal signified, that upon which everything else is signifier. In this view, law derives from on high, and trickles down to the subjects it creates. The Logos of the agora and Christian philosophy is the way to get to absolute truth, a means to get in touch with the ideal and universal verities of being (Kirk and Raven 1957). Through Logos, talk becomes logic. It is the way to truth and therefore a way to legitimize political decisions. Plato made this new basis for legitimacy the foundation of an entire, ideal political and social order in his *Republic*. There, he condensed power and legitimacy into politics (Arendt 1959). Aristotle codified this approach. Much later, in the face of the collapse of the polis, this time in its imperial Roman version, Augustine transferred the political ideal to that of the divine in *The City of God* (ca. 410). Augustine's vision set the template for much of Western thought for the next thousand years. His theory of the sign illustrates it best for present purposes. Jesse Gellrich (1985:44) noted that "the idea of the Book is perpetuated in a sense of writing as metaphor of the 'system of signified truth.'" In this tradition, the sign, the word, Scripture are metaphorical; they intervene between reality and consciousness, and Logos becomes a means to an end.

Immanent in the notion of Logos as legitimizing is a hierarchical model of truth given by the Phoenician Porphry in the fourth century CE and later elaborated by Boethius. The Porphyrian model structures the power of definition into a tree or taxonomy of superordinate and subordinate relations. The most general and abstract sits atop the tree; it encompasses all subordinate categories. In this system of thought, one understands the particular by reference to the general, token by type. The movement of knowledge goes from species to genera, instance to ideal. Agorian discourse operates in this way. One reasons from the specific and material instance, understanding it by going upward to greater abstractions. The logic of Logos locates the universal at the top of the tree with its fruits, truth and legitimacy.

Derrida and the Rabbinic tradition offer a very different viewpoint. The movement of understanding is in the reverse direction, down to the roots of the tree instead of up its branches. In Rabbinic and Derridean discourse the power to define is modeled on the encyclopedia, not the dictionary.

> If the so-called universals, or metatheoretical constructs, that work as markers within a dictionary-like representation are mere linguistic labels that cover more synthetic properties, an encyclopedia-like representation assumes that the representation of the content takes place only by means of *interpretants*, in a process of unlimited semiosis. These interpretants, being in their turn interpretable, there is no bidimensional tree able to represent the global semantic competence of a given culture. Such a global representation is only a semiotic postulate, a regulative idea, and takes the format of a multidimensional network. (Eco 1986:68)

In the Rabbinic tradition, Jewish identity entails adherence to the law, the Torah. "The Torah contains no ur-text; rather it has revision and decision all the way down" (Wheeler 2000:145). The Torah, the text of the law, *is* reality and morality. It needs interpretants and interpreters. Every interpretation admits of alternatives. Rabbinic and Derridean discourse replaces Aristotelian logic in which A equals A with a set of alternative A's equaling a set of alternative A's. There is no magic language, no final, definitive definition, because all definitions depend on circumstance and interpretation. The Rabbinic tradition has a universe always being created, which is the duty of human interpreters of the Torah. Creation was not completed; it is an ongoing process. The same is true of the law; it is continually in the making through discourse. In contrast to Habermas, where law sets the boundaries of discourse, Derridean discourse sets the meaning of laws.

Scandinavian Theorists

Derrida and the rabbis were not the only ones to point to the untenability of magic language. Wheeler specified the analytic philosophers Donald Davison, Willard Van Orman Quine, and Ludwig Wittgenstein. To these should be added Scandinavian jurists in the realist tradition dating from the first part of the twentieth century. The Scandinavian Realists were those strongly influenced by Axel Hägerström (Olivecrona 1971:174). In his *Der römische Obligationsbegriff im Lichte der allgemeinen römischen Rechtsanschauung* (2 volumes 1927–1941) he examined Greek and Roman law, where he found that many basic ideas such as "right," "property," and "duty" or "obligation" were merely codes for the exercise of supernatural powers. Vilhelm Lundstedt, his colleague, agreed, calling such entities "superstitious phantasms" (176).

The key to their reasoning lay in legal performatives, which they compared to magical incantations. The example was the ancient Roman sales ceremony, the *mancipatio*, in which the seller orally affirms ownership, and then says he allows the property to be purchased by the buyer. The buyer is a passive onlooker as this ritual is performed before witnesses, and according to a rigid formula. As Olivecrona noted about this procedure, "What else but magic is it to call forth an effect through words, solemnly recited during a ritual act in strict accordance with an ancient model?" (229–230). Various legal rituals abound even in contemporary societies, but their supernatural origin is obscured. Instead, personal "will" has taken the place of overt magic. This is, among other things, the foundation of contract law. "Words, and to some extent acts, are thought to be means of expressing the actor's will" (231). Of course a similar mystical "will" pervades criminal law with its principle of mens rea or criminal intent. With the advent of "the will" one harkens back to Edwin Hung's (2006) PIMs, persons-in-mirrors, discussed in the chapter on the nature of theory. As in the case of PIMs, an imagined entity gets interposed to explain observable facts. In this case, some mental-emotional entity explains social relations. According to Samuel von Pufendorf's (1682) theory of state and law, all legal transactions, including contracts and crimes, required a declaration of will by some outward sign, a declaration of will most commonly in words. In this theory, words are signs of a mental entity—the sovereign will. "In natural law theory these subjective feelings and views [will] are objectivised and transformed into entities in a supersensible sphere" (Olivecrona 1971:288–289).

More recent Scandinavian theorists of criminal justice derive their philosophical underpinnings from Axel Hägerström (1964) and their jurisprudence from Vihelm Lundstedt (1956) and Karl Olivecrona. Hägerström's materialist metaphysic, and social pragmatic epistemology help explain their affinity with lines of thought more familiar to American audiences, such as symbolic interactionism derived from George Herbert Mead and the Marxian-grounded political economics filtered through Frankfurt School thought. Thomas Mathiesen (1990) reiterated George Herbert Mead's 1918 arguments about punishment, with more recent empirical studies and discussions of particular national penal policies. Mead succinctly dismissed deterrence and retribution as excuses for punishment. He pointed out that the kind of moral weighing needed to make sense of retribution has never and can never find the exact equivalents between the pain of a crime and the pain of the punishment. Mathiesen echoed this insight.

> As we have now seen, those who end up in prison for such acts are also exposed to pain. The two "versions" of pain are, however, *not commensurable entities. Therefore, it is not possible to "weigh" one by another, as if we were operating with a pair of scales, in a construction of punishment values, punishment scales, and a final proportionality or balance.* (1990:131)

The project of proportionate punishment, given material form in the sentencing grids developed by the U.S. Sentencing Commission and, until *Blakely v. Washington* (2004), used by judges in state and federal courts to determine length of prison stays, fails the test of time and logic. Justice simply cannot justify punishment.

Proponents of punishment (in contemporary times this has mainly meant prison) use deterrence as another rationale. Mead pointed out that rather than preventing crime, penal policies have created a permanent class of criminals. Mathiesen reviewed the literature on prison starting with Donald Clemmer's 1940 study, then Gresham Sykes's (1958), and his own in Norway. His first argument pertains to rehabilitation. That is, can prison prevent crime by changing prisoners so that they no longer break criminal laws? "The overall reply to the main question posed in this chapter, 'does prison have a defense in rehabilitation?' may be put briefly: 'an overwhelming amount of material, historical as well as sociological, leads to a clear and unequivocal *no* to the question.'" He further observed, in agreement with Mead, that "Most likely we can also say that in fact it *de*habilitates" (Mathiesen 1990:47).

Regarding general deterrence, Mathiesen said that the deterrence argument rests on an embedded semiotic hypothesis that has little to recommend it. For punishment to prevent the masses from committing crime, they have to understand it as such. Comparing the criminal justice system to the school and the church as enterprises that transmit and generate meaning, he said that the criminal justice system, like the other two, does not just apprehend, prosecute, and punish, but "very strongly emphasizes a whole series of designations of reality." The system uses "guilt," "sentence," "legal procedure," and other locutions to designate a structure of legal signs, which collectively construct an ideology (61). Pointing out that the main way most people get information about the criminal justice system is through the mass media, Mathiesen said that mode of communication systematically distorts the message. Therefore, the general deterrent effects of criminal law, its enforcement, and punishment do not inform the populace accurately enough to have an efficient deterrent effect. In his discussion of both general and specific deterrence, Mathiesen referred to a number of empirical studies from the 1970s and 1980s. He concluded that severity of punishment has no measurable effects and that certainty of punishment could not have anything but a marginal influence on crime or repeat offending. Roughly 20 years later, after more data, more finely tuned statistical analyses, and a good deal of political support for showing a connection in an enforcement-punishment regime, the results remained the same. "The general pattern revealed in our meta-analysis is that empirical support for deterrence theory dwindles among studies that are the most rigorous methodologically" (Pratt et al. 2006:384). The only place where deterrence has a measurable, positive effect pertains to white-collar crime (384), an area with little enforcement and even less punishment.

Mathiesen also took up incapacitation as a deterrent policy. The concept violates a basic principle of penal law, which states that punishment must follow a violation, not precede it. He compared incapacitation regarding crime to that regarding war. "During war, most young men in the younger age groups are dangerous, or potentially dangerous. Perhaps we should incapacitate our youth, or parts of it?" (Mathiesen 1990:98). Objections to the analogy fall back into some of the core issues in criminal justice. An intuitive reaction to the analogy is that young men do not *cause* war, and therefore incapacitating them would not prevent it. Young men who stick up convenience stores do not *cause* crime. The problem is largely one of logic, as there are obscured reifications and a slippery level of abstraction involved. These problems go back to George Herbert Mead, who was trying to explain the popularity of punishment. He said that the populace saw criminals as enemies of society. Therefore, those who had a stake in the continuation of a particular society saw crime as an attack on that which gave them identity, esteem, status, predictability, and so on. They reacted as if criminals were enemy combatants attacking all those critical social goods, so their response favored treating criminals as enemies—hence the inclination to punish (Mead 1918). What Mead left out, but what the Scandinavian theorists acknowledged, were two important aspects of society. First, no modern society is egalitarian; they are all stratified by class and other divisions. Second, punishment regimes, and more generally criminal justice regimes, change over time along with changes in the political economy.

Crime and crime control are not excrescences of the reigning political economy; they are integral and necessary to it, as Nils Christie (2000 and 2004) has observed. These insights, very much in keeping with those of Rusche and Kirchheimer (1939) and Foucault (1975), point to the fact that crime serves a necessary function in society, something that Durkheim mentioned at the end of the nineteenth century. Christie treats the insight with a good deal more specificity, certainly more than Durkheim, but usefully more than the others also. His point locates the functions of crime and crime control inside the needs of late capitalism. Moreover, Christie remains sensitive to the different rates of capital development in an increasingly globalized economy. Therefore, crime and crime control look different in Malaysia than Japan, different in Norway than the United States, and different in Nigeria than Somalia. These differences take the form of differences in criminalization—who gets identified as criminals and for what. Consequently, differences in crime patterns emerge, and different forms of crime control take shape to deal with identified criminal populations in ways that benefit the political economic system and its leaders.

Perhaps the main difference between the work of Thomas Mathiesen, Nils Christie, and some other Scandinavian criminal justice theorists versus theorists in the United States and United Kingdom lies less in their ideas than in their influence. Mathiesen and Christie have served on government commissions and written reports that have affected policies, maybe not as much as they would have liked, but affected them nonetheless. Critical theorists in the Anglo-American world have been singularly ineffective in steering government policies, but their ideas still offer challenges to those who have an interest in criminal justice as a field of study.

British Theorists

One of the most influential British theorists was W. G. "Kit" Carson He taught at the London School of Economics, served on the Home Office Research Unit, and took part in the New Deviancy Conference at Cambridge University in 1968. Carson repudiated the rehabilitative, or "correctionalist" in British terminology, approaches regnant in the postwar period by stressing the determinative factor of criminalization. In addition to having a voice in British policy, he also affected many students, including David Garland, now at New York University. Carson's theoretical significance lies in bridging the gap between structural Marxian thought and symbolic interactionism, somewhat like the Scandinavian theorists. He also premised his approach on C. Wright Mills's sociological imagination (Pavlish and Brannigan 2007).

Another strain of influence, not unrelated to the Marx-Mead fusion at the conceptual level, stems from the British tradition of cultural Marxism found in the work of Raymond Williams, generally but more particularly in criminal justice; Stuart Hall; Tony Jefferson; and Stanley Cohen. The latter authors, among others, highlighted the role of moral panics on criminal justice policies. Stanley Cohen's 1972 study of the "Mods" and "Rockers" in 1960s Britain served as a model for the study of mugging in the mid-1970s (Hall et al. 1978). Two elements stand out in these studies. First, they emphasize that crime and crime control are epiphenomenal to some other social crisis such as class and race conflict. Second, the appearance of a crime crisis came about from deliberate, although not necessarily fully coordinated, efforts by elites to create a mask for their policy initiatives. Here, I use the word *mask* to underscore both of its functions—representation by appearance and concealment of what lies beneath it. In neither case, Mods versus Rockers or mugging, was there a genuine threat. Criminalization is the conceptual key to this approach. As Stanley Cohen noted in a later work, "Marx perhaps only slightly exaggerated the drama of criminalization: 'At the same time, when the English stopped burning witches at the stake, they began hanging forgers of bank notes'" (Cohen 1987:255). Cohen went on to define the term.

> Criminalization is the process of identifying an act deemed dangerous to the dominant social order and designating it in law as criminally punishable. This fateful decision produces a peculiar illusion (peculiar because we know very well that it is an illusion): that acts of conduct were divided originally into positive/negative, criminal/virtuous. (257)

The value of the focus by Cohen and others on criminalization lies in its attention to the more general problem of reification. Referring to the so-called left-realists in British criminology such as Jock Young, Cohen criticized their conversion of crime victims' conceptions of their problems into the language of crime. "This is to reify the very label that (still) has to be questioned and to legitimate the very system that needs to be weakened. We gain political realism but we lose visionary edge and theoretical integrity" (271).

In its simplest terms, reification turns a verb into a noun. Of course, the Marxian, social meaning has more to it, but grammar is a good place to start. A crime has to be some action by someone with respect to someone else. What kinds of actions qualify as crimes? Demanding money from someone might fit the bill, especially if the demand carries a threat. For example, a landlord might demand payment of rent from a tenant. If the landlord has any sense, she or he will deliver to the tenant a "quit-or-pay-rent" notice. The threat, ultimately, is that armed henchmen of the state will forcibly remove the tenant and all her or his belongings. When and where was this a crime? In certain locales, say the lower east side of Manhattan, during the depression of the 1930s in the United States politically active groups treated it as a crime so that when sheriffs' deputies came to evict their neighbors, people moved the furniture back into the abode. At least for that "community" the eviction was a crime. For a different "community"—for instance landlords' associations, bankers, real estate brokers, and the like—it was perfectly legal and legitimate. Crime, just like law and order as discussed in the introductory chapter, has become a commodity. Like all commodities, it consists of congealed social interactions, and social interactions do not occur randomly. They are shaped, quarantined, and determined by the prevailing structure of social relations, coming down to questions of who has power and influence and who does not. The social relations in Britain, beginning in the 1970s, began to tilt back toward the owners and away from the workers. The change in the political economy of the United Kingdom has eponymously come to be called Thatcherism, after the Tory prime minister Margaret Thatcher (1979–1990). During the next several decades, British criminal justice policy increasingly mirrored that of the United States, which experienced a similar tilt in social relations. In Britain, strong voices in criminology decried the "policy transfer" (Dolowitz et al. 2000). Nonetheless, American criminal justice policy was enormously politically attractive in the United Kingdom despite the fact that as Denis Rothman said, "the least controversial observation about American criminal justice today is that it is remarkably ineffective, absurdly expensive, grossly inhumane, and riddled with discrimination" (Newburn 2002:166 quoting Rothman 1995:29). Protests by British criminologists were of little or no avail. The same was true in the United States, as there the criminal justice juggernaut rolled on (Gordon 1990).

Theorists Marginalized: The USA

Criminologists in the United States tend to populate sociology departments; a few inhabit other places like law schools. Criminal justice departments are a different matter. Criminologists, a lot of them, maybe even a majority, have been writing and speaking against the criminal justice juggernaut since it began in the mid-1970s. They have been marginalized in policy making while their criminal justice colleagues have had far readier access.

Elliott Currie noticed the phenomenon, and he made several observations. First, he pointed out that criminologists know a lot about conditions that breed crime, what conditions inhibit crime, and what measures are effective and which ineffective in reducing crime (Currie 2007:176). He also said that policy makers had not been listening to criminologists.

"The truth is that if 35 years ago criminologists had been given the rather perverse assignment of dreaming up a set of social policies designed to work at cross-purposes to our goals of (a) reducing serious violent crime and (b) achieving an effective and humane justice system, we might have come up with something not unlike what, in fact we got" (Currie 2007:177). But what is Currie's solution? He recommends more serious scholarship in which criminologists try to explain "the data." They should abjure what C. Wright Mills called abstracted empiricism, worry less about their record of publications in peer-reviewed journals, and attend to the crucial issues of the day such as crimes against humanity and human trafficking. Currie espouses a naïve position. He appears to believe that if criminologists only work harder and smarter, they can influence policy. The problem is not, however, that they have not done the right kinds of things. Instead, no matter what the criminologists do, policy makers have no interest in their ideas and recommendations. The problem is not that policy makers are ill-informed. They are informed only too well. Political and economic power shape criminal justice policy, and criminal justice is the discipline designated to justify it with scholarly appearances.

Consider several recent examples of criminological work. Jonathan Simon's project to fill out, update, and adapt a Foucauldian critique culminated in his 2007 book *Governing Through Crime*. The thesis is that the crime control industry in all its aspects—legislative, enforcement, judicial, penal, administrative, and so on—has created a regime of crime, fear of crime, and a devastatingly inhumane enforcement and carceral apparatus for controlling the masses. The important objective is control. Simon is an academic in a law school, Boalt Hall at Berkeley. The book is descriptive theory. There are implicit prescriptive remedies. Their chances of implementation rival those of a snowball in Hades.

Following the advice of Elliott Currie, a group of leading criminologists wrote a report aimed at influencing criminal justice policy (Austin et al. 2007). The report includes theory and empirical findings about crime and its causes, and ways to reduce crime while also reducing the number of Americans behind bars. Its arguments are reasonable, verifiable, cogent, and eminently impossible politically.

Some other theoretical efforts also draw on Foucault or a Marxian-Meadian nexus of critical theory going back to the Frankfurt School. Murray Lee's 2007 *Inventing Fear of Crime* unabashedly used Foucault's concept that fear of crime is the result of discursive practices orchestrated through power-knowledge techniques and apparatuses, especially the criminal justice system. David C. Brotherton (2008) has argued for a new kind of gang theory that uses a counter-hegemonic analysis and, incidentally, a return to older criminological literature and research techniques on gangs. Katherine Beckett and Steve Herbert (2008) evaluated alternative social control strategies to control disenfranchised populations from the perspective of criminalization theory.

Harold Pepinsky and Richard Quinney (1991) documented another theoretical trajectory that they call peacemaking criminology. Its philosophical foundations rest on the humane traditions of justice such as the ancient Greek eunomia of Themis and the Judaic Tsedeka discussed by Herman Bianchi (1994). It also bears a resemblance to the more recent work of Nils Christie, especially his 2004 *A Suitable Amount of Crime*. This orientation takes seriously the goal of using criminal justice to increase justice for all with righteous and humane policies and practices. Therefore, it envisions less physical force, more support, and leveling of differences in power. In some ways, students of criminal justice can understand peacemaking criminology more clearly by contrasting it with the kind of control and retribution system taken for granted as the norm in the contemporary United States. The theoretical foundation opposite to peacemaking criminology is Benjamin's violent law of Yahweh (1921) and the justice of the ancient Greek Dike.

Another marginalized area of criminal justice theory remains feminist criminology. Dana Britton (2000) reflected on its outsider status in her review article. Little has changed since then. While a few researchers study women's roles in criminal justice, most disappointing has been the failure to develop a feminist critique of criminal justice in a way that resembles Marxian and social justice critiques.While decades ago feminist scholars in other social science fields such as anthropology and sociology questioned the basic assumptions of the disciplines, criminal justice feminism has mainly just added gender to the mix of variables.

There are many more works using critical theoretical approaches to understand crime, criminality, criminalization, and criminal justice policy and practice. As noted in the beginning of this book, the problem is not paucity among theoretical scholars of criminal justice. The problems lie elsewhere.

9

Frameworks for New Theories: Chaos and World Systems

Unlike previous chapters, this one benefits from a preliminary road map; nothing detailed, just a sketch. The following framework draws on Immanuel Wallerstein's world systems theory, especially as he applied it to contemporary conditions in his 2003 *The Decline of American Power*. Wallerstein has developed world systems theory since the 1970s. Others have also contributed, but he pioneered its modern version for the social sciences. According to world systems theory, one or several political economic systems dominate, or exert hegemony, over regions of the globe during given periods of history. Since about the beginning of the sixteenth century only one system has arisen—the capitalist world system. Other world systems theorists disagree about the beginning point, putting it much further back or seeing a more gradual, multiple-millennial development (Mielants 2007). Nonetheless, Wallerstein's conception, with its defined historical boundaries, has more utility for present purposes. The five-hundred-year world capitalist system is ending. The present moment, the early twenty-first century, is a time of transition. A new system will emerge, but its nature remains indeterminable (Wallerstein 2003:223). While indeterminable, the successor systems are susceptible to shaping, perhaps more so than during periods of system stability.

In addition to Wallerstein's analysis, two additional factors pertain to building a framework for new criminal justice theories. First, criminal justice as realized in the world and criminal justice as an academic discipline emerges from and in turn affects social conditions generally, and especially those parts of society most directly connected with the political economy. Second, the degree to which the successor to the world capitalist system can be shaped depends heavily on correct analyses of developing conditions and policies. Correct analyses need incisive theories. Incisive criminal justice theories can contribute to the ability to set the pattern for the next five hundred years.

The Moribund World Capitalist System

The dominant political economic system in the world ended September 11, 2001. While the precision is more metaphorical than objectively accurate, it helps the mind to grasp the issue. The system ending on that date began about 1492 after a period of transition beginning about 1450. Periods of transition are "chaotic" in the terminology of the sciences of complexity. Chaos refers to systems undergoing bifurcation consequent to deviation from states of equilibrium. Viable systems maintain a measurable degree of equilibrium, such as that measured by human body temperature. Variables affecting the human body system may change the temperature, but only within certain limits. For social systems, like the world capitalist system, bifurcation entails a period of chaos during which the "noise" in the system comes to the forefront. Those continual perturbations that previously affected the system—think of the typical capitalist boom and bust cycle—get so extreme that they disrupt basic systemic functions. Under chaotic conditions, the outcome of the perturbations is no longer predictable. There will be no certain return to business as usual.

The previous transition period in the last half of the fifteenth century also had historical markers, the significance of which came with hindsight. The invention and employment of movable type in printing, although important at the time to those few Europeans who produced and read books, remained veiled until much later for most people. Other markers, like the end of the Hundred Years' War or the more widely acknowledged Turkish capture of Constantinople, doubtless had different kinds of significance in 1453 than now. As Wallerstein quoted from a traditional Yugoslav aphorism, "the only absolutely certain thing is the future, since the past is constantly changing" (2003:219). Just as the end of the old system and beginning period of chaotic transition had its metaphorical markers, Columbus's voyage to the New World marks the beginning of the world capitalist system, not predictable at the time. So does 9/11 mark the transition phase.

Wallerstein described the reaction of the upper strata of the world system as taking two forms. The majority of those enjoying control of and the lion's share of the benefits from world capitalism will resort to "their traditional short-run politics, perhaps with a higher dose of repressiveness," (2003:232) much as elucidated by Dario Melossi, whose 1993 article offered a cogent account of the punitive binge of U.S. criminal justice.

Current U.S. government policies, not just in criminal justice, illustrate the basic strategy. The 2008 housing market collapse leading to a global financial crisis prompted the bailout of banks and brokerage houses. At the same time, U.S. imperialism took the form of military conquest, notably in the Middle East. Simultaneously, the U.S. government increasingly instituted police-state governmentality for its domestic population. While menacing for the great bulk of U.S. residents and portending ill for common denizens of much of the rest of the world, such efforts by the ruling class to keep their dominance cannot arrest, let alone reverse, the inevitable breakdown of the system.

That is because the reason for the breakdown resists such strategies. The falling rate of profit has done in the capitalist system at its heart. As profit approaches zero, capital accumulation comes to a standstill, even while some capitalists may increase their share of the total wealth, such as the Bank of America did in purchasing Merrill Lynch in 2008. Consequently there is increasing concentration of capital but little growth. The asymptotic rate of profit represents irreversible history, another characteristic of world capitalism (Debord 1967; Harvey 2005; Wallerstein 2003). The system has already bifurcated; equilibrium cannot be reestablished. As David Harvey pointed out, the current period combines contradictory approaches, neoliberalism and neoconservatism. As the upper classes struggle to keep their advantage, they act without allegiance to the system, which they gladly scuttle to save themselves. "[R]uling classes rarely, if ever, voluntarily surrender their power . . . . If the preferred policy of ruling elites is *après moi le deluge*, then the deluge largely engulfs the powerless and unsuspecting while elites have well-prepared arks in which they can, at least for a time, survive quite well" (Harvey 2005:153). Hence, they pursue both neoliberal policies so as to grasp as much wealth as they can lay their hands on, and neoconservatism to keep the masses contained. The contradictions be damned.

The academic discipline of criminal justice emerged at about the same time as the failed world revolutions of 1968. During that year uprisings with differing characters occurred in disparate parts of the world. The events surrounding the Democratic National Convention in Chicago exemplified the U.S. version. The Prague Spring, the Events of May in Paris, Mexico City, and other places all protested the established structures and practices. Armed state force contained and, in some cases, Prague for example, completely crushed the rebellions. Nonetheless, the upsurge of resistance set in motion changes clearly relevant for criminal justice institutions. The common outcome for all the rebellions was to overthrow what Wallerstein (2003, 2004) called the liberal consensus in politics. Noticeably in the United States and Great Britain, the challenge to the liberal consensus in 1968 marked a period of dismantling the main liberal political institutions.

The world capitalist system left plenty of malcontents in its wake. Following the end of the Second World War, the masses throughout the world had new hope, on the surface at least with good reason. The two triumphant states, the United States and the Soviet Union, both claimed and stood for freedom and equality. Decolonization, however sophistical it would turn out in the end, seemed a real possibility. Led by the United States, there was an enormous economic expansion. By the mid-1960s, these aspirations faltered.

Long-term anger against the system combined with disappointment over the failure of antisystem movements to change the world. The 1968 explosions had two common themes, whatever the local context. First, they rejected U.S. hegemonic power. Second, they recognized that the Soviet Union, supposedly the antagonist to U.S. leadership of world capitalism, actually colluded with it. Moreover, where antisystemic political movements, like various versions of socialist political parties, actually gained power in some states, they did not fulfill their promises.

> The cultural shock of 1968 unhinged the automatic dominance of the liberal center, which had prevailed in the world-system since the prior world revolution of 1848. The right and left were liberated from their role as avatars of centrist liberalism and were able to assert, or rather re-assert, their more radical values.... The immediate effect of the world revolution of 1968 seemed to be a legitimation of left values, most notably in the domains of race and sex. (Wallerstein 2004:85)

It was exactly these domains that helped undo the apparent triumph. The politics of the left fragmented into identity politics. Black nationalism and radical feminism are examples. Instead of unifying truly transformative movements in social, environmental, political, and economic issues, identity politics around status group interests inevitably competed with one another. In the meantime, the ruling classes, with their eye always on the ball of the political economy, devised strategies to fight back and regain total control. Furthermore, the radical movements' attack on liberalism meant the center consensus lost its allies on the left.

The formation of the liberal consensus goes back to 120 years before the failed 1968 world revolutions. In 1848 other convulsive uprisings shook Europe. The world capitalist system centered in Western Europe came under challenge from a new breed of democratic political ideas and movements. Karl Marx and Friedrich Engels named it. In their famous opening they said, "A spectre is haunting Europe—the spectre of communism" (1848:203). The only industrial country not to experience the uprising was England. The European ruling classes attributed England's immunity to the "mode of conservatism preached and practiced there between 1820 and 1850 by Sir Robert Peel, which consisted of timely (but limited) concessions aimed at undercutting the long-term appeal of radical action" (Wallerstein 2004:64). Peel was Tory home secretary (1822–1829), then prime minister (1834–1835; 1841–1846). Those versed in criminal justice literature, of course, associate Robert Peel with something else— establishing the model for professional policing, Scotland Yard. Although not realized in widespread practice until the second half of the twentieth century in the United States, Peel's so called Nine Principles (possibly apocryphally attributed to him) summarize much of liberalism's criminal justice policies. He said the basic mission for which the police exist is to prevent crime and disorder, which depends on a cooperative public. That is, policing needs legitimation. This further implies management of public opinion so as to secure approval for the state's use of force to maintain the existing political economic system. Peel's professional policing model combined with reformist penal policies and criminal adjudication that recognized, if often only in the breach, basic civil rights. As Friedrich Engels put it, this strategy means that "The lowest police officer of the civilized state has more 'authority' than all the organs of gentile society put together" (1891:156).

The high-water mark of the liberal consensus in the United States followed the Second World War. After 1968, neoliberalism and neoconservatism supplanted the liberal consensus in the global political economy and domestic governance. The process proceeded almost systematically. If the astute analyst did not know better, it would seem as if the rollback of liberalism followed a blueprint and timetable laid out beforehand. Of course real political change is never so predictable, but looking back to 1971 and Lewis Powell's memo, it looks as if his program took form much as he described it. In the 1970s the intellectual foundation took shape. Reaganism and Thatcherism gave it political reality in the 1980s. By the 1990s neoliberalism ruled the world through the dollar and its organizations, the World Bank and International Monetary Fund. All was backed up, of course, by U.S. militarism, as shown in the Balkan invasions.

Over the same period neoconservatism triumphed in the arena of social control. Criminal justice played a major role in dismantling liberalism in the United States. Police forces throughout the country received equipment and training in crowd control and military tactics to suppress mass protests. Criminal laws mushroomed, especially at the federal level. Penal reformism gave way to incapacitation, and the U.S. prison population increased geometrically. By the turn of the millennium, the land of the free and the home of the brave had the most incarcerated population on the planet, and a population that feared fellow citizens more than it did the armed force of the state.

The attacks of September 11, 2001, punctuated the structural crisis of the world capitalist system. The neoconservatives, having planned for the opportunity years in advance, for example with the Project for the New American Century (now available at http://www.newamericancentury. org), pursued a program centered on unilateral U.S. military power combined with attempts to undo the cultural revolutions of 1968, especially around race and sex. An interesting feature of the latter shows the contradictory nature of periods of chaos. While antiabortion, abstinence, Clarence Thomas, and the petty bourgeois messages of the Nation of Islam garnered political gains, segmented marketing to racial and ethnic groups and various levels of sexualized images permeated the commercial media markets. Neoliberal economics paralleled neoconservative politics.

Wallerstein named three empirical expectations of the transitional period of chaos. First, institutional systems throughout the world in all the main areas of social fundamentals—economic, educational, political, and reproductive—are subject to wild fluctuations. Second, the world economy suffers acute speculative pressures, which escape the control of the major financial institutions and bodies such as central banks. Third, a high degree of violence erupts everywhere, as state legitimacy declines precipitously. "No one has any longer the power to shut down such eruptions effectively. The moral constraints traditionally enforced by religious institutions are finding their efficacy considerably diminished" (Wallerstein 2004:87).

> In the struggle over the system (or systems) that will succeed our existing world-system, the fundamental cleavage will be between those who wish to expand both liberties—that of the majority and that of the minorities—and those who will seek to create a non-libertarian system under the guise of preferring either the liberty of the majority or the liberty of the minorities. In such a struggle, it becomes clear what the role of opacity is in the struggle. Opacity leads to confusion, and this favors those who wish to limit liberty. (89)

Three kinds of tasks confront those who favor greater liberty: intellectual, moral, and political. In at least one field of endeavor, that of criminal justice, the intellectual tasks need a theoretical foundation.

The Ideology of Criminal Justice

In an article that seemingly had nothing to do with theoretical frameworks for criminal justice, Anthony Lane wrote about conditions in China.

> China has taken the gamble of seeking to make people rich before it has made them free. By the standards of the Enlightenment, that is either an illusion or a cruel con, though a free marketer might argue that the liberties bestowed by trade and consumption—the strange half-freedom of the television commercial, for example, which enslaves us even as it promises the wealth of the world—are not to be sniffed at, and may, indeed, be what most of us ponder and pursue. (2008:72)

First a clarification: it is not China that has taken a gamble; it is the Chinese political leadership. The leaders of the Chinese Communist Party, of all things, have opted for a style of laissez-faire economic policies reminiscent of those in America's Gilded Age, the post – Civil War era when U.S. industry exploded to lead the world in industrial production by the turn of the century. China's criminal justice system, meanwhile, is a hodgepodge of revolutionary "people's law," Roman law traditions from the Manchu Dynasty and early republic, and international commercial law, all built on legal philosophies from the classical period.

A second clarification: by the standards of the Enlightenment, the Chinese are free. In fact they are no less free than Gilded Age Americans, a period of American history that in many ways corresponds to early twenty-first-century China with its raw industrial capitalism, extensive foreign investment, poorly controlled and relatively underdeveloped outer provinces, and corrupt and exploitive local elites. The percipience of Lane's observation lies not in its analytic accuracy but in the apparent goal of Chinese government policies—making (some) people rich. To encourage wealth accumulation, Chinese laws and customary economic practices have to change, much as the law and customary practices had to change in Europe on the threshold of modern world capitalism. In the historical case, the latter fifteenth century, the laws of property had to change from reflecting feudal social relations to what came to be modern society. Under the feudal system, property meant land. Ownership entailed various obligations to those above and those below (Tawney 1926). Capitalism required an expanded definition of property, curtailment if not elimination of its obligations, and the opening of possibilities for alienation. Land, in other words, had to be transformed into capital, and property had to be defined as that which could be owned and sold (Renner 1949).

The landmark criminal case during the period of transition was the Carrier's Case (Y. B. 13 Edw. IV. f. 9, pl. 5), initially decided in 1473 by the Star Chamber in England as a felony (Hall 1935). A merchant gave his servant bales of goods to deliver. The servant broke open the bales and took the contents for his own use. The problem, at the time, was that the crime of theft necessarily included trespass onto land. After tortuous reflection the court convicted the servant under novel if not downright disingenuous reasoning. The goods contained in the bales had to become property, and the merchant had to be their owner.

> Thus, the institution of property in the sense it came to have in bourgeois law posits a person (*persona*) and a thing (*res*), joined by the legal norm called property or ownership. Human society is dissolved into isolated individuals, and the world of goods split into discrete items. One can no longer speak of a duty to use property or behave toward others in a certain way: all such duties as may be imposed by law are *prima facie* derogations from the fundamental "right of property". (Tigar 1977:197)

Even in England, the first country to see the triumph of the bourgeoisie, it took centuries to transform feudal laws to fit the needs of modern capitalism. Land, for example, did not achieve transmissibility until the legislation of the English Revolution (198). The common law did not triumph until after the Glorious Revolution of 1689, and those fundamental rights associated with it—the right against self-incrimination, due process, habeas corpus, and trial by jury—appeared in actual practice only in the eighteenth century, despite claims of hoary lineage back to the Magna Carta. Freedom, under Anglo-American law and similar legal systems of the capitalist world system, means the freedom to organize property and people into the system of production (306–307).

The criminal law guards these freedoms as its paramount goal. "Once property had been officially deified, it became the measure of all things" (Hay 1975:19). A spate of new capital offenses protected bourgeois interests. Forgery became a heinous crime with the growth of promissory bank notes. Food riots and their kindred enclosure riots, traditionally rather formal affairs barely deserving the sobriquet of "riot," had the death penalty attached. By an act of 1764 Parliament declared capital punishment for those who would vandalize linen manufactures (20–21). Nonetheless, as Douglas Hay explained, the terror of England's criminal justice system did not just protect property. Its practice sought to legitimize the authority of the law. To that end, the law's practitioners gave punctilious attention to forms and procedure. "The law thereby became something more than the creature of a ruling class—it became a power with its own claims, higher than those of prosecutor, lawyers, and even the scarlet-robed assize judge himself. To them, too, of course, the law was The Law" (33). Another part of legitimation required equality before the law, so the occasional lord was executed, usually for murder. A third component of legitimacy included mercy. Despite the enormous increase in capital offenses, the number actually executed remained stable. Judges and great men intervened to save the lives of the lower classes, at least when such persons remained useful to them. The criminal law had to establish itself as an instrument of justice. "It became part of the untested general idea, the ideology which made it possible to stigmatize dissent as acts of individuals, of rogues and criminals and madmen" (56). When, therefore, Robert Peel demanded legitimacy if there were to be an English police force, he relied on the preexisting legitimacy of the English criminal law that appeared to guarantee freedom and equality, but in fact guaranteed property.

A Theoretical Framework for the Next World System

The intellectual task for a new theory of criminal justice has to take into account two immutable facts. First, whatever the form of the next world system, it will develop from the old one. Second, while social relations will change, they need not necessarily depart from the current trajectory. That trajectory opposes liberty. In the previous system, property defined liberty. The present task must define property in terms of liberty. In fact, all matters must revolve around liberty.

For the field of criminal justice, this means that its main areas of study—crime, criminality, criminalization, and policy and practice—have to be defined in terms of liberty. In simple terms, more as a point of departure, crime would be anything restricting liberty. This contrasts, for example, with the overriding principle of Beccaria (1764) that the ultimate crimes are those that disrupt social solidarity. The conception of laws and crime dominated by bourgeois property relations gave the greatest liberty to property, or more practically, to those who owned property, to do with it what they would, including restricting the freedom of other people. In this proposal, liberty for all is the test. While it seems a radical form of libertarianism, it can be tempered by communitarian values. The ultimate goal has to be justice. Democratic decision making and egalitarian deliberative processes help ensure expansive and profound social integration.

Several criminological schools would fit easily with such a definitional framework. Chief among them are peacemaking criminology and restorative justice with integrative shaming. Moreover, the framework does not exclude already-established theories such as life-course theories of criminality, feminist, and critical race theories. On the one hand, the framework provides a robust structure for the still vaguely grounded peacemaking and restorative justice orientations. On the other hand, for already well-founded theories, the framework opens different perspectives that eventually could enhance their explanatory power.

Peacemaking and restorative justice

Especially regarding peacemaking and restorative justice, theory and advocacy too often blend into one another. While both aim at more humane, rational, and just social outcomes, their theoretical value lies in their usefulness for analyzing crime, criminality, criminalization, and policy and practice. This is not to deny, like Ronald Akers (2000:214), the empirical validity of peacemaking criminology, but rather to distinguish its theory from its philosophy and advocacy.

John Wozniak (2002) summarized the peacemaking view of crime as social harms (217), and provided an analytic showing that existing social arrangements are the source of harms, with the bulk of them derived from law's service to the interests of the rich and powerful (218). Earlier Wozniak observed that "peacemaking criminology calls upon us to refuse to invest in a social ethic that separates us" (283). Further, citing Dennis Sullivan (1980), Wozniak (2000:271) said peacemaking criminology substitutes a needs-based model for the prevailing deserts-based market economical model of criminalization. Although Wozniak associated the concept of needs-based justice with anarchism, it fits better with the slogan for communism: from each according to his ability; to each according to his need. Peacemaking criminology fits into the category of distributive justice insofar as its advocacy goes. Teasing out its theoretical analytic requires closer scrutiny.

Richard Quinney (1991), among the first to write about peacemaking criminology, defined crime as suffering. He had in mind those conditions susceptible to human amelioration that, causing suffering, are left to continue to plague people. Where intervention to relieve suffering is possible but is not undertaken, that is crime. Peacemaking theory therefore encompasses most existing prohibitive regulations of predatory behavior, but would also treat everything from allowing hunger and starvation to persist in such places as central Africa to failure to provide perinatal care to mothers and children in America's urban ghettos. Informed by peacemaking theory, criminality concerns studies of those who allow, promote, and benefit from the suffering of others. What comes to mind easily in this category would be ascertaining the identity, character, motivations, and so on of corporate CEOs who profited from the mortgage crisis in the United States that came to light in 2008. Peacemaking theories of criminalization would generate hypotheses about how and why behavior that causes suffering for millions of people leads to rewards in the form of public monies devoted to corporate bailouts, golden parachutes for executives to the tune of tens of millions of dollars, and other emoluments, but prosecutes and punishes with violence those who provide services for pleasure, such as prostitutes. For policy and practice in criminal justice, peacemaking theories explain how existing criminal justice creates more victimization and more crime (Fuller and Wozniak 2006).

John Braithwaite (1989, 2002) has developed integrative shaming as a form of restorative justice. He explained that most people do not commit crimes most of the time because criminal acts remain largely unthinkable by social processes of shaming. From this perspective, the panoply of social controls, most of which remain informal, rely on self-imposed emotional discomfort to channel thoughts and behavior. In contrast, the current criminal justice system uses stigmatizing shame, usually with forms of physical violence and control. "Shame acknowledgement seems to prevent wrongdoing, while displacing shame into anger seems to promote wrongdoing . . . stigmatization is related to counterproductive shame management" (Braithwaite et al. 2006:397). The key to productive shaming lies in its link to guilt and maintenance of self-esteem through adequate narcissistic investment (Kohut 1971, 1977). Integrative shaming prevents crime; reintegrative shaming in a system of restorative justice prevents further deviance by "healing a damaged part of the self that is mostly good" (Braithwaite et al. 2006:401). Furthermore, reintegrative shaming as part of a formal system of restorative justice ramifies throughout social relations at large as a form of Durkheimian restitutive justice (1893). That is, reintegrative shaming encourages self-rehabilitation at the individual level and restores and strengthens social bonds at the societal level.

The program of integrative shaming proposed by Braithwaite presumes a basic, socially supportive environment for the development of healthy selves, because without fundamentally healthy selves reintegrative shaming has no psychological grounding. As George Herbert Mead (1934) pointed out, the self is a social phenomenon, and as such selves reflect patterns of social relations. Current conditions in the United States produce an ever-growing proportion of people who learn that their social worth is minimal and strictly depends on their ability to serve capital as producers and consumers. Those who do not measure up are redundant. In support, Braithwaite (2002:62–66) found that restorative justice approaches fare better with corporate crime than do adversarial approaches, perhaps because the people involved have sufficiently healthy selves to benefit from the restorative approaches. Social arrangements that produce healthy selves throughout all levels of social strata make for more effective reintegrative and restorative approaches. Although certainly capitalist, the Japanese enjoy far greater material equality and concomitantly far greater equality in social esteem. The same holds true for the Navajo. Both societies serve as models for the effectiveness of reintegrative shaming (Braithwaite et al. 2006:401).

The theoretical power of integrative shaming in restorative justice comes from its ability to critique current criminal justice sanctions and their relation to generalized social arrangements. The more traditional sanctions are imposed, the more counterproductive the criminal justice system becomes. Increasing incarceration, therefore, creates more stigmatization, increased likelihood of criminality throughout populations treated as redundant, and eventually therefore more incarceration. Breaking or even possibly reversing this vicious circle entails an understanding of the social function of shame and its potential for socially integrative effects.

Just as peacemaking and restorative justice theories gain from the framework of world systems analysis of capitalism, life course, feminist, and critical race theories are compatible and articulate with the world systems perspective. Very briefly, life course criminology recognizes the truth of the line from Bob Dylan's "Like a Rolling Stone" (1965): "When you got nothing, you got nothing to lose" (Laub et al. 2006:314). Similarly, the neuropsychologically grounded life course theory (Moffitt 2006) recognizes the deleterious effects of social inequality on the biopsychological factors affecting delinquency. Feminist and critical race theories add gender and race/ethnicity as foundational stratifications in U.S. society that crosscut and interact with class. World systems focuses on class because of its basically Marxian analysis, broadly understood. Therefore, these two theories fill out the critical power of the world systems analysis.

In addition to giving a more solid foundation to existing theories of criminal justice, world systems analysis can articulate with a discursive method. Putting the two together, world systems with a method produces a robust framework for theory building in law and criminal justice.

World Systems and Rabbinic Discourse

Rabbinic discourse is a style of discourse associated with a rabbinic tradition in Judaism. It exemplifies a core oppositional process of the persistent identity system of Jewish culture. Based in an interpretation of law as represented by Torah and Talmud, this style of discourse undermines central reifications of the Greco-Roman-Christian tradition, which constitutes the historical framework for contemporary Western cultural hegemony and punitive systems of justice. A central precept is that identity is contingent and not, as in the predominant Western tradition, something that is natural, transcendent, and absolute. The implicit critique of Western identity allows rabbinic discourse to deconstruct and challenge the authority of law and governmentality.

To be sure, asserting that something as vague as Jewish "culture" opposed Western hegemony is to assert nothing at all. The task is to find the factor in Jewish culture that maintained the oppositional process. This factor is a particular *way of symbolizing*. This way of symbolizing is found in rabbinic discourse, a tradition of discursive practices, rooted in historical circumstances, but overflowing historical particularity. This way of symbolizing has come to exceed anything that is necessarily part of the Jewish religion; rather it is a model for cultures of opposition. It is the oppositional quality, coupled with historical tradition, that has led to relatively contemporary discourses of opposition found within Western hegemony.

For several thousand years Jewish culture has not only survived but grown through a kind of process Barbara Myerhoff (1982) called "re-membering." Re-membering is an active, purposive process of unifying the self through the recollection of other figures in one's life and of one's past selves. It is the reaggregation of the members that make up the corpus of identity, and the reestablishment of one's membership in corporate groups and the traditions of those groups. It is through this process that Jews have survived.

Jewish culture has done more than survive. It has resisted the hegemony of Western culture rooted deep in the Greco-Roman-Christian tradition. Through that resistance it has become the epitome of cultures of opposition. And even more, it has so influenced Western culture that people write of a Judeo-Christian tradition as a fundamental part of the West. Jewish culture runs like a red thread through the warp and woof of the West even while it resisted domination.

Rabbinic discourse is the obverse of Agorian discourse. The movement of knowledge and understanding flows in the reverse direction, down to the roots of the tree instead of up to its branches. In the process of discourse, but not necessarily in terms of the substance or object of discourse, the Rabbinic and Agorian modes act as dialectical antitheses.

When viewing the text of the Torah and Talmud, in the tradition of rabbinic discourse, reality is before the student. It is the student's task to spread it out, undo the condensation. This spreading out is an enormous task because if the text, Scripture, embodies reality, then the text must be extremely condensed. Think of the universe shortly after the big bang. Students of Talmud and Scripture do not merely have to decode the text by following certain technical procedures to get to the truth. That way of understanding the text depends on a correspondence theory of truth in which accurate signs stand for real things and conditions in the world. That theory of truth derives from an essentialist and Platonic viewpoint. Instead, the rabbinic tradition calls upon the student to view reality as encyclopedic and use a semiotic analysis to realize it.

A hierarchical social order is always clothed in condensed symbols of authority. To analyze the condensations is to break apart what appears to be the univocality of authority into a cacophony of competing voices and ideologies (Bakhtin 1981). This is precisely what rabbinic discourse does. Its intellectual strategy plays the role of Hegel's bondman's influence on the consciousness of the master. Historically situated, they have carried on the influence of elements of Judaic culture on Western dominance. Rabbinic discourse is part of the social amnesia of the West (Jacoby 1975), which can have a liberating effect if used strategically. "All reification is forgetting" said Max Horkheimer and Theodore Adorno in the *Dialectic of Enlightenment*, quoted by Jacoby (1975:4). The translation by John Cumming is (1972:230) "All *objectification* is forgetting." The original is "*alle Verdinglichung ist ein Vergessen.*" Jacoby pointed out in his footnote that translating Verdinglichung in this context as "objectification" is to lose the distinction between Marx and Hegel. The rabbinic tradition, in contrast to the Agorian tradition and its dominant Western successors, offers an analytic for comprehending identity while treating it as in-process and continually problematizing it. The problem of identity, in the rabbinic tradition, is not solved by a reification that smooths over contradictions; rather identity is a process of human reason and labor with no appeal to a higher authority.

In the Talmudic view, the Torah, the law of the universe, is up to people to construe as a common enterprise. In so doing, the law is realized; the universe depends on people constantly to make it manifest. In contrast, consider Plato's description of the death of Socrates. According to Plato, only Socrates' identification with the abstract, overarching ideals of the polis justifies his moral identity. In the Agorian tradition, people achieve identity through identification with a superordinate authority. This identification makes identity absolute, not merely contingent. In this view, individual identity does not come from people in their particular historical circumstances; it is an unbreachable and natural given.

Law: Physis, Dike, Themis, and Torah

The law consists of texts. In the case of nonliterate societies, the texts are oral, maintained by memory, and often performative. Literate societies maintain the law in written texts. Both kinds of legal texts express, formally, normative aspects of ideology. As ideologies change through time, the texts of laws may change, or the texts may stay the same, but receive different interpretations. Whatever kind of texts, oral or written, the legal expression of ideology is made of signs, as is ideology as a whole. "*Without signs, there is no ideology*" (Vološinov 1973:9). Ideological, and therefore legal, signs partake of the ongoing social semiotic, and consequently they express meaning. The signs are material, whether performative or written. That is, they have a physical, observable form. They are not *mere* ideas, not Platonic forms.

This fungibility of ideological signs makes them refracting and distorting media. Ruling elites strive to impart an eternal character to such signs, to extinguish or occlude the social value of struggles indexed by the sign, and to make the sign uniaccentual (23).

> In actual fact, each living ideological sign has two faces, like Janus.... This *inner dialectic quality* of the sign comes out fully in the open only in times of social crises or revolutionary changes. In the ordinary conditions of life, the contradiction embedded in every ideological sign cannot emerge fully because the ideological sign in an established, dominant ideology is always somewhat reactionary... so accentuating yesterday's truth as to make it appear today's. (23–24)

William Chambliss (1964) showed that what appeared to be a relatively stable law of vagrancy—certain definitional and penal aspects varied according to historical circumstance—became, on analysis, a story of class struggle over how to get the poor to work.

Herman Bianchi's Tsedeka, Robert Cover's paideic strategy, and rabbinic discourse share important precepts. They all treat law as pedagogic instead of controlling and punitive. "Obedience is correlative to understanding.... Interpersonal commitments are characterized by reciprocal acknowledgment" (Cover 1983:13). During the chaotic period between the old world capitalist system and its successor, instruments of forceful subordination have to be dismantled lest the successor system turn into a new version of repressive capitalism almost realized by Mussolini, Hitler, and the fascist regimes of twentieth-century Europe. The uncontrolled character of meaning in rabbinic discourse "exercises a destabilizing influence upon power" (18).

Bianchi (1994) described a eunomic approach to crime control that contrasts with the current repressive system. He maintains that the repressive system is anomic. Anomia, according to Bianchi, is not normlessness, as Durkheim's usage is usually interpreted. Citing the rabbinic tradition about the Torah and reminding the reader that Durkheim's father, grandfather, and great-grandfather were rabbis, Bianchi likened anomia to ignorance of the law. He then contrasted the anomic with the eunomic approach to criminal justice on 13 axes: disruptive versus communicative, vertical versus horizontal, inquisitorial versus responsive, informative versus educative, provocative versus invocative, servomechanic versus organic, frustrative versus therapeutic, irrational versus rational, enemy versus opponent, criminalization versus real law, dysfunctional versus functional, stigmatization versus liberation, and ritualism versus expiatory (58–70).

The repressive anomic system disrupts all social relations by removing offenders. A eunomic system promotes communication like that envisioned by restorative justice. The anomic repressive system organizes justice vertically. A eunomic system supports horizontal social relations. The anomic system rationalizes threats, incarceration, and even torture in a disingenuous search for a limited and heavily rationalized version of the truth. Eunomic criminal justice avoids making truth claims and instead demands responsibility from all citizens. The repressive system partly justifies punishment as deterrence, whereas the eunomic system aims at education: "The normative learning process cannot be fostered by fear of pain, only by identification with good examples" (61). Psychologically, punishment provokes anger and resentment. A eunomic system does not seek to provoke but invokes offenders to resolve the conflicts they have caused.

One of Bianchi's most relevant contrasts is that of the servomechanic versus organic. Servomechanisms are control devices in which smaller devices control larger ones. "A repressive crime-control system is a kind of servomechanism in a large political power system, the modern state" (62). The eunomic approach is organic in that it seeks resolution of social conflicts, dissolves stratifications, and neutralizes class and status divisiveness.

The frustrative versus therapeutic distinction refers to the same kind of personal change among victims and offenders as that sought by restorative justice. The repressive system treats criminals as enemies in ways stated by George Herbert Mead in 1918. Eunomic systems treat lawbreakers as opponents whose humanity cannot be doubted. In a similar vein, the criminalization versus real law contrast notes that the repressive system does not aim to control crime but to sustain the status quo of the hierarchic system of social stratification. A eunomic system avoids this class-based control system by demanding broad participation in every aspect of justice. The anomic repressive approach has long been identified as dysfunctional for crime control. Eunomic approaches are more likely to be functional because they appeal to people's capacity for conflict resolution. The repressive system unabashedly stigmatizes criminals. Eunomic systems liberate offenders from guilt because they get a chance to make reparations. Finally, the repressive system relies on ritual to legitimize its actions. Eunomic criminal justice demands expiation.

In keeping with Wallerstein's libertarian goal and his warning about how opacity militates against liberty, Bianchi's version of eunomic justice provides an orientation for criminal justice theorizing. The overall objective of criminal justice has to work against hierarchy and authoritarianism to avoid a dystopian future. The more meaning-centered the law, the more egalitarian the mechanisms of justice, the more humane the social control, and the more justice institutions encourage the realization of human potential for everyone, the less likely will be a dystopia.

10

An Iconic Theory of Criminal Justice

Even mildly critical appraisals of American criminal justice around the turn of the twenty-first century mention Willie Horton. Horton, a convicted murderer serving time in Massachusetts, committed rape and armed robbery while out of prison on a state furlough. The advisers to George H. W. Bush's 1988 run for the presidency created an advertising campaign based on Horton's story. Far more important than the narrative was the image of Horton. It graced national television thousands of times and became one of the most important factors in Bush's defeat of his rival, Michael Dukakis, who was governor of Massachusetts. The advertising campaign pinned Horton's picture on Dukakis. It is not necessary to be one of the political cognoscenti to be unsurprised. By 1988 imagery had become politics, or as Murray Edelman put it, "most of the time politics is a series of pictures in the mind" (Edelman 1985:5). Willie Horton became an icon, or more precisely, his television visage did. Icons should not be confused with symbols, except in the most casual kind of meaning. Icons differ from symbols, and the distinction can provide the framework for a different kind of social theory, particularly, a different kind of theory about criminal justice.

Charles Sanders Peirce introduced iconicity as an element of semiosis, his general theory of signs. He distinguished three kinds of sign relations—icon, index, and symbol. In indexical sign relations the sign and object relate contiguously, as in smoke and fire, wind and weather vanes, or disease and symptoms. Symbolic sign relations are arbitrary and conventional. A symbol "refers to the Object that it denotes by virtue of a law, usually an association of general ideas" (Peirce 1958:2.249). Iconic sign relations are those in which the sign represents the object "by virtue of a character which it possesses in itself... [it] does not draw any distinction between itself and its object" (volume 5, 73–74). The sign represents itself "by virtue of its being an immediate image, that is to say by virtue of characters which belong to it in itself as a sensible object, *and which it would possess just the same were there no object in nature that it resembled*" (4.447 emphasis added). A shorthand version denotes icons as based on resemblance, indexes as pointers, and symbols as meaningful.

The visage of Willie Horton on television screens was an icon of "the Criminal Black Man," despite the absence of such a thing in nature. The point is that Willie Horton's television image did not represent Willie Horton, who was a real person, but represented something else, which was a political construction. The Horton icon was a copy without an original, a simulacrum (Baudrillard 1981).

Mythos to Logos to Iconos: An Evolutionary History

Eric Havelock argued for an epochal shift in communication and consciousness among Greeks of the classical age. He placed it sometime in the fifth century BCE. The dominant form of discourse before the shift he called mythos. Its paradigm was the performances of the great epics, the *Iliad* and *Odyssey*. Poets and their entourages recited the mythic stories. These performances constituted the primary form of socialization. Havelock argued that performance characterized discourse and consciousness using mythic history. It was an oral culture in a tribal social order.

Adopting an alphabetic writing system in the seventh or eighth century BCE, the ancient Greeks employed it gradually and increasingly to record the poetic epics, along with more pedestrian uses such as recording tax receipts and the other ancient applications of writing. Adoption of writing as the main form for the ruling epics signified the shift from mythos to logos, a shift from an oral to a written culture, from the performative to the lexical. Whereas Homer exemplified mythos, Plato became the exemplar of logos. The shift in classical Greece set the stage for a logocentric Western culture (Derrida 1967a). It had particular application to law and criminal justice. Indeed it was in those institutions that the shift took some of its most dramatic forms.

In 406 BCE, toward the end of the Peloponnesian War, the great court of Athens, the *Ecclesia*, the assembly of all citizens, considered the case against certain Athenian naval commanders. These commanders had left sailors to drown during the sea battle of Arginoussai (Xenophon 370 BCE:I.i. 7–37). Before voting on the commanders' guilt, an ally of the accusers demanded that ballots should bear tribal designations so that each tribe could be held accountable for their vote. The commanders' defenders objected, saying that the case should be heard by the courts, not the assembly, according to the constitution. The majority of the assembly shouted down the defenders, saying that the people should be able to decide as they pleased (I.vii. 2–15). The defenders gave in to popular sentiment, all except Socrates "who said he would not do anything except according to law" (I.vii. 15). The assembly voted for putting the commanders to death, and the execution was carried out forthwith. Later, the Athenians repented and made complaints against those who had argued for the commanders' condemnation (I.vii. 35). What is salient for present purposes in this story is the conflict between the written constitution versus popular will responding to oral rhetoric in the *Ecclesia*.

Another aspect of the conflict pits democracy against authority, and here it is significant that Socrates was the sole opponent of the procedure, referring to the (written) constitution, the laws of Athens. "The courts, like the Assembly, ran on a fuel of sophisticated rhetoric which the Athenians recognized was potentially corrosive to the machinery of the state" (Sennett 1994:64 quoting Ober 1989:175–176). In its early stages logos came associated with authority and the state. For Plato, the antidemocrat and follower of Socrates, logos was that rational understanding available only to the elite of society who should rule the masses (Gouldner 1965:351). On the one side was popular decision making and rhetorical performance; on the other was state authority and written laws embodying rational understanding.

It took the Enlightenment, more than two millennia later, to begin to democratize logos. After the revolutionary era in the late eighteenth through early nineteenth centuries, printed documents integrated with liberal governmentality in Europe and North America. The written word supported a literate public and opened laws to public scrutiny. Lawmaking and administration cloaked themselves in the logos of rational understanding and rationalized public administration so admired by Cesare Beccaria and Jeremy Bentham. The liberal consensus held sway throughout the nineteenth and the first two-thirds of the twentieth centuries. Its end came with the worldwide uprising of 1968, although the seeds of its destruction had already started to germinate.

Without inferring simple causality, television's emergence in the middle of the twentieth century marked the shift from logos to iconos. Ideas, personalities, and narratives merged into images on the screen. A truism of political history has it that John F. Kennedy defeated Richard M. Nixon for the presidency in 1960 because of the effects of their television images, especially in the first-ever televised debates.

Shifts in the dominant mode of representation, mythos-logos-iconos, do not imply complete breaks, as the previous mode persists. Just as performative representation did not disappear when writing came to dominate, so the written word does not disappear in a regime of iconos. To illustrate, the advertising industry in the 1920s invented a new approach. Instead of selling a product based on aggrandizing its virtues, the new advertising sold a way of life, an image of a desirable lifestyle. To quote from a 1926 internal newsletter from the J. Walter Thompson advertising agency: "To sell *goods* we must also sell *words*. In fact we have to go further: we must sell *life*" (Marchand 1985:20 citing *JWT News Letter*, Nov. 11, 1926, p. 261). In 1926 words created the image. Moreover, the favored advertising technique was "dramatic realism," which imitated the style of romantic novels soon to be translated to radio soap operas (Marchand 1985:24). The technique relied on dramatizations or tableaux created by words. Thus in the 1920s and 1930s the world was still logocentric. Performances usually relied on verbalization, and even when they did not, as in mime or silent movies, audiences understood them verbally. Beginning around 1950, images began to displace words.

The first generation of American children who grew up with television constituted the youth rebellion of the 1960s and played a major role in the world uprising of 1968. Concomitantly, that same generation grew up with a United States as standing for justice and equality—"truth, justice, and the American way," in the words of Superman. Their understanding depended heavily on the construction of imagery in a deliberate public relations campaign by the Advertising Council (1951) designed to promote "Americanism" and counter the Communist menace. Impetus for their rebellion emerged with their discovery that the imagery did not fit with lived experience (Ayers 2003). By the beginning of the twenty-first century, iconos was well established: no one who used a computer could avoid icons.

Iconos–mythos–logos: Their different characteristics

The iconic relies most heavily on metaphor, or more exactly, metaform, compared to mythos and logos. Metaform is a connective kind of modeling resulting from representing abstractions in concrete terms (Sebeok and Danesi 2000:38). Willie Horton gave concrete representation to abstractions. In fact the Willie Horton image illustrates another characteristic of the metaformic process, that of combining disparate signifiers into a single one. Since the principle of metaphor depends on similarity, combining different signifiers implies that they have commonalities. So, an image combining Black, male, criminal, and violence has the implicating force that makes them seem related. Part of the metaphorical maneuver uses domain transference, as in the metaphor "fishing" for information. One domain of a food-gathering activity transfers to the domain of communication (Geeraerts 2002). The metaphor naturalizes the transfer, making it seem inherently logical. The image makes the connections concrete and condenses fields of meaning into one.

Condensation is another characteristic of iconos. Each step in the mythos-logos-iconos evolution increasingly condensed the representation of information. The old saw that a picture has a thousand words catches the sense of condensation. Although aural icons abound, onomatopoeia for example, visual icons carry more power. They exert power because they carry a heavy informational load and because their impact involves more intense emotional responses. The destruction of the World Trade Center on September 11, 2001, illustrates the emotional impact. The two kinds of power can operate independently. The emotional power of images does not depend on extensive cognitive knowledge, unlike mythic and symbolic representations. For instance, the O. J. Simpson criminal trial of 1995 generated widespread emotion-laden interest, but that performance, in typical mythos mode, depended on observers absorbing what occurred in the trial. They had to process it cognitively. The reactions of people to the repeated images of the World Trade Center on 9/11 needed little in the way of higher-level intellectual work.

Icons' ability to bring forth emotional responses makes them especially suited to entertainment or infotainment (Postman 1985). Icons increasingly formed the structure of journalism as television replaced print media as the main source of news. Imagine a nightly news program without images. While a mythos-based public discourse also involves entertainment (Bevan 1936), its performative character includes an element largely lacking in electronically mediated discourse: immediate social interaction. Ancient Greek theater, or for that matter Athenian trial courts, performed informational and entertainment functions, but they depended on physically present audiences. Indeed, their effectiveness partly arose from their affirming and intensifying effects of ancient social structure and social relations. Today's mediated observers often engage alone or with a few intimates. Audience engagement by contemporary, electronically mediated observers is virtual.

Iconos also differs from mythos and logos in that the latter two require linear perception. In contrast, people perceive icons synchronously. Although several icons can follow a linear arrangement, which produces linear perceptions and consciousness—say a series of photographs, statues, or even motion pictures—each one in the series has a synchronic effect.

Viewing the stars illustrates the difference between linear and synchronic perception. We see the image of a star years after its visible light originated from its body. A linear perception of the star would perceive the stream of light as it made its way to earth. When it has arrived, we perceive the star as a steady image, even when the star may have flamed out and died centuries ago. Performances typical of mythos present their narratives in a linear way. Talking and reading both use linear presentations. Some kinds of knowledge are better suited to linear representations; others fit better with the synchronous style. For instance, baseball is a linear sport well suited to radio reportage, but radio coverage of football and basketball suffers in comparison to televised games. Radio, of course, is a quintessential linear medium; television largely a synchronous one.

Icons and Criminal Justice

Critical criminologists have made a truism of the observation that the authoritarian turn in late-twentieth-century Britain and the United States owes much to electronically mediated imagery. Richard L. Fox and Robert W. Van Sickel (2001:3) made a typical comment: "...the United States has entered an era of *tabloid justice*, in which the mass media in both their traditional and emerging forms now tend to focus on sensationalistic, personal, lurid, and tawdry details...." Television takes the brunt of the criticism, as its increasing tabloidization plays out in infotainmet, where journalism blends with dramatized fiction. This is not limited to television or criminal justice, as Neil Gabler (1998:3–10) argued that all the mass media present fact as if it were fiction, life as entertainment. Nonetheless, the consequences of the late modern or postmodern trends have powerful effects on criminal justice policies, according to the critics. Much of the effect comes from imagery appearing on television, which has replaced print media as the main source of news for 80 percent of U.S. adults (Fox and Van Sickel 2001:61).

Kevin Glynn (2000:17–18) gave the most comprehensive description of tabloid culture, linking it to postmodernity:

- media and image saturation
- prioritization of images over "the real"
- instability and uncertainty over modernist categories—e.g., public versus private and reality versus representation
- pluralization, relativization, and fragmentation of discourses
- cultural products marked by stylistic eclecticism and bricolage
- incredulity about narratives, especially those claiming universality and scientific objectivity and rationalism

According to Glynn, tabloid culture "is immersed in image rearticulation and appropriation" (2000:18 citing Collins 1992:333). Furthermore, Glynn said, tabloid media exemplify the commodification of culture lying at the heart of postmodernity. Finally, Glynn, relying on Frederick Jameson, argued that the postmodern news media relegate recent historical experiences to the past. The logic of " 'you are there' is taken to the nth degree" (Glynn 2000:18 citing Jameson 1983:125). Once relegated to the past, media representations deposit residual collective memory traces preparing the way for subsequent media reappropriation. The built-in obsolescence of popular media "thwart precisely those forms of understanding that are needed" (Glynn 2000:19). Consider the fact that the U.S. government never presented any clear and convincing evidence that Osama bin Laden and his organization, which they dubbed "al Qaeda," planned and carried out the attacks of 9/11, although today the media treat the speculation as established fact based on continual reappropriation of the televised images.

Once the images of 9/11 became established as iconic signs, they contributed to ideological formations.

> In actual fact, each living ideological sign has two faces, like Janus . . . any current truth must inevitably sound to many other people as the greatest lie. This *inner dialectic quality* [sic] of the sign comes out fully in the open only in times of social crises or revolutionary changes. In the ordinary conditions of life, the contradiction embedded in every ideological sign cannot emerge fully because the ideological sign in an established, dominant ideology is always somewhat reactionary . . . so accentuating yesterday's truth as to make it appear today's. And that is what is responsible for the refracting and distorting peculiarity of the ideological sign within the dominant ideology. (Vološinov 1973:23–24)

In trials of those accused of terrorism, the prosecution regularly has introduced images and film footage of the 9/11 attacks as part of its evidence. The image, having been embedded in an ideological formation, subsequently proves the truth of the ideology.

Imagery, iconic signs, suffuse throughout all aspects of criminal justice, just as they do in every corner of twenty-first-century culture. Instead of an exhaustive list, two areas of criminal justice serve to illustrate: race and contraband images. U.S. criminal justice has long contributed to racial projects, shoring up racial formations (Omi and Winant 1994). Mainly, criminal justice apparatuses—police, courts, and prisons—maintain racial boundaries, in effect ensuring racial minorities "know their place." They have achieved this both informally as in the "street justice" meted out by police and formally through selective criminalization, enforcement, and incarceration. As for contraband, the long history of turning certain kinds of images into contraband became a major federal criminal matter with the advent of the Internet. Before that, pornography of all kinds had been banned from the U.S. mails. After the Second World War comic books became the subject of congressional investigation and almost became contraband.

Racial iconography in criminal justice

Although the authoritarian turn had already begun in U.S. criminal justice, the Reagan years brought masterful expertise to the construction of a political culture. "Race and television were the twin pillars that anchored Ronald Reagan's decade of 'feel-good politics'" (Gray 1995:14). Herman Gray connected the Reagan success to the larger project of what he called "the new right." The new right deliberately set out to shift discourse to the right in politics and culture. As part of the effort they made race a political issue, using signs of blackness in "an explosion of television images, photo opportunities, and campaign pledges" (15). Much of Reagan's success came from making his persona into a "key signifier of the 'authentic America' and the glory days of 'American national preeminence'" (Gray 1995:16 citing Rogin 1987). The construction of an authentic America, which was remarkably White, built on recouped images of television programs such as *The Adventures of Ozzie and Harriet* (ABC 1952–1956) and *Little House on the Prairie* (NBC 1974–1983). That such programs made no claim to documentary accuracy made no difference, as their importance lay in the images they had deposited in American collective memory (Coontz 1992).

In contrast to the Reaganesque authentic America, "blackness was constructed along a continuum ranging from menace on one end to immorality on the other with irresponsibility located somewhere in the middle" (Gray 1995:17). Such images of blackness appealed to the long-established racism in Euro-American culture going back to the earliest colonization, which depicted the indigenous population as hostile savages and employed kidnapped and enslaved Africans to turn the invaded territory into economically productive capital. The masterstroke engineered by new-right Republicans in the United States and Thatcherite Tories in the United Kingdom appealed to White racism without appearing racist (18–19). Part of the trick involved spotlighting right-wing African Americans such as Clarence Thomas, Colin Powell, and Condoleeza Rice.

By far the more important part of the strategy relied on complicit mass media, which continually overemphasized individuals' risks from personal violence and associated criminal violence with blackness. Unlike risks stemming from public health hazards such as pollution, unsafe consumer products, or working conditions—all of which present far greater risks to personal safety—risks from personal criminal violence offer the possibility of anthropomorphized blame. Somebody is the threat. Somebody can be blamed. Mass-mediated imagery shows the body and the face, which are more commonly Black, Latin, or more recently Middle Eastern. As Mary Douglas (1985) has pointed out, the propensity to blame victims is not associated only with the United States or Britain. It is a social pattern everywhere. Internal victim blaming facilitates social control while blaming external enemies enhances group loyalty. Three conditions contribute to such scapegoating. First, fear of criminal assault personalizes risk with identifiable victims and offenders. Second, offenders are easy prey to state police power. Finally, state criminal justice apparatuses make claims of effectiveness so that blaming offenders makes the risk seem controllable, despite the never-ending supply of criminals (Hollway and Jefferson 1997:260). Since claims about risk depend on political morality (Cohen 2002: xxvi), allocation of blame,—that is, scapegoating—achieves central prominence in political projects (Douglas 1992). In a culture of control (Garland 2001), "the focus shifts from the *crime* problem to the *criminal* problem" (Welch 2006:41), and the constructed image of the criminal assumes the visage of a racial minority.

Racialization of criminality and politicization of crime go hand in hand. Cinema and television contribute to the partnership. Movies and television programs play major roles in shaping political sensibilities because of the postmodern blending of fact and fiction. Crime has been a staple fare for both movies and television since their inception. Crime movies of the 1930s through the 1970s and crime television programs from the 1950s through the same period reveal a stark racial contrast with these electronically mediated images of the last few decades. Black criminality rarely showed up on the big screen in the past. When it did, African Americans, and sometimes other minorities, were as often portrayed as victims, for example in *To Kill a Mockingbird* (1962) or *Twelve Angry Men* (1957). Television crime programs also excluded Black criminals. Some of the most popular, such as *Dragnet* (1951–1959), *Highway Patrol* (1955–1959), *Peter Gunn* (1958–1961), *Naked City* (1958–1963), *77 Sunset Strip* (1958–1964), and *The Untouchables* (1959–1963) rarely had non-White criminals. In contrast, movies such as *Colors* (1988), *Boyz N the Hood* (1991), and *Menace II Society* (1993) depend largely on the dramatization of minority criminality. Perhaps most often mentioned in this regard by critical criminologists are television programs such as *America's Most Wanted* (first aired 1988), *Cops* (first aired 1989), or *Law & Order* (first aired 1990). Black and Latin criminals and gangs did not first appear on U.S. streets in the 1980s, but the national political need for the minority criminal icon emerged only in the last decades of the twentieth century. When it did, lo, there they were, *mirabile dictu*!

Criminalizing images: Comics

Racist portrayal of criminality fits easily into the political category of right-wing authoritarianism. In contrast, the moral entrepreneurs who succeeded in outlawing certain kinds of images do not lend themselves to placement on the political spectrum so easily. Comics and child pornography offer two revealing case studies. In the case of comics, the critics included conservative political and cultural interests, but also liberal reformers such as Frederic Wertham, possibly the best-known advocate for comic book censorship, and C. Wright Mills, who supported him. The same left-right political mix applies to those who have favored making child pornography contraband.

Both comics and child pornography show the importance of iconography that emerged in the twentieth century: comics at the beginning and child pornography with the advent of the postmodern, digital age.

Comics recommend themselves in two ways. First, they represent a transitional form, combining the verbal with contrived images. The two forms create their effect interdependently. It is their interdependence that distinguishes them from photojournalism. Second, the moral entrepreneurs who sought to criminalize them singled out crime comics because, they argued, crime comics encouraged juvenile delinquency. In the United States comics began with comic strips in the populist press. The original strip, *Hogan's Alley* with the Yellow Kid, depicted urban working-class life at the turn of the twentieth century. Some commentators associated the pejorative term "yellow journalism" with the two papers featuring the Yellow Kid—the *New York World* of Joseph Pulitzer and William Randolph Hearst's *New York Journal* (Campbell 2001:32). Two features of the early strips defined comics: drawings combined with dialogue balloons.

The mass media provided comics their home. Books combining collections of strips appeared in the early twentieth century, but stand-alone books with their own story lines became a major industry after the Second World War. They put the comic format into books in the tradition of cheap pulp penny dreadfuls and dime novels. Their commercial success owed much to the postwar prosperity that allowed children their own spending money. Usually selling for a dime, they were within the fiscal range of ten-year-olds. From the first, comics appealed to populist, working-class, and juvenile readership. The crime comic books, and later horror comics, also carried a subversive subtext against the adult establishment. These characteristics added comics to the postwar anxieties about communism, juvenile delinquency, and organized crime.

The U.S. Senate began the Army-McCarthy hearings, and the Subcommittee on Juvenile Delinquency began its hearings on comics virtually simultaneously in spring 1954. Estes Kefauver, who had held the televised hearings on organized crime a few years before, spearheaded the comic book investigation. The psychiatrist Frederic Wertham had published a series of books and articles in popular magazines as part of his campaign against comics. He was convinced that comics contributed to delinquency. According to him, much of their effect came from the amoral plots combined with images, thus inordinately affecting the minds of impressionable youths. He was a chief expert witness before the committee. In the end, no flurry of federal or state legislation ensued because the comic book publishers decided to self-censor (Hajdu 2008; Nyberg 1998).

Pornography

Whereas self-censorship preempted criminalization of comics, pornography has long benefited commercially from criminal regulation at local, state, and federal levels in the United States. Most recently the federal child pornography statute, Title 18 § 2252A of the U.S. Code, criminalizes receipt and possession of child pornography, not just its production or sale. The preceding statute, Title 18 § 2251, criminalizes the act of child sexual abuse, but images are the target of § 2252A. Images, in the child pornography statute, receive the same treatment as other kinds of contraband like narcotics or certain kinds of firearms. The law deems possession of contraband criminal because of its potential use. In the case of firearms, the connection is obvious. For illegal drugs, it is less obvious, since the immediate victims of drugs' harmful potential are the possessors. Still, the immediate effect of drugs presumably acts physically, producing undesirable physical and mental changes. With pornographic images, the effect is semiotic. The ostensible harm is their power of representation, the spectacle. Spectacles, according to Debord (1967), are reified social relations—that is, commodities. When represented they are icons. So, the logic of child pornography laws prohibits not child sexual abuse or exploitation, since another statute covers that crime, but their semiosis. Moreover, recent legislation has tried to outlaw virtual images of child pornography, with an ambiguous Supreme Court ruling still leaving it constitutionality vague (*United States v. Williams* 2008).

Spatial Theory and the Iconic Shift in Criminal Justice

Peter Kraska (2006) identified two problems for theorizing criminal justice. First, theories of crime, and its corollary, criminality, have served as the presumptive framework for criminal justice research. Second, while it is true that theorists have concentrated on the components of the criminal justice apparatus—Kraska cited police, courts, corrections, and juvenile justice—so far no overarching theoretical infrastructure has encompassed all the components, along with the substantive elements of criminal justice: crime, criminality, criminalization, and criminal justice administration and policy. Kraska did note that eight theoretical orientations operating as metaphors have routinely appeared in criminal justice scholarship. The eight include (1) Rational-Legalism; (2) System; (3) Crime Control versus Due Process; (4) Politics; (5) Social Constructivism; (6) Growth Complex; (7) Oppression; (8) Late Modernity (2006:176–178). Kraska called these theoretical "orientations." Nonetheless, orientations themselves cannot serve as a framework for theory building, since they are analytic proclivities as opposed to structures.

Spatial theory can provide a rich new framework, and spatial theory fits with the iconic shift. Space, after all, is nothing if not iconic in its form of representation. The most fruitful theoretical framework of space comes from Henri Lefebvre as he developed it in *The Production of Space*, first published in French in 1974 and translated into English in 1991. Of course, Spatial theory is not new in social science. Georg Simmel's "Metropolis and Mental Life" (1900) drew together geography, capitalism, social relations, and the modern, urban character. Arguably the most formidable criminological theories for the middle years of the twentieth century built on the human ecology model of the Chicago School of sociology (Park et al. 1925), resulting in the studies of Clifford Shaw and Henry McKay (1942) and the current work of Robert J. Sampson and his collaborators on collective efficacy theory (Sampson 2006). In a more metaphorical sense, the Bogardus (1926) social distance scale used spatial theory. Lefebvre's spatial theory has the advantage of connecting the older spatial models in social science with neo-Marxist analyses of late modern capitalism, contemporary theories in geography and architecture, and C. S. Peirce's semiotics. The following describes the spatial framework.

> When we evoke "space," we must immediately indicate what occupies that space and how it does so: the deployment of energy in relation to "points" and within a time frame. When we evoke "time," we must immediately say what it is that moves or changes therein. Space considered in isolation is an empty abstraction; likewise energy and time. (Lefebvre 1974: 12)

Lefebvre went on to note that physical and mental space overlap so that physical space, ideational space, and practical space each "involves, underpins, and presupposes the other" (14). Having been produced, space can be decoded or read, although there is no general code of space. Each space needs decoding on its own terms and with its own unique history and context in mind. Therefore, Lefebvre argued, a spatial theory must operate at the level of abstraction of a "supercode." Such a supercode, and the codes of particular spaces, should be understood dialectically, as part of practical relationships and interactions among subjects who inhabit the spaces they produce.

Since the middle of the twentieth century, three developments stand out. First, the state is consolidating on a world scale. It "weighs down on society (on all societies) in full force," planning and organizing, promoting itself as the stable center (Lefebvre 1974: 23). The implications for criminal justice follow directly from activities of the state, since criminal justice apparatuses are main tools the state uses to organize and control. Second, other forces are "on the boil" (23), because the control activities provoke opposition so that the "violence of power is answered by the violence of subversion" (23). Third, the working class continues as does the class struggle. Social conflict, which always goes on with class struggle as its substratum, continues within social space shaped by the conflict. "The space thus produced also serves as a tool of thought and action; that in addition to being a means of production it is also a means of control, and hence domination.... The social and political forces seek, but fail, to master it completely" (26). For example, the spaces of prisons dominate, but also reflect and take part in the means of production in the broadest sense. Their economic role takes several forms as centers of capital in usually remote terrain away from major urban centers, since most prisons are located in the hinterlands. They often act as the main employer in local regions. Productivity within prisons connects to the wider economy through prison industries, and it connects to the wider underground economy by means of importing illicit drugs and other contraband. Similarly, policing urban ghettos dominates portions of urban space, but also provokes, channels, and engages conflict through gang wars.

Nonetheless, Lefebvre pointed out, the production of social space is concealed by a double illusion. The first of these is the illusion of transparency whereby space appears as a given and as intelligible. "The illusion of transparency goes hand in hand with a view of space as innocent, as free of traps and secret places.... Comprehension is thus supposed, without meeting any insurmountable obstacles" (28). The transparency illusion owes much to the iconic character of space, which presents itself as if it were an immediate object, rather than what it is—a representation of the object world. The confusion arises because of an unexamined assumption that mental space unmediatedly reflects social space. The machinery by which this occurs can only be magic, since there is no account of the process by which the two kinds of space come to coincide. The other part of the dual illusion is that of natural simplicity. In effect, space is treated as autochthonously real. This naïve realism, oddly enough, refers to some of the most abstracted models available—Euclidean geometry and Newtonian physics. In this conception, space conforms to Euclidean geometry's parameters set in infinite space, and the Newtonian model of motion, with its three laws, which presuppose an external and unmoved observer. Despite the fact that modern mathematics and modern physics since the beginning of the twentieth century have discarded the assumptions of infinite space and uninvolved observers, conceptions of space in the social sciences remain bound to the old-fashioned assumptions.

Lefebvre built his spatial theory on a conceptual triad:

- Spatial practice
- Representations of space
- Representational spaces

Although Lefebvre's terminology remains as in the original (Lefebvre 1974:33), bullets are substituted for numbers to emphasize the dialectical character of the elements of the triad. No one of them takes precedence or primacy. In this they act as C. S. Peirce's semiotic triad of object, sign, and interpretant. Semiosis is impossible without all three. All three act in a truly triadic dynamic, and they are best conceived as movements in the process of semiosis in the case of Peirce's model, and spatialization in the case of that of Lefebvre.

People produce space through social action, but they produce it with knowledge of space within which they act, and they produce it according to rules for conceptualizing space. None of these can exist without the other, and none preexists the other two. Therefore, "spatial practice of a society secretes that society's space; it propounds and presupposes it, in a dialectical interaction; it produces it slowly and surely as it masters and appropriates it ... the spatial practice of a society is revealed through deciphering it" (Lefebvre 1974:38).

Representations of space are conceptualized spaces as scientists, planners, and social engineers conceive it according to sets of rules. "This is the dominant space in any society (or mode of production). Conceptions of space tend ... towards a system of verbal (and therefore intellectually worked out) signs". A scene in the movie *Falling Down* illustrates the rule-governed exercise of power. Michael Douglas wanders into a small park or abandoned tract in a Los Angeles ghetto area. Several gang members approach him, pointing to some graffiti written on a rock, which they tell him means outsiders should keep out. They mock him, rhetorically asking him if he can "read." Of course he cannot read the gang graffiti, and therefore has no idea of the space. The scene dramatically shows both the effectiveness of representations of space, and how local representations, the gang turf, oppose the representations of space imposed by the wider society.

Representational space is the experiential, possibly phenomenological, moment in the production of space. Lefebvre used the heart to illustrate, but another organ, the liver, serves even better. Much of representational space is unconscious, just like the functioning of the liver; it proceeds beyond the consciousness of most people. Great swathes of representational space are subterranean. To get back to the Willie Horton icon, its political effectiveness depended on tapping into denied and rationalized racism; vague, barely conscious and largely unconscious imagery of the ghetto; fears, prejudices, and anger rarely articulated in cogent discourses, but lived, felt, and experienced by many Americans.

Spatial Theory for Criminal Justice

An effective theoretical framework should support theories of crime, criminality, criminalization, and criminal justice policy and administration. In addition, particular theories derived from the framework should offer accounts of the elements of criminal justice apparatuses: cops, courts, and corrections. The pertinent question, therefore, is whether spatial theory can provide such a framework, keeping in mind the shift from logos to iconos. Can spatial theory support theoretical work about contemporary and emerging developments in criminal justice while at the same time providing cogent explanations for persistent issues?

Lefebvre (1974:53) recounted the construction of abstract space under capitalism: Capitalist abstract space "includes the 'world of commodities,' its 'logic' and its worldwide strategies, as well as the power of money and that of the political state." Although Lefebvre did not focus much on criminal justice issues, he used the following to illustrate the rules of capitalist abstract space:

> [Abstract space] has something of a dialogue about it, in that it implies a tacit agreement, a non-aggression pact . . . of non-violence. It imposes reciprocity and a communality of use. In the street, each individual is supposed not too attack those he meets; anyone who transgresses this law is deemed guilty of a criminal act. A space of this kind presupposes the existence of a "spatial

economy" closely allied, although not identical, to the verbal economy.... As for the denotative (i.e. descriptive) discourses in this context, they have a quasi-legal aspect which also works for consensus: there is to be no fighting over who should occupy a particular spot. (56)

This small example goes a long way toward qualifying spatial theory as a fruitful framework for criminal justice. It implies an explanation for the overwhelming emphasis on street crime as opposed, for instance, to the far more destructive suite crime relegated to the white-collar margins of concern. It frames the orientation toward territoriality in police policy and administration so admirably described and analyzed by Steven Herbert in his case study of the Los Angeles Police Department (1997). It makes sense of the political effectiveness of decrying street crime as a national problem so successfully by Richard Nixon, then carried on by Ronald Reagan and subsequent national figures. Still, there is more to theoretical utility.

The real test of the value of spatial theory in the context of the iconic shift is whether it can supply the "supercode" Lefebvre cited for the dynamic relations among crime, criminality, criminalization, policy, and administration. In addition, a broadly useful theoretical framework should provide the groundwork for theories of functioning criminal justice apparatuses—cops, courts, and corrections. Finally, it must not only explain past and current practices, but also provide the basis for new developments and trends. Since this discussion only aims at evaluating the potential value of the spatial framework, not propounding an exhaustive list of specific theories, the following discussion relies on illustration and exemplification, rather than thorough review.

Spatial theory as supercode for criminal justice

In his 2006 article on criminal justice theory, or more precisely, the lack of it, Kraska named five late-modern social conditions to which criminal justice adapts. They are as follows:

- the rise of "actuarial justice" and the influence of the "risk society;"
- neo-liberal shift in macro-politics;
- increasing contradictions and incoherence in crime control policy;
- the decline of the sovereign state's legitimacy; and
- the ascendance of an "exclusion" paradigm for "managing" those perceived as posing a "safety" threat in an increasingly security-conscious society. (2006:179)

Several overarching developments in late modernity, which now quali-
fies as postmodernity, embed these five conditions. First and foremost
is the declining rate of profit for global capitalism, now approaching its
asymptote of zero profit, thus slowing global capital growth and fostering
neoliberal policies aimed at wealth transfer instead of wealth production.
Second, and of course related to the first, is the collapse of the world capitalist system with its replacement not yet discernible. Third is the entry into
a period of chaos between the old world capitalist system and its replacement as suggested by Immanuel Wallerstein and discussed in more detail
in the previous chapter. Finally, there is the shift to a regime of collective
consciousness and communication in which iconos replaces logos as the
dominant kind of sign relation.

Beginning with Kraska's last condition first, placing the operation of
criminal justice in postmodern America means applying a spatial understanding for managing and excluding perceived social threats. Settlement
patterns in the urbanized United States have long followed the main frac-
tures of race and class. Thus, the ghettoization of post-Second World
War America followed traditional sociospatial divisions. It was, however,
exacerbated by the frequently noted deindustrialization, first of the urban
Northeast, Midwest, and West Coast, and then nationally as productive
industries relocated to low-wage, low-tax, and low-environmental-control
sectors of the "developing" world. The residue population thereby acquired
its iconic representation of threats to domestic tranquility through criminalization of ghetto lifestyles and devices such as the "war on drugs."
Extraction and sequestration of the most potentially rebellious elements in
the residue population called for coordination of cops, courts, and corrections so that by 2007 the United States locked up 2.3 million of its citizens,
and a secret number of detainees for immigration offenses. Iconicity played
a crucial role in these processes as public acquiescence, still a prerequisite
for social control programs, depended on creating the imagery of criminal ghettos. These processes also reveal the dynamic dialectic of spatial
practice, representations of space, and representational spaces whereby the
practice is ghettoization; laws, rules, and criminal justice policies and practices represent the ghetto; and ghetto imagery connects with subterranean
and often collectively unconscious ideas and judgments of race, class, law,
and crime.

In addition to the venerable criminal justice practices of criminalization, the criminal justice apparatuses serve a sort of ethnic cleansing function by clearing nonghetto, economically prime or potentially politically
contested spaces. Gated communities appeared decades before the twenty-
first century marked by postmodernity, but their logic has been employed
in urban areas. Katherine Beckett and Steve Herbert (2008) examined new

methods of social control by municipal governments in furtherance of neoliberal macropolitics. They discussed several techniques including Broken Windows policing linked to so-called civility laws: "In some cases, these ordinances have enabled authorities to relocate marginal populations away from what David Snow and Michael Mulcahy call 'prime' urban spaces to more peripheral and less visible areas" (9). Removing undesirables from the view of the constituent mass public, whose support the authorities need, has several crucial consequences. First, by removing their real physical presence, their representations and especially their iconic representations become subject to easier manipulation. Another consequence is that undesirables' voices fade from hearing. They cannot protest the treatment or their plight. Both consequences allow scapegoating whereby the undesirables bear the burden of the risks of late and postmodern capitalism—nuclear, chemical, environmental, biological, and medical risks (Hollway and Jefferson 1997; Ungar 2001:272–273)—through personification of otherwise vaguely defined fears. For example, the real risks of industrial toxins get shunted away from consciousness and placed onto images of ghetto dwellers, homeless people, and similar residues of the neoliberal economy.

Kraska's mention of increasing contradictions and incoherence in crime control policy brings together several developments explicable by a spatial framework. The most visible of these contradictions arise from the twin effects of neoliberal globalization and neoconservative militaristic imperialism. Immigration enforcement stands out as a particularly egregious example of incoherence and contradiction. The Transactional Records Access Clearinghouse reported that by 2008, immigration prosecutions made up over half of all federal prosecutions, overshadowing white-collar crime, corruption, drugs, and gun violations (TRAC 2008). This shift in prosecutorial zeal remains ambiguously motivated, as the great expansion of immigration control came from a supposed reaction to the attacks of 9/11, but the great majority of defendants remain the usual workers from Mexico. They are employed in low-wage industries, often located in rural areas away from the main urban centers in the United States. Food processing lately seems to be a favored locus for both such employment practices, and raids and prosecutions of the workers. While contradictions and incoherence traditionally have characterized U.S. immigration policies and practices, the involvement of the criminal justice apparatus has come about only recently. The connection with borders as a mechanism of social, political, and economic control seems obvious. So should the connection with neoliberal economics and neoconservative politics.

Not only does immigration highlight incoherence, but the related development of increasing overlap between domestic policing and international military adventures also connects with the underlying issues of immigration. For example, the mercenary military force Blackwater USA garnered federal contracts and was among the earliest responders to New Orleans in the wake of Hurricane Katrina. Their job, unlike past deployments of National Guard and Red Cross workers to previous disaster areas, seemed more to control and confine the denizens of New Orleans. Instead of blankets, food, and water, Blackwater personnel came armed with M-4 automatic rifles, Glock 17 automatic pistols, and Mossberg M590A shotguns with slug and 00 buck ammunition (Scahill 2007:323–324). Of course part of the reason for Blackwater's deployment to New Orleans in 2005 resulted from the deployment of so many National Guard units to fight foreign wars in the Middle East.

The longer-term trends of militarization of local police forces (Kraska 1999; Kraska and Cubellis 1997) have transformed into mixed forces of all kinds and at all levels. Private, mercenary armies like Blackwater get into domestic social control while at the same time they carry out military operations in sites of U.S. imperialism such as Iraq, Afghanistan, and Colombia. Crowd control at national political conventions employs forces operationalized under Joint Terrorism Task Forces with arrestees prosecuted under terrorism-related charges (Huffstutter 2008; Kall 2008). As the legitimacy of the state declines, another postmodern condition cited by Kraska, it relies more on physical force, and as private capital no longer derives acceptable profit margins from traditional industrial manufacture, it relies more on government contracts to provide public services, such as policing. In every case, the issue is control and pacification of space—whether workplace space in food processing plants, political space around national conventions, or disaster sites such as New Orleans.

The second-longest serving Speaker of the House, Thomas 'Tip' O'Neill (1977–1987) is reputed to have said "All politics are local." In the same vein, all policing is local—especially in the broad sense of the police power of the state for regulating social life. Concomitant implications follow. First, not only is all policing local, but courts and corrections are local. Each depends on principles of territoriality and the production of special places. As George Herbert Mead observed about courts (1918), for example, the characteristics of their locale, their space, reveals the main purpose of punishment, which is to enforce the majesty of the state and secure regulated social functioning. Furthermore, the four analytic areas of criminal justice—crime, criminality, criminalization, and policy and administration—are local. All crime is defined locally. Think of almost any kind of crime, from murder to fraud; its definition depends on where it occurs, which of course largely determines the human actors who are involved. The sale of certain commodities, say opium products or firearms, is a crime on ghetto streets, but rarely if ever in Wall Street suites.

Although few theories have yet explicitly built on a spatial theoretical framework, many existing theories would fit, and by putting them into such a framework, their explanatory power increases. An obvious example is so-called routine activities theory, which as it stands does not really qualify as theory but merely an empirical regularity. Put in a spatial framework, the routine activities part of the theory becomes spatial practice, the rest of the details of routine activities then relate to representations of spaces and representational spaces, all of which are produced in a dynamic dialectic of the changing political economy and practices of the state for administering justice. That is, by linking routine activities to a spatial framework as proposed here, the theory takes into account the interactions of patterns of crime, policing, and law that Leroy Gould (1969, 1971) said was essential for a full theoretical development.

Two discourses masquerading as theories—Broken Windows and Self-Control—gain some theoretical traction if put into a spatial framework. Needless to say, they also lose much of their propaganda value for the reactionary program of authoritarianism. The policy prescriptions of Broken Windows reveal themselves as blatant control of marginal populations in public and semipublic spaces. And the policy prescribes ways to insulate populations needed for their economic productivity, white- and blue-collar workers along with their political acquiescence. Under a spatial theory framework, the Self-Control discourse's basic focus on an imaginary middle-American home comes to light. This imaginary single-family home is the site of child-rearing practices designed to reproduce a mass public according to a version of the Reaganesque authentic America. It is unattainable for the 20–30 percent of the U.S. population who have been marginalized by the twenty-first-century economy. For the upper classes, the authentic American lifestyle is undesirable.

In sum, the spatial theoretical framework offers a fruitful and robust grounding for criminal justice theory development. It rehabilitates reactionary quasi theories, and it gives new life to older theories that came from the Chicago School.

Bibliography

Abraham, David. 1986. *The Collapse of the Weimar Republic: Political Economy and Crisis*, second edition. New York, NY: Holmes & Meier.

Abrahamsen, David. 1960. *The Psychology of Crime*. New York, NY: Columbia University Press.

Advertising Council. 1951. *Basic Elements of a Free, Dynamic Society: Condensed Record of a Round Table Discussion*. New York, NY: Macmillan.

Agamben, Giorgio. 1995 (1998). *Homo Sacer: Sovereign Power and Bare Life*, translated by Daniel Heller-Roazen. Stanford, CA: Stanford University Press.

Agnew, Robert. 1985. "A Revised Strain Theory of Delinquency." *Social Forces* 64(1): 151–167.

———. 1992. "Foundations for a General Strain Theory of Crime and Delinquency." *Criminology* 30(1): 47–87.

———. 2001. "Building on the Foundation of General Strain Theory: Specifying the Types of Strain Most Likely to Lead to Crime and Delinquency." *Journal of Research in Crime and Delinquency* 38(4): 319–361.

Aichhorn, August. 1925 (1935/1954). *Wayward Youth*. New York, NY: World Publishing Co.

———. 1965. *Delinquency and Child Guidance: Selected Papers*, edited by Otto Fleishman, Paul Kramer, and Helen Ross. New York, NY: International Universities Press.

Akers, Ronald L. 1985. *Deviant Behavior: A Social Learning Approach*. Belmont, CA: Wadsworth Publishing.

———. 1990. "Rational Choice, Deterrence, and Social Learning Theory in Criminology: The Path Not Taken." *Journal of Criminal Law and Criminology* 81(5): 653–678.

———. 2000. *Criminological Theories: Introduction, Evaluation, and Application*, third edition. Los Angeles, CA: Roxbury.

——— and Gary F. Jensen (eds.). 2003. *Social Learning Theory and the Explanation of Crime: A guide for the New Century*. New Brunswick, NJ: Transaction Publishers.

Allard, Patricia and Malcolm Young. 2002. "Prosecuting Juveniles in Adult Court." The Sentencing Project. Online at http://www.sentencing-project.org/Admin%5CDocuments%5Cpublications%5Csl_prosecuting juveniles.pdf.

American Bar Association. 1997. *The Federalization of Criminal Law*. Online at http://www.nacdl.org/public.nsf/legislation/over criminalization/$file/fedcrimlaw2.pdf.

American Friends Service Committee. 1971. *Struggle for Justice*. New York, NY: Hill & Wang.

Amnesty International and Human Rights Watch. 2005. *The Rest of Their Lives: Life Without Parole for Child Offenders in the United States*. Online at http://hrw.org/reports/2005/us1005/TheRestofTheirLives.pdf.

Ancient History Sourcebook: The Code of the Assura, ca. 1075 BCE. Online at http://www.fordham.edu/halsall/ancient/1075assyriancode.html.

Ancient History Sourcebook: Code of Hammurabi, ca. 1780 BCE, translated by L. W. King. Online at http://www.fordham.edu/halsall/ancient/hamcode.html.

Applegate, Brandon, Francis Cullen, Bonnie Fischer, and Thomas VanderVen. 2000. "Forgiveness and Fundamentalism: Reconsidering the Relationship Between Correctional Attitudes and Religion." *Criminology* 38(3): 719–754.

Apter, David E. 1965. *The Politics of Modernization*. Chicago, IL: University of Chicago Press.

Aravamudan, Srivinas. 2005. "Carl Schmitt's *The Nomos of the Earth*: Four Corollaries." *South Atlantic Quarterly* 104(2): 227–236.

Arendt, Hannah. 1959. *Power and the Human Condition*. Chicago, IL: University of Chicago Press.

Aronowitz, Stanley. 1986. "Introduction." In *Critical Theory: Selected Essays, Max Horkheimer*. New York, NY: Continuum Publishing.

Arsenault, Raymond. 2006. *Freedom Riders: 1961 and the Struggle for Racial Justice*. New York, NY: Oxford University Press.

Aschaffenburg, Gustave. 1913. *Crime and Its Repression*, translated by Adalbert Albrecht. Boston, MA: Little, Brown and Co.

Augustine. ca. 410 (1972). *The City of God*, translated by Henry Bettenson with an introduction by David Knowles. Hammondsworth, UK: Penguin Books.

Austin, James, Todd Clear, Troy Duster, David F. Greenberg, John Irwin, Candace McCoy, Barbara Owen, and Joshua Page. 2007. *Unlocking America*. Washington, DC: JFA Institute. Online at http://www.jfa-associates.com.

Austin, John. 1832. *The Province of Jurisprudence Determined*. London, UK: John Murray.

Ayers, William. 2003. *Fugitive Days: A Memoir*. New York, NY: Penguin Books.

Bahrani, Zaina. 2003. *The Graven Image: Representations in Babylonia and Assyria*. Philadelphia, PA: University of Pennsylvania Press.

Bailyn, Bernard. 1967. *The Ideological Origins of the American Revolution*. Cambridge, MA: Belknap Press.

Bakan, David. 1958 (1965). *Sigmund Freud and the Jewish Mystical Tradition*, with a new preface by the author. New York, NY: Schocken Books.

Bakhtin, Mikhail M. 1981. *The Dialogic Imagination*, edited by Michael Holquist, translated by Caryl Emerson and Michael Holquist. Austin: University of Texas Press.

Balakrishnan, Gopal. 2000. *The Enemy: An Intellectual Portrait of Carl Schmitt*. New York, NY: Verso.

Balkan, Sheila, Ronald Berger, and Janet Schmidt. 1980. *Crime and Deviance in America: A Critical Approach*. Monterey, CA: Wadsworth.

Banfield, Edward C. and James Q. Wilson. 1963. *City Politics*. Cambridge, MA: Harvard University Press.

Barlow, David E. and Melissa Hicks Barlow. 2000. *Police in a Multicultural Society*. Prospect Heights, IL: Waveland.

Bartolovich, Crystal. 2002. "Introduction." In *Marxism, Modernity, and Postcolonial Studies*, edited by Crystal Bartolovich and Neil Lazarus, pp. 1–17. New York, NY: Cambridge University Press.

Bateson, Gregory. 1979. *Mind and Nature: A Necessary Unity*. New York, NY: E. P. Dutton.

Baudrillard, Jean. 1981 (1994). *Simulacra and Simulation*, translated by Sheila Faria Glaser. Ann Arbor, MI: University of Michigan Press.

Beccaria, Cesare. 1764 (1995). *Of Crimes and Punishments*, translated by Richard Bellamy, Richard Davies, and Virginia Cox. New York, NY: Cambridge University Press.

Becker, Gary S. 1968. "Crime and Punishment: An Economic Approach." *Journal of Political Economy* 76(2): 169–217.

Becker, Howard S. 1963 (1973). *Outsiders: Studies in the Sociology of Deviance*, revised edition. New York, NY: Free Press.

Beckett, Katherine. 1997. *Making Crime Pay: Law and Order in Contemporary American Politics*. New York, NY: Oxford University Press.

———— and Steve Herbert. 2008. "Dealing with Disorder: Social Control in the Post-Industrial City." *Theoretical Criminology* 12(1): 5–30.

———— and Theodore Sasson. 2004. *The Politics of Injustice: Crime and Punishment in America*, second edition. Thousand Oaks, CA: Sage Publications.

Beirne, Piers. 1993. *Inventing Criminology: Essays on the Rise of 'Homo Criminalis'*. Albany, NY: SUNY Press.

Bellesiles, Michael. 2000. *Arming America: The Origins of a National Gun Culture*. New York, NY: Knopf.

Bendersky, Joseph W. 1983. *Carl Schmitt: Theorist for the Reich*. Princeton, NJ: Princeton University Press.

Benjamin, Walter. 1921 (1978). "Critique of Violence." In *Walter Benjamin Reflections: Essays, Aphorisms, Autobiographical Writings*, translated by Edmund Jephcott, edited by Peter Demetz, pp. 277–300. New York, NY: Harcourt Brace Jovanovich.

Bennett, William J, John J. DiIulio, and John P. Walters. 1996. *Body Count: Moral Poverty—and How to Win America's War Against Crime and Drugs*. New York, NY: Simon & Schuster.

Bentham, Jeremy. 1789/1823 (1948). *An Introduction to the Principles of Morals and Legislations*, with an introduction by Laurence J. Lafleur. New York, NY: Hafner Publishing, reprint of 1823 edition.

Berger, Peter L. 1967. *The Sacred Canopy: Elements of a Sociological Theory of Religion*. Garden City, NY: Doubleday.

Bernard, Thomas J. 1992. *The Cycle of Juvenile Justice*. New York, NY: Oxford University Press.

Bevan, Edwyn R. 1936. "Rhetoric in the Ancient World." In *Essays in Honour of Gilbert Murray*, pp. 189–214. London: George Allen & Unwin.

Bianchi, Herman. 1994. *Justice as Sanctuary: Toward a New System of Crime Control*. Bloomington, IN: Indiana University Press.

Bittner, Egon. 1967. *The Functions of Police in Modern Society*. Chevy Chase, MD: National Institutes of Health.

Black, Donald. 1976. *The Behavior of Law*. New York, NY: Academic Press.

———. 1998. *The Social Structure of Right and Wrong*, revised edition. New York, NY: Academic Press.

Blackstone, William. 1765–1769. *Commentaries on the Laws of England*. Oxford, UK: Clarendon Press.

Blakely v. Washington. 2004. 542 U.S. 296; 124 S. Ct. 2531; 159 L. Ed. 2d 403.

Blomley, Nicholas. 2003. "Law, Property, and the Geography of Violence: The Frontier, the Survey, and the Grid." *Annals of the Association of American Geographers* 93(1): 121–141.

Bloom, Allan. 1974. "Leo Strauss: September 20, 1899 – October 18, 1973." *Political Theory* 2(4): 372–392.

Bogardus, Emory S. 1926. "Social Distance in the City." *Proceedings and Publications of the American Sociological Society* 20: 40–46.

Bogus, Carl T. (ed.). 2000. *The Second Amendment in Law and History*. New York, NY: The New Press.

Bohannon, Paul. 1968. "Law and Legal Institutions." In *International Encyclopedia of the Social Sciences*, volume 9, edited by David L. Stills, pp. 73–78. New York, NY: Macmillan Co. and The Free Press.

Borges, Jorge Luis. 1952 (1964). "The Analytical Language of John Wilkins." In *Other Inquisitions, 1937–1952*, translated by Ruth L. C. Simms, introduction by James E. Irby, pp. 101–105. Austin, TX: University of Texas Press.

Bourdieu, Pierre. 1985. "The Social Space and the Genesis of Groups." *Theory and Society* 14(6): 723–744.

———. 1997 (2000). *Pascalian Meditations*, translated by Richard Nice. Stanford, CA: Stanford University Press.

Bowman, Thorlief. 1954 (1960). *Hebrew Thought Compared with Greek*, translated by Jules L. Moreau. Philadelphia, PA: Westminster Press.

Boynton v. Virginia. 1960. 364 U.S. 454; 81 S. Ct. 182; 5 L. Ed. 2d 206. Decided December 5, 1960.

Braithwaite, John. 1989. *Crime, Shame and Reintegration*. New York, NY: Cambridge University Press.

———. 2002. *Restorative Justice and Responsive Regulation*. New York, NY: Oxford University Press.

———, Eliza Ahmed, and Valerie Braithwaite. 2006. "Shame, Restorative Justice, and Crime." In *Taking Stock: The Status of Criminological Theory*, edited by Francis T. Cullen, John Paul Wright, and Kristie R. Blevins, pp. 397–417. New Brunswick, NJ: Transaction Publishers.

Breitman, George. 1967. *Last Year of Malcolm X: The Evolution of a Revolutionary*. New York, NY: Pathfinder Press.

Britton, Dana M. 2000. "Feminism in Criminology: Engendering the Outlaw." *Annals of the American Academy of Political and Social Science* 571: 57–76.

Bronowski, Jacob. 1978. *Magic, Science, and Civilization*. New York, NY: Columbia University Press.

Brotherton, David C. 2008. "Beyond Social Reproduction: Bringing Resistance Back in Gang Theory." *Theoretical Criminology* 12(1): 55–77.

Bureau of Justice Statistics. 2007. "Adult Correctional Populations, 1980–2006." Online at http://www.ojp.usdoj.gov/bjs/correct.htm.

Butler, Judith. 1990. *Gender Trouble: Feminism and the Subversion of Identity*. New York, NY: Routledge.

Campbell, Joseph W. 2001. *Yellow Journalism: Puncturing the Myths, Defining the Legacies*. Westport, CT: Praeger.

Carawan, Edwin. 1998. *Rhetoric and the Law of Draco*. New York, NY: Oxford University Press.

Chambliss, William. 1964. "The Law of Vagrancy." *Social Problems* 12: 67–77.

———. 1966. "The Deterrent Influence of Punishment." *Crime and Delinquency* 12(1):70–75.

Christie, Nils. 2000. *Crime Control as Industry*, third edition. New York, NY: Routledge.

————. 2004. *A Suitable Amount of Crime*. New York, NY: Routledge.

Cicourel, Aaron V. 1968. *The Social Organization of Juvenile Justice*. New York, NY: John Wiley & Sons.

Cleaver, Eldridge. 1967. *Soul on Ice*. New York, NY: McGraw-Hill.

————. 1969. *Eldridge Cleaver: Post-Prison Writings and Speeches*, edited by Robert Scheer. New York, NY: Random House/Ramparts Books.

Clemmer, Donald. 1940. *The Prison Community*. New York, NY: Holt, Rinehart & Winston.

Cloward, Richard A. and Lloyd E. Ohlin. 1960. *Delinquency and Opportunity*. Glencoe, IL: Free Press.

Cockburn, Alexander and Jeffrey St. Clair. 1998. *Whiteout: The CIA, Drugs, and the Press*. New York, NY: Verso.

Cohen, Albert K. 1955. *Delinquent Boys: The Culture of the Gang*. Bloomington, IN: Indiana University Press.

Cohen, Lawrence E. and Marcus Felson. 1979. "Social Change and Crime Rate Trends: A Routine Activities Approach." *American Sociological Review* 44 (August): 588–607.

———— and Frederick C. Land. 1980. "Property Crime Rates in the United States: A Macrodynamic Analysis, 1947–1977." *American Journal of Sociology* 86(1): 90–118.

Cohen, Stanley. 1972 (1980). *Folk Devils and Moral Panics: The Creation of the Mods and Rockers*. New York, NY: St. Martin's Press.

————. 1987/1988. *Against Criminology*. New Brunswick, NJ: Transaction Books.

————. 2002. *Folk Devils and Moral Panics: The Creation of the Mods and Rockers*, third edition. New York, NY: Routledge.

Collins, Jim. 1992. "Television and Postmodernism." In *Channels of Discourse Reassembled: Television and Contemporary Criticism*, edited by Robert C. Allen, second edition, pp. 327–353. Chapel Hill, NC: University of North Carolina Press.

Coontz, Stephanie. 1992. *The Way We Never Were: American Families and the Nostalgia Trap*. New York, NY: Basic Books.

Cornish, Derek B. and Ronald V. Clarke (eds.). 1986. *The Reasoning Criminal: Rational Choice Perspectives on Offending*. New York, NY: Springer-Verlag.

Cover, Robert. 1983. "Nomos and Narrative." *Harvard Law Review* 97: 4–68.

Crank, John P. 2003. *Imagining Justice*. Cincinnati, OH: Anderson Publishing.

Critchley, T. A. 1967. *A History of Police in England and Wales, 900 to 1966*. London, UK: Constable and Co.

Cummins, Eric. 1994. *The Rise and Fall of California's Radical Prison Movement.* Stanford, CA: Stanford University Press.

Currie, Elliott. 2007. "Against Marginality: Arguments for a Public Criminology." *Theoretical Criminology* 11(2): 175–190.

Davis, Kingsley. 1935. *Youth in the Depression.* Chicago, IL: University of Chicago Press.

Davis, Maxine. 1936. *The Lost Generation: A Portrait of American Youth Today.* New York, NY: Macmillan.

De Ste. Croix, Geoffrey E. M. 1972. *Origins of the Peloponnesian War.* London, UK: Duckworth.

———. 2004. *Athenian Democratic Origins and Other Essays,* edited by David Harvey and Robert Parker with Peter Thonemann. New York, NY: Oxford University Press.

Debord. Guy. 1967 (1992/1995). *The Society of the Spectacle,* third edition, translated by Donald Nicholson-Smith. New York, NY: Zone Books.

Deck v. Missouri. 2005. 544 U.S. 622; 125 S. Ct. 2007; 161 L. Ed. 2d 953. Decided May 23, 2005.

Derrida, Jacques. 1967a (1976). *Of Grammatology,* translated by Gayatri Chakravorty Spivak. Baltimore, MD: Johns Hopkins University Press.

———. 1967b (1973). *Speech and Phenomena and Other Essays on Husserl's Theory of Signs,* translated with an introduction by David B. Allison. Evanston, IL: Northwestern University Press.

———. 1967c (1978). *Writing and Difference,* translated with an introduction by Alan Bass. Chicago, IL: University of Chicago Press.

———. 1992. "Force of Law: The Mystical Foundation of Legal Authority." In *Deconstruction and the Possibility of Justice,* edited by Drucilla Cornell, Michel Rosenfeld, and David Gray Carlson, pp. 3–67. New York, NY: Routledge.

Diamond, Arthur S. 1971. *Primitive Law Past and Present.* London, UK: Methuen.

Diamond, Stanley. 1971. "The Rule of Law Versus the Order of Custom." In *The Sociology of Law: A Conflict Perspective,* edited by Charles E. Reasons and Robert M. Rich, pp. 239–262. Toronto, Canada: Butterworth & Co. reprinted from *Social Research* 38 (Spring 1971): 42–72.

Dobzhansky, Theodore. 1951. *Genetics and the Origin of Species,* third edition. New York, NY: Columbia University Press.

Dohrn, Bernardine. 2005. "Preface." In *Letters from Young Activists,* edited by Dan Berger, Chesa Boudin, and Kenyon Farrow, pp. xiii–xxiii. New York, NY: Nation Books.

Dolowitz, David P., Rob Hulme, Mike Nellis, and Fiona O'Neill (eds.). 2000. *Policy Transfer and British Social Policy: Learning From the USA?* Philadelphia, PA: Open University Press.

Domhoff, G. William. 1967. *Who Rules America?* Englewood Cliffs, NJ: Prentice-Hall.

————. 1979. *The Powers That Be: Processes of Ruling-Class Domination in America.* New York, NY: Vintage Books.

————. 1983. *Who Rules America Now? A View for the '80s.* New York, NY: Simon & Schuster.

Douglas, Mary. 1966 (2002). *Purity and Danger: An Analysis of Concepts of Pollution and Taboo,* with a new preface by the author. New York, NY: Routledge.

————. 1985. *Risk Acceptability According to the Social Sciences.* New York, NY: Russell Sage.

————. 1992. *Risk and Blame: Essays in Cultural Theory.* New York, NY: Routledge.

Dray, W. H. 1970. *Laws and Explanation in History.* Oxford, UK: Clarendon Press.

Drury, Shadia B. 1988. *The Political Ideas of Leo Strauss.* New York, NY: St. Martin's Press.

————. 1997. *Leo Strauss and the American Right.* New York, NY: St. Martin's Press.

Dugdale, Richard L. 1877. *"The Jukes": A Study in Crime, Pauperism, Disease and Heredity.* New York, NY: G. P. Putnam's Sons.

Duménil, Gérard and Dominique Lévy. 2002. "The Profit Rate: Where and How Much Did It Fall? Did It Recover? (USA 1948–2000)." *Review of Radical Political Economics* 34: 437–461.

Durkheim, Emile. 1893 (1964). *The Division of Labor in Society,* translated by George Simpson. New York, NY: Free Press.

————. 1895 (1982). *Rules of the Sociological Method,* edited with an introduction by Steven Lukes, translated by W. D. Hall. New York, NY: Free Press.

————. 1896 (1951). *Suicide,* translated by John A. Spaulding and George Simpson, edited by George Simpson. New York, NY: Free Press.

————. 1901 (1983). "Two Laws of Penal Evolution." In *Durkheim and the Law,* edited by Steven Lukes and Andrew Scull, translated by T. Anthony Jones and Andrew Scull, pp. 102–132. New York, NY: St. Martin's Press.

Dworkin, Ronald M. 1986. *Law's Empire.* Cambridge, MA: Belknap Press.

Dylan, Bob. 1965. "Like a Rolling Stone." New York, NY: Columbia Records.

Eco, Umberto. 1986. *Semiotics and the Philosophy of Language.* Bloomington, IN: Indiana University Press.

Edelman, Murray. 1985. *The Symbolic Uses of Politics.* Chicago, IL: University of Chicago Press.

Eisenhower, Dwight D. 1961. "Farewell Address to the Nation." Online at http://www.yale.edu/lawweb/avalon/presiden/speeches/eisenhower001. htm.http://mcadams.posc.mu.edu/ike.htm.

Engels, Friedrich. 1891 (1942). *The Origin of the Family, Private Property and the State.* New York, NY: International Publishers.

Estabrook, Arthur H. 1916. *The Jukes in 1915.* Washington, DC: Carneigie Institution of Washington.

Euripides. 405 BCE (1978). *Iphigenia at Aulis,* translated by W. S. Merwin and George E. Dimrock, Jr. New York, NY: Oxford University Press.

Evans-Pritchard, E. E. 1937. *Witchcraft, Oracles, and Magic Among the Azande.* Oxford, UK: Oxford University Press.

Faur, Jose. 1986. *Golden Doves With Silver Dots.* Bloomington, IN: University of Indiana Press.

Feeley, Malcolm M. 2003. "Crime, Social Order and the Rise of Neo-Conservative Politics." *Theoretical Criminology* 7(1): 111–130.

———— and Jonathan Simon. 1992. "The New Penology: Notes on the Emerging Strategy of Corrections and Its Implications." *Criminology* 30(4): 449–474.

Ferri, Enrico. 1896. *Criminal Sociology.* New York, NY: D. Appleton and Co.

Feyerabend, Paul. 1975. *Against Method.* London, UK: New Left Books.

Fisher, Dorothy Canfield. 1943. *Our Young Folks.* New York, NY: Harcourt, Brace and Co.

Flyvbjerg, Bent. 2000. "Ideal Theory, Real Rationality: Habermas Versus Foucault and Nietzsche." Paper presented at the Fiftieth Annual Conference, Political Studies Association. London: London School of Economics. Online at http://flyvbjerg.plan.aau.dk/IdealTheory.pdf.

Fones-Wolf, Elizabeth A. 1994. *Selling Free Enterprise: The Business Assault on Labor and Liberalism, 1945–1960.* Urbana, IL: University of Illinois Press.

Ford, Richard T. 1999. "Law's Territory (A History of Jurisdiction)." *Michigan Law Review* 97: 843–930.

Foucault, Michel. 1965. *Madness and Civilization: A History of Insanity in the Age of Reason,* translated by Richard Howard. New York, NY: Random House.

————. 1966 (1973). *The Order of Things.* New York, NY: Vintage Books.

————. 1975 (1979). *Discipline and Punish,* translated by Alan Sheridan. New York, NY: Vintage Books.

Fox, Richard L. and Robert W. Van Sickel. 2001. *Tabloid Justice: Criminal Justice in an Age of Media Frenzy.* Boulder, CO: Lynne Rienner.

France, Anatole. 1930. *The Red Lilly.* New York, NY: Grosset & Dunlap.

Freeland, Richard M. 1974. *The Truman Doctrine and the Origins of McCarthyism: Foreign Policy, Domestic Politics, and Internal Security, 1946–1948.* New York, NY: Schocken Books.

Freeman, Kathleen. 1963. *The Murder of Herodes and Other Trials from the Athenian Law Courts.* New York, NY: W. W. Norton.

Frege, Gottlob. 1892 (1960). "On Sense and Reference." In *Translations from the Writings of Gottlob Frege,* edited and translated by Peter Geach and Max Black. Oxford, UK: Basil Blackwell.

Freud, Sigmund. 1895 (1974). "A Reply to Criticisms of My Paper on Anxiety Neurosis." In *The Standard Edition of the Complete Psychological Works of Sigmund Freud,* volume 3, translated and edited by James Strachey, pp. 121–140. London, UK: Hogarth Press.

———. 1900 (1955). *The Interpretation of Dreams,* translated by James Strachey. New York, NY: Basic Books.

———. 1939. *Moses and Monotheism,* translated by Katherine Jones. New York, NY: Vintage Books.

Friedman, Lawrence M. 1977. "The Devil Is Not Dead: Exploring the History of Criminal Justice." *Georgia Law Review* 11(2): 257–274.

Friedrichs, David O. 1979. "The Law and the Legitimacy Crisis." In *Critical Issues in Criminal Justice,* edited by R. G. Iacovetta and Dae H. Chang, pp. 290–311. Durham, NC: Carolina Academic Press.

Fromm, Erich. 1930 (2000). "The State as Educator: On the Psychology of Criminal Justice." In *Erich Fromm and Critical Criminology: Beyond the Punitive Society,* edited by Kevin Anderson and Richard Quinney, translated by Heinz D. Osterle and Kevin Anderson, pp. 123–128. Urbana, IL: University of Illinois Press.

———. 1931 (2000). "On the Psychology of the Criminal and the Punitive Society." In *Erich Fromm and Critical Criminology: Beyond the Punitive Society,* edited by Kevin Anderson and Richard Quinney, translated by Heinz D. Osterle and Kevin Anderson, pp. 129–156. Urbana, IL: University of Illinois Press.

Fuller, John Randolph and John F. Wozniak. 2006. "Peacemaking Criminology: Past, Present, and Future." In *Taking Stock: The Status of Criminological Theory,* edited by Francis T. Cullen, John Paul Wright, and Kristie R. Blevins, pp. 251–276. New Brunswick, NJ: Transaction Publishers.

Fussell, Paul. 1983. *Class: A Guide Through the American Status System.* New York, NY: Simon & Schuster.

Gabler, Neil. 1998. *Life: The Movie.* New York, NY: Knopf.

Garland, David. 2001. *The Culture of Control: Crime and Social Order in Contemporary Society.* Chicago, IL: University of Chicago Press.

————. 2006. "Concepts of Culture in the Sociology of Punishment." *Theoretical Criminology* 10(4): 419–447.

Geeraerts, Dirk. 2002. "The Interaction of Metaphor and Metonymy in Composite Expressions." In *Metaphor and Metonymy in Comparison and Contrast*, edited by Renée Diren and Ralf Pörings, pp. 435–465. Berlin, Germany: Mouton de Gruyter.

Geertz, Clifford. 1965. The Impact of the Concept of Culture on the Concept of Man. In *New Views of the Nature of Man*, edited by J. R. Platt, pp. 93–118. Chicago, IL: University of Chicago Press.

Gellrich, Jesse M. 1985. *The Idea of the Book in the Middle Ages: Language Theory, Mythology, and Fiction.* Ithaca, NY: Cornell University Press.

Gennep, Arnold van. 1909 (1960). *The Rites of Passage*, translated by Monica B. Vizedom and Gabrielle L. Caffee. Chicago, IL: University of Chicago Press.

Gibbs, Jack P. 1975. *Crime, Punishment, and Deterrence.* New York, NY: Elsevier.

Gibson, H. B. 1970. "Review of *Causes of Delinquency*." *Sociological Review* 18(3): 452–454.

Gilbert, James. 1986. *A Cycle of Outrage: America's Reaction to the Juvenile Delinquent in the 1950s.* New York, NY: Oxford University Press.

Girard, René. 1972 (1977). *Violence and the Sacred*, translated by Patrick Gregory. Baltimore, MD: Johns Hopkins University Press.

Glueck, Sheldon and Eleanor Glueck. 1930. *500 Criminal Careers.* New York, NY: A. A. Knopf.

————. 1943 (1966). *Criminal Careers in Retrospect.* New York, NY: Krause Reprint Corp.

————. 1950. *Unraveling Juvenile Delinquency.* New York, NY: Commonwealth Fund.

————. 1956. *Physique and Delinquency.* New York, NY: Harper & Row.

————. 1968. *Delinquents and Nondelinquents in Perspective.* Cambridge, MA: Harvard University Press.

Glynn, Kevin. 2000. *Tabloid Culture: Trash Taste, Popular Power, and the Transformation of American Television.* Durham, NC: Duke University Press.

Goddard, Henry H. 1912 (1919). *The Kallikak Family: A Study in the Heredity of Feeblemindedness.* New York, NY: Macmillan, reprint.

Goebel, Julius. 1937 (1976). *Felony and Misdemeanor: A Study in the History of Criminal Law*, with an introduction by Edward Peters. Philadelphia, PA: University of Pennsylvania Press.

Gordon, Diana R. 1990. *The Justice Juggernaut: Fighting Street Crime, Controlling Citizens.* New Brunswick, NJ: Rutgers University Press.

Goring, Charles B. 1913 (1972). *The English Convict: A Statistical Study.* Montclair, NJ: Patterson Smith, reprint.

Gould, Leroy C. 1969. "The Changing Structure of Property Crime in an Affluent Society. *Social Forces* 48(1): 50–59.

———. 1971. "Crime and Its Impact in an Affluent Society." In *Crime and Justice in American Society*, edited by Jack Douglas, pp. 81–118. Indianapolis, IN: Bobbs Merrill.

Gouldner, Alvin W. 1954. *Wildcat Strike.* Yellow Springs, OH: Antioch Press.

———. 1965. *Enter Plato: Classical Greece and the Origins of Social Theory.* New York, NY: Basic Books.

———. 1976. *The Dialectic of Ideology and Technology.* New York, NY: Seabury Press.

Gottfredson, Michael R. and Travis Hirschi. 1990. *A General Theory of Crime.* Stanford, CA: Stanford University Press.

Gottwald, Norman. 1985. *The Hebrew Bible—A Socio-Literary History.* Philadelphia, PA: Fortress Press.

Grasmick, Harold, Elizabeth Davenport, Mitchell Chamlin, and Robert Bursik, Jr. 1992. "Protestant Fundamentalism and the Retributive Doctrine of Punishment." *Criminology* 30(1): 21–25.

Gray, Herman. 1995. *Watching Race: Television and the Struggle for "Blackness."* Minneapolis, MN: University of Minnesota Press.

Green, Kenneth Hart. 1997. *Jewish Philosophy and the Crisis of Modernity: Essays and Lectures in Modern Jewish Thought by Leo Strauss.* Albany, NY: SUNY Press.

Gramsci, Antonio. 1971. *Selections From the Prison Notebooks of Antonio Gramsci*, edited and translated by Quentin Hoare and Geoffrey Nowell Smith. New York, NY: International Publishers.

Grice, H. Paul. 1975. "Logic and Conversation." In *Syntax and Semantics: Speech Acts*, volume 3, edited by Peter Cole and Jerry L. Morgan, pp. 41–58. New York, NY: Academic Press.

Guerry, André-Michel. 1833 (2002). *Essay on the Moral Statistics of France*, edited and translated by Hugh P. Whitt and Victor W. Reiking. Lewiston, NY: Edwin Mellon Press.

Gusfield, Joseph R. 1981. *The Culture of Public Problems: Drinking-Driving and the Symbolic Order.* Chicago, IL: University of Chicago Press.

Haack, Susan. 2006. *Defending Science—Within Reason: Between Scientism and Cynicism.* Amherst, NY: Prometheus Books.

Habermas, Jürgen. 1985 (1987). *The Philosophical Discourse of Modernity: Twelve Lectures.* Cambridge, MA: MIT Press.

———. 1992 (1996). *Between Facts and Norms: Contributions to a Discourse Theory of Law and Democracy*, translated by William Rehg. Cambridge, MA: MIT Press.

Haffner, Sebastian. 2000 (2002). *Defying Hitler; A Memoir*, translated by Oliver Pretzel. London, UK: Weidenfeld & Nicolson.

Hägerström, Axel. 1927–1941. *Der römische Obligationsbegriff im Lichte der allgemeinen römischen Rechtsanschauung*. Uppsala, Sweden: Alqvist & Wiksell.

———. 1964. *Philosophy and Religion*, translated by Robert T. Sandin. London, UK: George Allen & Unwin.

Hajdu, David. 2008. *The Ten-Cent Plague: The Great Comic-Book Scare and How It Changed America*. New York, NY: Farrar, Strauss, and Giroux.

Hall, Jerome. 1935. *Theft, Law, and Society*, second edition. Indianapolis, IN: Bobbs Merrill.

——— and Tony Jefferson (eds). 2006. "Once More Around Resistance Through Rituals." In *Resistance Through Rituals: Youth Sub-Cultures in Post-War Britain*, pp. vii–xxxii. New York, NY: Routledge.

Hall, Stuart, Chas Critcher, Tony Jefferson, John Clarke, and Brian Roberts. 1978. *Policing the Crisis: Mugging, the State, and Law and Order*. New York, NY: Holmes & Meier Publishers.

Hallsworth, Simon. 2002. "The Case for a Postmodern Penology." *Theoretical Criminology* 6(2): 145–163.

Hamdan v. Rumsfeld. 2006. 548 U.S. 557; 126 S. Ct. 2749; 165 L. Ed. 2d 723. Decided June 9, 2006.

Hamm, Theodore. 2001. *Rebel and a Cause: Caryl Chessman and the Politics of the Death Penalty in Postwar California, 1948–1974*. Berkeley, CA: University of California Press.

Handelman, Susan. 1982. *Slayers of Moses: The Emergence of Rabbinic Interpretation in Modern Literary Theory*. Albany, NY: SUNY Press.

Hardt, Michael and Antonio Negri. 2004. *Multitude: War and Democracy in the Age of Empire*. New York, NY: Penguin Press.

Harper's Index. 2007. April, p. 17.

Harrington, Michael. 1973. *Fragments of the Century*. New York, NY: Saturday Review Press.

Harvey, David. 2005. *A Brief History of Neoliberalism*. New York, NY: Oxford University Press.

Havelock, Eric. 1983. "The Linguistic Task of the Presocratics." In *Language and Thought in Early Greek Philosophy*, edited by Kevin Robb, pp. 7–82. La Salle, IL: Hegler Institute.

Hay, Douglas. 1975. *Albion's Fatal Tree: Crime and Society in Eighteenth-Century England*. New York, NY: Pantheon Books.

Hempel, Carl G. 1965. "Aspects of Scientific Explanation." In *Aspects of Scientific Explanation and Other Essays in the Philosophy of Science*, pp. 331–496. New York, NY: Free Press.

Herbert, Steven K. 1997. *Policing Space: Territoriality and the Los Angeles Police Department*. Minneapolis, MN: University of Minnesota Press.

————. 2001. "Policing the Contemporary City: Fixing Broken Windows or Shoring Up Neo-Liberalism?" *Theoretical Criminology* 5(4): 445–466.

Hesiod. ca. 700 BCE (1973). *Theogony*, translated by Dorothea Wender. New York, NY: Penguin Books.

————. ca. 700 BCE (1996). *Works and Days*, translated with commentary for the social sciences by David W. Tandy and Walter C. Neale. Berkeley, CA: University of California Press.

Hesse, Mary. 1980. *Revolution and Reconstructions in the Philosophy of Science*. Bloomington, IN: Indiana University Press.

Hilliard, David (ed.). 2007. *The Black Panther Inter-Communal News Service, 1967–1980*. New York, NY: Simon and Schuster.

Hinds, Lyn. 2006. "Challenging Current Conceptions of Law and Order." *Theoretical Criminology* 10(2): 203–221.

Hirschi, Travis. 1969. *Causes of Delinquency*. Berkeley, CA: University of California Press.

————. 2002. *Causes of Delinquency*. New Brunswick, NJ: Transaction Publishers.

Hobbes, Thomas. 1651. *Leviathan, or, The Matter, Forme, and Power of a Common Wealth, Ecclesiasticall and Civil*. London, UK: Printed for Andrew Cook.

Hoffner, Harry Angier Jr. 1997. *The Laws of the Hittites: A Critical Edition*. New York, NY: Brill.

Hollway, Wendy and Tony Jefferson. 1997. "The Risk Society in an Age of Anxiety: Situating Fear of Crime." *British Journal of Sociology* 48(2): 255–266.

Holmes, Oliver Wendell Jr. 1881 (1991). *The Common Law*, with an introduction by Sheldon M. Novick. Mineola, NY: Dover Publications. Reprint.

Horkheimer, Max and Theodore W. Adorno. 1944 (1972). *Dialectic of Enlightenment*, translated by John Cumming. New York, NY: Herder and Herder.

Huffstutter, P. J. 2008. "Terrorism Charges Filed in Alleged Plot to Disrupt GOP Convention." *Los Angeles Times*, September 4, 2008. Online at http://www.latimes.com/news/nationworld/nation/la-na-terror4-2008 sep04,0,7911659.story.

Hume, David. 1748 (1955). *An Inquiry Concerning Human Understanding*. Indianapolis, IN: Bobbs Merrill.

Hung, Edwin Hin-Chung. 2006. *Beyond Kuhn: Scientific Explanation, Theory Structure, Incommensurability and Physical Necessity*. Burlington, VT: Ashgate Publishing.

Irwin, John. 1970 (1987). *The Felon*, second edition with a new introduction. Berkeley, CA: University of California Press.

Jackson, George. 1970. *Soledad Brother: The Prison Letters of George Jackson*. New York, NY: Coward McCann.

———. 1972. *Blood in My Eye*. New York, NY: Random House.

Jacoby, Russell. 1975. *Social Amnesia*. Boston, MA: Beacon Press.

Jameson, Frederick. 1983. "Postmodernism and Consumer Society." In *The Anti-Aesthetic: Essays on Post-modern Culture*, edited by Hal Foster, pp. 111–125. Port Townsend WA: Bay Press.

Kafka, Franz. 1919 (1961). "In the Penal Colony." In *The Penal Colony: Stories and Short Pieces*, translated by Willa and Edwin Muir, pp. 191–227. New York, NY: Schocken Books.

Kall, Rob. 2008. "Police State in Republican Convention City." Online at http://www.opednews.com/articles/Police-State-In-Republican-by-Rob-Kall-080831-839.html.

Kennedy, Ellen. 1985. "Introduction: Carl Schmitt's *Parliamentarismus* in Its Historical Context." In Carl Schmitt, *The Crisis of Parliamentary Democracy*, edited and translated with an Introduction by Ellen Kennedy, pp. xiii-l. Cambridge, MA: MIT Press.

Kierkegaard, Søren. 1843 (1968). *Fear and Trembling*, translated by Walter Lowrie. Princeton, NJ: Princeton University Press.

———. 1849 (1968). *Sickness Unto Death*, translated by Walter Lowrie. Princeton, NJ: Princeton University Press.

Killias, Martin 2006. "The Opening and Closing of Breaches: A Theory on Crime Waves, Law Creation and Crime Prevention." *European Journal of Criminology* 3(1): 11–31.

Kirchheimer, Otto. 1940 (1996). "Criminal Law in National Socialist Germany." In *The Rule of Law Under Siege: Selected Essays of Franz L. Neumann and Otto Kirchheimer*, edited by William E. Scheuerman, pp. 172–191. Berkeley, CA: University of California Press.

Kirk, Geoffrey Stephen and J. E. Raven. 1957. *The Presocratic Philosophers: A Critical History with a Selection of Texts*. Cambridge, UK: Cambridge University Press.

Kofsky, Frank. 1995. *Harry S. Truman and the War Scare of 1948*. New York, NY: Schocken Books.

Kohut, Heinz. 1971. *The Analysis of the Self: A Systematic Approach to the Psychoanalytic Treatment of Narcissistic Personality Disorders*. New York, NY: International Universities Press.

———. 1977. *The Restoration of the Self*. New York, NY: International Universities Press.

Korzybski, Alfred. 1958. *Science and Sanity: An Introduction to non-Aristotelian Systems and General Semantics*, fourth edition. Lakeville, CT: International Non-Aristotelian Publishing.

Kovel, Joel. 1981. *The Age of Desire: Reflections of a Radical Psychoanalyst.* New York, NY: Pantheon.

Kraska, Peter B. 1999. "Militarizing Criminal Justice: Exploring the Possibilities." *Journal of Political and Military Sociology* 27 (winter): 205–215.

———. 2004. *Theorizing Criminal Justice: Eight Essential Orientations.* Long Grove, IL: Waveland Press.

———. 2006. "Criminal Justice Theory: Toward Legitimacy and an Infrastructure." *Justice Quarterly* 23(2): 167–185.

Kraska, Peter B. and Louis J. Cubellis. 1997. "Militarizing Mayberry and Beyond: Making Sense of American Paramilitary Policing." *Justice Quarterly* 14(4): 607–629.

Kristol, Irving. 1995. *Neoconservatism: Autobiography of an Idea.* New York, NY: Free Press.

Kuhn, Thomas S. 1970. *The Structure of Scientific Revolutions,* second edition. Chicago, IL: University of Chicago Press.

LaBarre, Weston. 1978. "The Clinic and the Field." In *The Making of Psychological Anthropology,* edited by George D. Spindler, pp. 258–299. Berkeley, CA: University of California Press.

Lane, Anthony. 2008. "Letter from Beijing: Fun and Games: Week Two at the Olympics." *The New Yorker,* September 1: 68–72.

Langworthy, Robert. 1985. "Wilson's Theory of Police Behavior: A Replication of the Constraint Theory. *Justice Quarterly* 2(1): 89–98.

Lapham, Lewis. 2008. "Notebook: Company Policy." *Harper's Magazine* 317(1898, July): 8–10.

Laski, Harold. 1921 (1968). "The Foundations of Sovereignty." In *The Foundations of Sovereignty and Other Essays.* Freeport, NY: Books for Libraries Press.

Laub, John H. 2006. "Edwin H. Sutherland and the Michael-Adler Report: Searching for the Soul of Criminology Seventy Years Later." *Criminology* 44(2): 235–256.

——— and Robert J. Sampson. 2003. *Shared Beginnings, Divergent Lives: Delinquent Boys to Age 70.* Cambridge, MA: Harvard University Press.

———, Robert J. Sampson, and Gary A. Sweeten. 2006. "Assessing Sampson and Laub's Life-Course Theory of Crime." In *Taking Stock: The Status of Criminological Theory,* edited by Francis T. Cullen, John Paul Wright, and Kristie R. Blevins, pp. 313–333. New Brunswick, NJ: Transaction Publishers.

Leach, Edmund R. 1977. *Custom, Law, and Terrorist Violence.* Edinburgh, UK: Edinburgh University Press.

Lee, Murray. 2007. *Inventing Fear of Crime.* Portland, OR: Willan Publishing.

Lefebvre, Henri. 1974 (1991). *The Production of Space*, translated by Donald Nicholson-Smith. Cambridge MA: Blackwell Publishers.

Lemert, Edwin M. 1951. *Social Pathology: A Systematic Approach to the Theory of Sociopathic Behavior*. New York, NY: McGraw-Hill.

———. 1967. *Human Deviance, Social Problems, and Social Control*. Engelwood Cliffs, NJ: Prentice-Hall.

——— and Judy Rosberg. 1948. *The Administration of Justice to Minority Groups in Los Angeles County*. Berkeley, CA: University of California Press.

Lewis, Sinclair. 1920. *Main Street: The Story of Carol Kennicott*. New York, NY: Harcourt, Brace and Howe.

———. 1922. *Babbitt*. New York, NY: Harcourt, Brace.

Lienhardt, Godfrey. 1961 (1987). *Divinity and Experience: The Religion of the Dinka*. New York, NY: Oxford University Press, reprint.

Lincoln, Bruce. 1989. *Discourse and the Construction of Society: Comparative Studies of Myth, Ritual, and Classification*. New York, NY: Oxford University Press.

Lindner, Robert Mitchell. 1944. *Rebel Without a Cause: The Hypnoanalysis of a Criminal Psychopath*. New York, NY: Grune and Stratton.

Lindesmith, Alfred and Yale Levin. 1937. "The Lombrisian Myth in Criminology." *American Journal of Sociology* 42(5): 653–671.

Llewellyn, Karl N. and E. Adamson Hoebel. 1941. *The Cheyenne Way: Conflict and Case Law in Primitive Jurisprudence*. Norman, OK: University of Oklahoma Press.

Lombroso-Ferrero, Gina. 1911 (1972). *Criminal Man, According to the Classification of Cesare Lombroso*, with an introduction by Cesare Lombroso, reprinted with a new introduction by Leonard D. Savitz. Montclair, NJ: Patterson Smith.

Loraux, Nicole. 1979. "L'Autochthonie: Une Topique Athenienne." *Annales* 34(1): 3–26.

———. 1993. *The Children of Athens: Athenian Ideas About Citizenship and the Division Between the Sexes*, translated by Caroline Levine. Princeton: Princeton University Press.

Loveman, Brian and Thomas M. Davies Jr. 1997. "Introduction." In *Che Guevara: Guerilla Warfare*, third edition, pp. 1–37. Wilmington, DE: Scholarly Resources.

Lowie, Robert H. 1927. *The Origin of the State*. New York, NY: Harcourt Brace and Co.

Lundstedt, Anders Vilhelm. 1956. *Legal Thinking Revised; My Views on Law*. Stockholm, Sweden: Almqvist & Wiksell.

Lyotard, Jean-François. 1979 (1984). *The Postmodern Condition: A Report on Knowledge*. Minneapolis, MN: University of Minnesota Press.

MacCormack, Geoffrey. 1990. *Traditional Chinese Penal Law*. Edinburgh, UK: Edinburgh University Press.

MacDowell, Douglas M. 1963. *Athenian Homicide Law in the Age of the Orators*. Manchester, UK: Manchester University Press.

MacLeod, William C. 1927. "Police and Punishment Among Native Americans of the Plains." *Journal of the American Institute of Criminal Law and Criminology* 28: 181–201.

Mahajan, Gupreet. 1997. *Explanation and Understanding in the Human Sciences*. Delhi: Oxford University Press.

Maine, Henry Sumner. 1861 (1986). *Ancient Law*. New York, NY: Dorset Press. Reprint.

Malinowski, Bronislaw. 1926 (1966). *Crime and Custom in Savage Society*. Totowa, NJ: Littlefield, Adams & Co. Reprint.

———. 1948 (1954). *Magic, Science, and Religion, and Other Essays*. Garden City, NY: Doubleday.

———. 1965. *Coral Gardens and Their Magic*. Bloomington, IN: Indiana University Press.

Marchand, Roland. 1985. *Advertising the American Dream: Making Way for Modernity, 1920–1940*. Berkeley, CA: University of California Press.

Marcuse, Herbert. 1964. *One-Dimensional Man*. Boston, MA: Beacon Press.

———. 1965. "Repressive Tolerance." In *A Critique of Pure Tolerance*, pp. 81–117. Boston, MA: Beacon Press.

———. 1966. *Eros and Civilization: A Philosophical Inquiry into Freud*. Boston, MA: Beacon Press.

———. 1969. *An Essay on Liberation*. Boston, MA: Beacon Press.

———. 1972. *Counter-Revolution and Revolt*. Boston, MA: Beacon Press.

Martinson, Robert. 1974. "What Works?—Questions and Answers about Prison Reform." *Public Interest* 35(1): 22–54.

Marx, Karl. 1844 (1983). "Contribution to the Critique of Hegel's *Philosophy of Right*: -Introduction." In *The Portable Karl Marx*, edited by Eugene Kamenka, pp. 115–124. New York, NY: Viking Press and Penguin Books.

———. 1845 (1983). "Theses on Feuerbach." In *The Portable Karl Marx*, edited by Eugene Kamenka, pp. 155–158. New York, NY: Viking Press and Penguin Books.

———. 1852/1869 (1963). *The Eighteenth Brumaire of Louis Bonaparte*. New York, NY: International Publishers.

———. 1867 (1967). *Capital, Volume 1: The Process of Capitalist Production*, edited by Frederick Engels, translated from the third German edition by Samuel Moore and Edward Aveling. New York, NY: International Publishers.

———— and Friedrich Engels. 1848 (1888/1967). *The Manifesto of the Communist Party*, translated by Samuel Moore. In *The Portable Karl Marx*, edited by Eugene Kamenka, pp. 203–241. New York, NY: Viking Press and Penguin Books

———— 1864 (1976). "The German Ideology". In *Collected Works*, volume 5. New York, NY: International Publishers.

Mathiesen, Thomas. 1990. *Prison on Trial: A Critical Assessment*. London, UK: Sage Publications.

Matza, David. 1964. *Delinquency and Drift*. New York, NY: John Wiley & Sons.

Mauer, Marc. 2006. *Race to Incarcerate*. Revised edition. New York, NY: The New Press.

McCormick, John P. 2004. "Identifying or Exploiting the Paradoxes of Constitutional Democracy?" In Carl Schmitt, *Legality and Legitimacy*, translated and edited by Jeffrey Seitzer, pp. xii–xliii. Durham, NC: Duke University Press.

————. 2007. *Weber, Habermas, and the Transformation of the European State*. New York, NY: Cambridge University Press.

Mead, George Herbert. 1918. "The Psychology of Punitive Justice." *American Journal of Sociology* 23(5): 577–602.

————. 1934. *Mind, Self, and Society*, edited with an introduction by Charles W. Morris. Chicago, IL: University of Chicago Press.

————. 1936. *Movements of Thought in the Nineteenth Century*. Chicago, IL: University of Chicago Press.

Meier, Heinrich (ed.). 1988 (1995). *Carl Schmitt and Leo Strauss: The Hidden Dialogue*, translated by J. Harvey Lomax. Chicago, IL: University of Chicago Press.

Melossi, Dario. 1993. "Gazette of Morality and Social Whip: Punishment, Hegemony and the Case of the USA, 1970–1992." *Social and Legal Studies* 2: 259–279.

————. 2000. "Changing Representations of the Criminal." *British Journal of Criminology* 40: 296–320.

————. 2003. "A New Edition of Punishment and Social Structure Thirty-five Years Later: A Timely Event." (Book Review.) *Social Justice* 30: 248–264.

————. 2004. "Neoliberalism's 'Elective Affinities': Penality, Political Economy and International Relations," pp. 1–21. San Francisco, CA: Conference Papers, American Sociological Association Annual Meeting. Online at http://www.asanet.org.

Merton, Robert K. 1938. "Social Structure and Anomie." *American Sociological Review* 3(5): 672–682.

————. 1968. *Social Theory and Social Structure*, enlarged edition. Glencoe, IL: Free Press.

————. 1995. "The Thomas Theorem and the Mathew Effect." *Social Forces* 74(2): 379–422.

Mielants, Eric H. 2007. *The Origins of Capitalism and the "Rise of the West."* Philadelphia, PA: Temple University Press.

Miller, Arthur I. 2001. *Einstein, Picasso, and the Beauty That Causes Havoc.* New York, NY: Basic Books.

Miller, Walter B. 1958. "Lower Class Culture as a Generating Milieu of Gang Delinquency." *Journal of Social Issues* 14(3): 5–19.

Military Commissions Act. 2006. P.L. 109–366.

Mills, C. Wright. 1956. *The Power Elite.* New York, NY: Oxford University Press.

————. 1959. *The Sociological Imagination.* New York, NY: Oxford University Press.

Moffitt, Terrie E. 2006. "A Review of Research on the Taxonomy of Life-Course Persistent Versus Adolescent-Limited Delinquent Behavior." In *Taking Stocj: The Status of Criminological Theory*, edited by Francis T. Cullen, John Paul Wright, and Kristie R. Blevins, pp. 277–311. New Brunswick, NJ: Transaction Publishers.

Morn, Frank. 1995. *Academic Politics and the History of Criminal Justice Education.* Westport, CT: Greenwood Press.

Mosher, Clayton J, Terance D. Miethe, and Dretha M. Phillips. 2002. *The Mismeasure of Crime.* Thousand Oaks, CA: Sage Publications.

Mounce, H. O. 1973. "Understanding a Primitive Society." *Philosophy* 48(186): 347–362.

Mousourakis, George. 2003. *The Historical and Institutional Context of Roman Law.* Burlington, VT: Ashgate Publishing.

Müller, Jan-Werner. 2003. *A Dangerous Mind: Carl Schmitt in Post-War European Thought.* New Haven, CT: Yale University Press.

Myerhoff, Barbara. 1982. "Life History Among the Elderly: Performance, Visibility, and Re-Membering." In *A Crack in the Mirror: Reflexive Perspectives in Anthropology*, edited by Jay Ruby, pp. 99–117. Philadelphia, PA: University of Pennsylvania Press.

National Advisory Commission on Civil Disorders. 1968. *Report.* New York, NY: E. P. Dutton & Co.

Nelson, Clifford C. 1973. "Preface." In *Prisoners in America*, edited by Lloyd E. Ohlin. Engelwood Cliffs, NJ: Prentice-Hall.

Neumann, Franz. 1944 (1963). *Behemoth: The Structure and Practice of National Socialism, 1933–1944*, second edition. New York, NY: Octagon Books, reprint of Oxford University Press.

Neusner, Jacob. 1976. *Talmudic Judaism in Sasanian Babylonia*. Leiden, Netherlands: E. J. Brill.

Newburn, Tim. 2002. "Atlantic Crossings: 'Policy Transfer' and Crime Control in the USA and Britain." *Punishment and Society* 4(2): 165–194.

Newman, Graeme R. 1978. *The Punishment Response*. Philadelphia, PA: Lippincott.

Nietzsche, Friedrich. 1878. *Human, All Too Human*, translated by Helen Zimmern, R. J. Hollingdale, and Marion Faber. Online at http://www.davemckay.co.uk/philosophy/nietzsche/nietzsche.php?name=nietzsche.1878.humanalltoohuman.zimmern.index.

———. 1883–1885 (1954). *Thus Spake Zarathustra*. In *The Portable Nietzsche*, translated and edited by Walter Kaufmann, pp. 103–439. New York, NY: Vintage Books.

———. 1886 (1968). *Beyond Good and Evil: Prelude to a Philosophy of the Future*, translated and edited by Walter Kaufmann. New York, NY: Modern Library.

Nonet, Philippe. 2006. "Antigone's Law." *Law, Culture and the Humanities* 2: 314–335.

Novick, Sheldon M. 1991. "Introduction." In *The Common Law* by Oliver Wendell Holmes Jr. Mineola, NY: Dover Publications.

Nyberg, Amy Kist. 1998. *Seal of Approval: The History of the Comics Code*. Jackson, MS: University Press of Mississippi.

Oakes, Guy. 1986. "Translator's Introduction." In Carl Schmitt, *Political Romanticism*, translated and with an Introduction by Guy Oakes. Cambridge MA: MIT Press.

Ober, Josiah. 1989. *Mass and Elite in Democratic Athens: Rhetoric, Ideology, and the Power of the People*. Princeton, NJ: Princeton University Press.

O'Connor, Alice. 2008. "Financing the Counterrevolution." In *Rightward Bound: Making America Conservative in the 1970s*, edited by Bruce J. Schulman and Julian E. Zelizer, pp. 148–168. Cambridge, MA: Harvard University Press.

Ohlin, Lloyd E. (ed.). 1973. *Prisoners in America*. Engelwood Cliffs, NJ: Prentice-Hall.

OJJDP (Office of Juvenile Justice and Delinquency Prevention). 2006. *Juvenile Offenders and Victims: 2006 National Report*. Washington, DC: Office of Justice Programs, U.S. Department of Justice. Online at http://ojjdp.ncjrs.gov/ojstatbb/nr2006/index.html.

Olivecrona, Karl. 1971. *Law as Fact*. London, UK: Stevens & Sons.

Omi. Michael and Howard Winant. 1994. *Racial Formation in the United States*, second edition. New York, NY: Routledge.

Packer, Herbert. 1968. *The Limits of the Criminal Sanction*. Palo Alto, CA: Stanford University Press.

Park, Robert E., Ernest W. Burgess, and Roderick D. McKenzie. 1925 (1967). *The City*. Chicago, IL: University of Chicago Press.

Parkinson, Cyril Northcote. 1958. *Parkinson's Law: The Pursuit of Progress*. London, UK: John Murray.

Pavlish, George and Augustine Brannigan (eds). 2007. "The Shift From Crime Control to Governance in the Sociology of Law." In *Governance and Regulation in Social Life: Essays in Honour of W. G. Carson*. New York, NY: Routledge-Cavendish.

Peirce, Charles Sanders. 1955. *Philosophical Writings of Peirce*, edited by Justus Buchler. New York, NY: Dover Publications.

———. 1958. *Collected Papers*, 8 volumes. Cambridge, MA: Harvard University Press.

Pepinsky, Harold E. 1976. *Crime and Conflict*. New York, NY: Academic Press.

———. 2000. *A Criminologist's Quest for Peace*. Online at http://www.critcrim.org/critpapers/pepinsky-book.htm

——— and Richard Quinney (eds). 1991. *Criminology as Peacemaking*. Bloomington, IN: Indiana University Press.

Peukert, Detlev. 1987 (1989). *The Weimar Republic*, translated by Richard Deveson. New York, NY: Hill and Wang.

Pew Center on the States. 2008. *One in 100: Behind Bars in America 2008*. Online at www.pewcenteronthestates.org/report_detail.aspx?id=35904.

Piketty, Thomas and Emmanuel Saez. 2004. "Income Inequality in the United States, 1913–2002." Online at http://emlab.berkeley.edu/users/saez/piketty-saezOUP04US.pdf.

Piven, Frances Fox. 1981. "Deviant Behavior and the Remaking of the World." *Social Problems* 28(5): 489–508.

Plato. ca. 307 BCE. *The Republic*, translated by R. E. Allen. New Haven, CT: Yale University Press.

Popper, Karl R. 1959. *The Logic of Scientific Discovery*. London, UK: Hutchinson.

Postman, Neil. 1985. *Amusing Ourselves to Death: Public Discourse in the Age of Show Business*. New York, NY: Viking.

Powell, Lewis. 1971. "Attack on American Free Enterprise System." Online at http://www.mediatransparency.org/story.php?storyID=21, http://reclaimdemocracy.org/corporate_accountability/powell_memo_lewis.html.

Pratt, Travis C., Francis T. Cullen, Kristie R. Blevins, Leah E. Daigle, and Tamara D. Madensen. 2006. "The Empirical Status of Deterrence Theory: A Meta-Analysis." In *Taking Stock: The Status of Criminological Theory*, edited by Francis T. Cullin, John Paul Wright, and Kristie R. Blevins. New Brunswick, NJ: Transaction Publishers.

President's Commission on Law Enforcement and the Administration of Justice. 1967a. *The Challenge of Crime in a Free Society*. Washington, DC: U.S. Government Printing Office.

———. 1967b. *Task Force Assessment: Crime and Its Impact—An Assessment*. Washington, DC: U.S. Government Printing Office.

———. 1967c. *Task Force Report: The Police Crime*. Washington, DC: U.S. Government Printing Office.

———. 1967d. *Task Force Report: Science and Technology*. Washington, DC: U.S. Government Printing Office.

Provinse, J. R. 1937 (1955). "The Underlying Sanctions of Plains Indians Culture." In *Social Anthropology of North American Tribes*, second edition, edited by Fred Egan. Chicago, IL: University of Chicago Press.

Pufendorf, Samuel von. 1682 (1964). *On the Duty of Man and Citizen According to the Natural Law*, translated by Herbert F. Wright. New York, NY: Oceana Publications. Online at http://www. constitution.org/puf/puf-dut.htm.

Quetelet, L. Adolphe. 1835/1842 (1968). *A Treatise on Man and the Development of His Faculties*, edited and translated by R. Knox and Thomas Smibert, reprint. New York, NY: Burt Franklin.

Quine, Willard V. O. 1960. *Word and Object*. New York, NY: Technology Press of MIT and John Wiley.

Quinney, Richard. 1970a. *The Social Reality of Crime*. Boston, MA: Little, Brown & Co.

———. 1970b. *The Problem of Crime*. New York, NY: Dodd, Mead & Co.

———. 1980. *Class, State, and Crime*, second edition. New York, NY: Longman.

———. 1991. "The Way of Peace: On Crime, Suffering, and Service." In *Criminology as Peacemaking*, edited by Harold E. Pepinsky and Richard Quinney. Bloomimgton, IN: Indiana University Press.

Rabinowitz, Avi and Herman Branover. 1985? "Is Halakhah Related to Quantum Physics? The Role of the Observer in Halakhah and Quantum Physics." Online at http://www.dvar.org/jstudies/observer.html.

Rasul v. Bush. 2004. 542 U.S. 466; 124 S. Ct. 2686; 159 L. Ed. 2d 548. Decided June 28, 2004.

Renner, Karl. 1949. *The Institutions of Private Law and their Social Functions*, translated by Agnes Schwarzchild, edited with an introduction and notes by O. Kahn-Freund. London, UK: Routledge & Kegan Paul.

Robinson, Cyril D. and Richard Scaglion. 1987. "The Origin and Evolution of the Police Function in Society: Notes Toward a Theory." *Law & Society Review* 21(1): 109–153.

Rogin, Michael. 1987. *Ronald Reagan: The Movie*. Berkeley, CA: University of California Press.

Rosch, Joel. 1985. "Crime as an Issue in American Politics." In *The Politics of Crime and Criminal Justice*, edited by Erika S. Fairchild and Vincent J. Webb. Beverly Hills, CA: Sage Publications.

Rostow, Walter W. 1960. *The Stages of Economic Growth: A Non-Communist Manifesto*. Cambridge, UK: Cambridge University Press.

Rothman, Denis J. 1995. "More of the Same: American Criminal Justice Policies in the 1990s." In *Punishment and Social Control: Essays in Honour of Sheldon L. Messinger*, edited by Sheldon L. Messinger, Thomas Blomberg, and Stanley Cohen. New York, NY: Aldine de Gruyter.

Roux, Georges. 1966. *Ancient Iraq*. Harmondsworth, Middlesex, UK: Penguin Books.

Rusche, Georg and Otto Kirchheimer. 1939. *Punishment and Social Structure*. New York, NY: Columbia University Press.

Russell, Bertrand. 1910 (1983). "The Theory of Logical Types." In *Logical and Philosophical Papers, 1909–1913*, volume 6 of *The Collected Papers of Bertrand Russell*, edited by J. G. Slater, pp. 3–31. New York, NY: Routledge.

———. 1913 (1983). "On the Notion of Cause." In *Logical and Philosophical Papers, 1909–1913*, volume 6 of *The Collected Papers of Bertrand Russell*, edited by J. G. Slater, pp. 190–210. New York, NY: Routledge.

Rutland, Robert A. 1955. *The Birth of the Bill of Rights*. Chapel Hill, NC: University of North Carolina Press.

Sampson, Robert J. 1986. "Effects of Socioeconomic Context on Official Reaction to Juvenile Delinquency." *American Sociological Review* 51(6): 876–885.

——— 2006. "Collective Efficacy Theory: Lessons Learned and Directions for Future Inquiry." In *Taking Stock: The Status of Criminological Theory*, edited by Francis T. Cullen, John Paul Wright, and Kristie R. Blevins, pp. 149–169. New Brunswick, NJ: Transaction Publishers.

——— and Jacqueline Cohen. 1988. "Deterrent Effects of the Police on Crime: A Replication and Theoretical Extension." *Law and Society Review* 22(1): 163–189.

——— and John H. Laub. 1993. *Crime in the Making: Pathways and Turning Points Through Life*. Cambridge, MA: Harvard University Press.

Saussure, Ferdinand de. 1959. *Course in General Linguistics*, translated by Wade Baskin, edited by Charles Bally and Albert Sechehaye with Albert Riedlinger. New York, NY: Philosophical Library.

Savelsberg, Joachim J. and Robert J. Sampson. 2002. "Introduction: Mutual Engagement: Criminology and Sociology?" *Crime, Law and Social Change* 37(2): 99–105.

Scahill, Jeremy. 2007. *Blackwater: The Rise of the World's Most Powerful Mercenary Army*. New York, NY: Nation Books.

Scheingold, Stuart A. 1991. *The Politics of Street Crime: Criminal Process and Cultural Obsession*. Philadelphia, PA: Temple University Press.

Scheuerman, William E. 1997. "The Unholy Alliance of Carl Schmitt and Friedrich A. Hayek." *Constellations* 4(2): 172–188.

———. 2006. "Carl Schmitt and the Road to Abu Ghraib." *Constellations* 13(1): 108–124.

Schmitt, Carl. 1919/1925 (1986). *Political Romanticism*, translated and with an introduction by Guy Oakes. Cambridge, MA: MIT Press.

———. 1920. "*Politische Theorie und Romantik*." *Historische Zeitschrift* 123: 377–397.

———. 1922/1934 (1985). *Political Theology: Four Chapters on the Concept of Sovereignty*, translated from the revised 1934 edition by George Schwab. Cambridge, MA: MIT Press.

———. 1923/1926 (1985). *The Crisis of Parliamentary Democracy*, translated and with an introduction by Ellen Kennedy. Cambridge, MA: MIT Press.

———1927/1932 (1976). *The Concept of the Political*, translated by George Schwab with comments by Leo Strauss. New Brunswick, NJ: Rutgers University Press.

———. 1932 (2004). *Legality and Legitimacy*, edited and translated by Jeffrey Seitzer with an introduction by John P. McCormick.

———. 1938 (1996). *The Leviathan in the Political Theory of Thomas Hobbes: The Meaning and Failure of a Political Symbol*, translated, edited, and with an introduction by George Schwab. Westport, CT: Greenwood Press.

———. 1950 (2003). *The* Nomos *of the Earth in the International Law of the* Jus Publicum Europaeum, translated by G. L. Ulmen. New York, NY: Telos Press.

———. 1975 (2004). *Theory of the Partisan: Intermediate Commentary on the Concept of the Political (1963)*, translated by A. C. Goodson. East Lansing, MI: Michigan State University Press. Online at http:// www.msupress.msu.edu/journals/cr/Schmitt.pdf.

Schulman, Bruce J. 2001. *The Seventies: The Great Shift in American Culture, Society, and Politics*. New York, NY: The Free Press.

——— and Julian E. Zelizer (eds). 2008. *Rightward Bound: Making America Conservative in the 1970s*. Cambridge, MA: Harvard University Press.

Schutz, Alfred. 1932 (1967). *The Phenomenology of the Social World*, translated by George Walsh and Frederick Lehnert with an introduction by George Walsh. Evanston, IL: Northwestern University Press.

———. 1962–1966. *Collected Papers*, 3 volumes, edited by Maurice Natanson. The Hague, Netherlands: M. Nijhoff.

Schwartz, Bernard. 1977. *The Great Rights of Mankind: A History of the American Bill of Rights*. New York, NY: Oxford University Press.

Schwendinger, Julia R. and Herman Schwendinger. 1983. *Rape and Inequality*. Beverly Hills, CA: Sage Publications.

Seale, Bobby. 1970. *Seize the Time*. New York, NY: Random House.

Sebeok, Thomas A. (ed.). 1968. *Animal Communication: Techniques of Study and Results of Research*. Bloomington, IN: Indiana University Press.

———— and Marcel Danesi. 2000. *The Forms of Meaning: Modeling Systems Theory and Semiotic Analysis*. New York, NY: Mouton de Gruyter.

Sellars, Wilfrid. 1961. "The Language of Theories." In *Minnesota Studies in the Philosophy of Science*, edited by Herbert Feigl and Grover Maxwell. Minneapolis, MN: University of Minnesota Press.

Sellin, Thorsten. 1939. *Culture Conflict and Crime*. New York, NY: Social Science Research Council.

Sennett, Richard. 1994. *Flesh and Stone: The Body and the City in Western Civilization*. New York, NY: W. W. Norton.

Shaw, Clifford R. and Henry D. McKay. 1942. *Delinquency in Urban Areas: A Study of Rates of Delinquents in Relation to Differential Characteristics of Local Communities in American Cities*. Chicago, IL: University of Chicago Press.

Simmel, Georg. 1900 (1950). "The Metropolis and Mental Life." In *The Sociology of Georg Simmel*, translated and edited by Kurt H. Wolff, pp. 409–426. New York, NY: The Free Press.

————. 1908a. "How is Society Possible?" In *Georg Simmel On Individuality and Social Forms*, edited by Donald N. Levine, pp. 6–22. Chicago, IL: University of Chicago Press.

————. 1908b. "The Problem of Sociology." In *Georg Simmel On Individuality and Social Forms*, edited by Donald N. Levine, pp. 23–35. Chicago, IL: University of Chicago Press.

Simon, Jonathan. 2007. *Governing Through Crime: How the War on Crime Transformed American Democracy and Created a Culture of Fear*. New York, NY: Oxford University Press.

Slater, Philip. 1970. *The Pursuit of Loneliness: American Culture at the Breaking Point*. Boston, MA: Beacon Press.

Smith, Paul. 2007. *Primitive America: The Ideology of Capitalist Democracy*. Minneapolis, MN: University of Minnesota Press.

Snodgrass, Jon. 1972. *The American Criminological Tradition: Portraits of the Men and Ideology in a Discipline*. Ph.D. dissertation, University of Pennsylvania.

Snow, David A. and Michael Mulcahy. 2001. "Space, Politics, and the Survival Strategies of the Homeless." *American Behavioral Scientist* 45(1): 149–169.

Spector, Malcolm and John Kitsuse. 1977 (2001). *Constructing Social Problems*, with a new introduction by John Kitsuse. New Brunswick, NJ: Transaction Publishers.

Spitzer, Steven. 1975. "Toward a Marxian Theory of Deviance." *Social Problems* 22(5): 641–651.

Spradley, James P. and Michael A. Rynkiewich (eds.). 1975. *The Nacirema: Readings in American Culture*. Boston, MA: Little, Brown & Co.

Steelworkers Trilogy. 1960. *United Steelworkers v. American Mfg. Co.*, 363 U.S. 564; 80 S. Ct. 1343; 4 L. Ed. 2d 1403; *United Steelworkers v. Warrior & Gulf Navigating Co.*, 363 U.S. 574; 80 S. Ct. 1347; 4 L. Ed. 2d 1409; *United Steelworkers v. Enterprise Wheel & Car Corp.*, 363 U.S. 593; 80 S. Ct. 1358; 4 L. Ed. 2d 1424. Decided June 20, 1960.

Steinsaltz, Adin. 1976. *The Essential Talmud*, translated by Chaya Galai. New York, NY: Basic Books.

Stern, Fritz. 2006. *Five Germanies I Have Known*. New York, NY: Farrar, Strauss and Giroux.

Stone, Isidor F. 1988. *The Trial of Socrates*. New York, NY: Doubleday.

Story, Joseph. 1987. *Commentaries on the Constitution of the United States*. Abridged in one volume, 1833, reprinted with an introduction by Ronald D. Rotunda and John E. Nowak. Durham, NC: Carolina Academic Press.

Strauss, Leo. 1932a (1988/1995). "Notes on the Concept of the Political." In *Carl Schmitt and Leo Strauss: The Hidden Dialogue*, edited with an introduction by Heinrich Meier, translated by J. Harvey Lomax, pp. 91–119. Chicago, IL: University of Chicago Press.

———. 1932b. Strauss to Schmitt, Hohenzollernkorso 11, Berlin-Neutenemlhof, 4 September 1932. In *Carl Schmitt and Leo Strauss: The Hidden Dialogue*, edited with an introduction by Heinrich Meier, translated by J. Harvey Lomax, pp. 124–126. Chicago, IL: University of Chicago Press.

———. 1952. *Persecution and the Art of Writing*. Glencoe, IL: Free Press.

———. 1953. *Natural Right and History*. Chicago, IL: University of Chicago Press.

———. 1958. "Freud on Moses and Monotheism." In *Jewish Philosophy and the Crisis of Modernity: Essays and Lectures in Modern Jewish Thought by Leo Strauss*, edited by Kenneth Hart Green, pp. 285–309. Albany, NY: SUNY Press.

Sugrue, Thomas J. and John D. Skrentny. 2008. "The White Ethnic Strategy." In *Rightward Bound: Making America Conservative in the 1970s*, edited by Bruce J. Schulman and Julian E. Zelizer, pp. 171–192. Cambridge, MA: Harvard University Press.

Sullivan, Dennis. 1980. *The Mask of Love: Corrections in America Toward a Mutual Aid Alternative*. Port Washington, NY: Kennikat.

Sullivan, Harry Stack. 1953. *The Interpersonal Theory of Psychiatry*, edited by Helen Swick Perry and Mary Ladd Gawell. New York, NY: W. W. Norton.

Sykes, Gresham M. 1958. *The Society of Captives: A Study of a Maximum Security Prison*. Princeton, NJ: Princeton University Press.

——— and David Matza. 1957. "Techniques of Neutralization." *American Sociological Review* 22 (Dec.): 664–670.

Talmon, Jacob L. 1957. *The Nature of Jewish History: Its Universal Significance*. London, UK: Hillel Foundation.

Tarde, Gabriel. 1890 (1912/2001). *Penal Philosophy*, translated by Rapelje Howell with a new introduction by Piers Beirne. New Brunswick, NJ: Transaction Publishers.

Tarski, Alfred. 1933/1956. "The Concept of Truth in Formalized Languages." In *Logic, Semantics, Mathematics: Papers from 1923 to 1938*, translated by J. H. Woodger, pp. 152–278. Oxford, UK: Clarendon Press.

Tawney, Richard H. 1912 (1967). *The Agrarian Problem in the Sixteenth Century*, with an introduction by Lawrence Stone. New York, NY: Harper & Row.

———. 1926 (1962). *Religion and the Rise of Capitalism: A Historical Study*. Gloucester, MA: P. Smith.

Thomas, William I. and Dorothy Swaine Thomas. 1928. *The Child in America: Behavior Problems and Programs*. New York, NY: Alfred A. Knopf.

Thrasher, Frederick Milton. 1927. *The Gang: A Study of 1,313 Gangs in Chicago*. Chicago, IL: University of Chicago Press.

Tigar, Michael E. and Madelein R. Levy. 1977. *Law and the Rise of Capitalism*. New York, NY: Monthly Review Press.

——— 2000. *Law and the Rise of Capitalism*, second edition. New York, NY: Monthly Review Press.

Tonry, Michael. 2007. "Looking Back to See the Future of Punishment in America." *Social Research* 74(2): 353–378.

TRAC. 2008. "Immigration Overshadows All Other Administration Enforcement Efforts." July 17, 2008. Online at http://trac.syr.edu/.

Troeltsch, Ernst. 1922 (1934/1957). "Troeltsch on Natural Law and Humanity." In Otto Gierke, *Natural Law and the Theory of Society, 1500 to 1800*, translated with introduction by Ernest Barker. Boston, MA: Beacon Press, originally published by Cambrdge University Press in two volumes.

Turk, Austin T. 1976. "Law as a Weapon in Social Conflict." *Social Problems* 23(3): 276–291.

Turner, Victor W. 1968. *The Drums of Affliction: A Study of Religious Processes Among the Ndembu of Zambia*. Oxford, UK: Clarendon Press.

————. 1969 (1977). *The Ritual Process: Structure and Anti-Structure.* Ithaca, NY: Cornell University Press.

Ungar, Sheldon. 2001. "Moral Panic Versus the Risk Society: The Implications of Changing Sites of Social Anxiety." *British Journal of Sociology* 52(2): 271–291.

U.S. Census Bureau. 2008. "Population Clocks." Online at http://www.census.gov.

Valentine, Douglas. 2004. *The Strength of the Wolf: The Secret History of America's War on Drugs.* New York, NY: Verso.

Vološinov, Valentine Nikolaevič. 1973 (1930). *Marxism and the Philosophy of Language,* translated by Ladislav Mateka and I. R. Titunik. New York: Seminar Press.

von Hirsch, Andrew. 1976. *Doing Justice: The Choice of Punishment.* New York, NY: Hill & Wang.

————. 1985. *Past or Future Crimes: Deservedness and Dangerousness in the Sentencing of Criminals.* New Brunswick, NJ: Rutgers University Press.

————. 1993. *Censure and Sanctions.* Oxford, UK: Oxford University Press.

Waldron, Jeremy. 1991. "Homelessness and the Issue of Freedom." *UCLA Law Review* 39: 295–324.

Walker, Daniel. 1968. *Rights in Conflict: The Violent Confrontation of Demonstrators and Police in the Parks and Streets of Chicago During the Week of the Democratic National Convention of 1968.* New York, NY: Bantam Books.

Walker, Jeffery T. 2006. "Advancing Science and Research in Criminal Justice/Criminology: Complex Systems Theory and Non-Linear Analyses." *Justice Quarterly* 24(4): 555–581.

Walker, Samuel. 1992. "Origins of the Contemporary Criminal Justice Paradigm: The American Bar Foundation Survey, 1953–1969." *Justice Quarterly* 9(1): 47–76.

Wallerstein, Immanuel M. 2003. *The Decline of American Power: The U.S. in a Chaotic World.* New York, NY: The New Press.

————. 2004. *World-Systems Analysis: An Introduction.* Durham, NC: Duke University Press.

Weber, Max. 1925 (1967). *Law in Economy and Society,* second edition, edited by Max Rheinstein, translated by Edward Shils and Max Rheinstein. Chicago, IL: University of Chicago Press.

————. 1952. *Ancient Judaism,* translated and edited by Hans Gerth and Don Martindale. Glencoe, IL: Free Press.

————. 1958a. *The Protestant Ethic and the Spirit of Capitalism,* translated by Talcott Parsons. New York, NY: Scribner.

———. 1958b. *The Religion of India: The Sociology of Hinduism and Buddhism*, translated and edited by Hans Gerth and Don Martindale. Glencoe, IL: Free Press.

Welch, Michael. 2006. *Scapegoats of September 11th: Hate Crimes & State Crimes in the War on Terror.* New Brunswick, NJ: Rutgers University Press.

Wetzell, Richard F. 2000. *Inventing the Criminal: A History of German Criminology, 1880–1945.* Chapel Hill, NC: University of North Carolina Press.

Wheeler, Samuel C. III. 2000. *Deconstruction as Analytic Philosophy.* Stanford, CA: Stanford University Press.

Whit, Hugh P. 2002. "Inventing Sociology: André-Michel Guerry and the *Essai sur la statistique morale de la France*." In *Essay on the Moral Statistics of France*, edited and translated by Hugh P. Whit and Victor W. Reinking, pp. ix–xxxvii. Lewiston, NY: Edwin Mellon Press.

Whitehead, Alfred North and Bertrand Russell. 1913 (1960). *Principia Mathematica*, volume 1, second edition. Cambridge, UK: Cambridge University Press.

Williams, Frank P. 1984. "The Demise of Criminological Imagination: A Critique of Recent Criminology." *Justice Quarterly* 1(1): 91–106.

Wilson, James Q. (ed.). 1968a. *City Politics and Public Policy.* New York, NY: John Wiley.———. 1968b. *Varieties of Police Behavior.* Cambridge, MA: Harvard University Press.

——— 1975. *Thinking About Crime.* New York, NY: Basic Books.

———. 1993. *The Moral Sense.* New York, NY: Free Press.

———. 1996. "Foreword." In *Fixing Broken Windows: Restoring Order and Reducing Crime in Our Communities*, by George L. Kelling and Catherine M. Coles. New York, NY: Free Press.

——— and Barbara Boland. 1978. "The Effects of Police on Crime." *Law and Society Review* 12(3): 367–390.

——— and George Kelling. 1982. "Broken Windows: The Police and Neighborhood Safety." *Atlantic Monthly* 249(3) March: 29–38.

Winch, Peter. 1964. "Understanding a Primitive Society." *American Philosophical Quarterly* 1(4): 307–324.

Wittgenstein, Ludwig. 1953. *Philosophical Investigations*, translated by G. E. M. Anscombe. New York, NY: Macmillan.

Wolfgang, Marvin E. 1967. "The Culture of Youth." In *New Light on Juvenile Delinquency*, edited by Ronald Steel, pp. 101–107. New York, NY: H. H. Wilson Co.

Wozniak, John F. 2000. "The Voices of Peacemaking Criminology: Insights into a Perspective with an Eye Toward Teaching." *Contemporary Justice Review* 3(3): 267–289.

———. 2002. "Toward a Theoretical Model of Peacemaking Criminology: An Essay in Honor of Richard Quinney." *Crime & Delinquency* 48(2): 204–231.

Xenophon. ca. 370 BCE (2006). *Helenica*, translated by Donald F. Jackson and Ralph E. Doty. Lewiston, ME: Edwin Mellen Press.

Index